An Essay on Divine Authority

A volume in the series
Cornell Studies in the Philosophy of Religion
EDITED BY WILLIAM P. ALSTON

A full list of titles in the series appears at the end of the book.

Mark C. Murphy

An Essay on Divine Authority

Cornell University Press, *Ithaca and London*

First published 2002 by Cornell University Press

Printed in the United States of America

Library of Congress Cataloging-in-Publication Data

Murphy, Mark C.
  An essay on divine authority / Mark C. Murphy
    p. cm. — (Cornell studies in the philosophy of religion)
Includes bibliographical references and index.
  ISBN 0-8014-4030-0 (cloth : alk. paper)
  1. Authority—Religious aspects—Christianity. 2. Philosophical
theology. 3. God. I. Title. II. Series.
  BT88 .M85 2002
  231.7—dc21

2002003511

Cornell University Press strives to use environmentally responsible suppliers and materials to the fullest extent possible in the publishing of its books. Such materials include vegetable-based, low-VOC inks and acid-free papers that are recycled, totally chlorine-free, or partly composed of nonwood fibers. For further information, visit our website at www.cornellpress.cornell.edu.

Cloth printing   10 9 8 7 6 5 4 3 2 1

for Flannery Jane,
divine subject

Contents

Preface

The questions that this essay aims to answer are questions about God. Obviously they arose for me not in a vacuum but in the context of my own religious beliefs. I am a Roman Catholic, and the conception of God that I take for granted in this essay is thus a Christian conception. For the most part, though, my arguments do not appeal to claims about God that are affirmed by Christianity but denied by either of the other Abramic faiths, and I take it that for the most part my arguments could be as easily addressed to those whose conception of God is that of Judaism or Islam as to those whose conception of God is that of Christianity. Indeed, so long as the reader is willing to work with a conception of God on which God is omniscient, omnipotent, perfectly good, and the creator of the world, the arguments that I offer will engage him or her on familiar ground.

I received a great deal of help in writing this book. Terence Cuneo, Trenton Merricks, Phil Quinn, Joe Shaw, and two referees for Cornell University Press were good enough to read and comment on the entire manuscript. John Hare, Matt McAdam, Lucas Swaine, and Thomas Williams offered critical remarks on portions of the text. I also owe thanks to audience members at colloquia at Georgetown University and at the Gifford Bequest International Conference on Natural Theology, who early on discussed with me some of the ideas presented here. I am indebted to all of these generous people.

I began this essay while on a research leave at the Erasmus Institute at the University of Notre Dame: I am grateful to the anonymous donors who funded that institute, and to its director, Jim Turner. I am grateful also to Georgetown University, which provided me with a junior faculty research leave to think and write about natural law and related matters. Special thanks are due to my department chair, Wayne Davis, for his ingenious efforts, which have made the philosophy department at Georgetown a wonderful environment in which to work.

Parts of Chapters 1 and 3 were previously published as "Divine Authority and Divine Perfection," *International Journal for Philosophy of Religion* 49 (2001), pp. 155–177; my thanks to Kluwer Academic Publishers for kindly granting permission to use that material here. Parts of Chapter 4 previously appeared as "A Trilemma for Divine Command Theory," *Faith and Philosophy* 19 (2002), pp. 23–31; I am grateful to that journal as well for permission to reprint.

I am most indebted to my wife, Jeanette, who is to me both a model of God's abundant grace and an instance of it.

M. C. M.

Herndon, Virginia

An Essay on Divine Authority

The Problem of
Divine Authority

Influence of Cambridge Platonists

God is a rational being, and we are rational beings. Rational beings are, in large measure, self-directing: capable of coming to an understanding of what reasons for action there are, of assessing the features of those reasons for action relevant to deliberation, and of deciding what course of action is to be carried out in light of those reasons. Thus, whenever it is suggested that one rational being is practically authoritative over another, that suggestion merits investigation to determine whether it is true. And so the suggestion that God is authoritative over us humans, and indeed over any other created rational beings that there are, is a claim that merits investigation. To determine whether it is true that God is authoritative over created rational beings, and to provide an adequate explanation of the extent of God's authority, together constitute the *problem of divine authority*.

The problem of divine authority does not figure prominently in current philosophy of religion. There appear to be two reasons that the problem has received so little attention. The first is that there is a tendency to think that the notion that God is authoritative is obviously true and that, since its truth is trivial, it requires no explanation. The second is that there is a tendency to think that the notion that God is authoritative is obviously false and that, since its falsity is so well established, it requires no further discussion. Let me say something about each of these tendencies in turn.

The tendency to think that the claim that God is authoritative[1] is trivially true arises from the fact that there is broad agreement among theists and nontheists that any being that counts as God must be authoritative: if God gives one a command to perform some action, then that command is a reason to perform that action, even a decisive reason. (I will say more about the precise connection between authority and reasons for action in 1.1.) If God exists, so the common wisdom goes, then God has extensive practical authority over all of us created rational beings, and would have had extensive practical authority over any rational beings that God had chosen to create.

One tendency to dismiss the problem of divine authority results from philosophers thinking not only that the claim 'God is authoritative' is commonly affirmed, but also that this claim is *true by definition*. God is, by definition, such that each created rational being has decisive reason to obey God. Here, for example, is James Rachels:

> To bear the title 'God' . . . a being must have certain qualifications. He must, for example, be all-powerful and perfectly good in addition to being perfectly wise. And in the same vein, to apply the title 'God' to a being is to recognise him as one to be obeyed. . . . And to recognise any being as God is to acknowledge that he has *unlimited* authority, and an unlimited claim on one's allegiance. . . . That God is not to be judged, challenged, defied, or disobeyed, is at bottom a truth of logic. (Rachels 1971, pp. 43–44; emphasis in original)

To think that there is a substantive question about whether God is practically authoritative over created rational beings would be, on this view, just like thinking that there is a substantive question about whether bachelors are really unmarried. One who wonders whether God should be obeyed fails to grasp the meaning of the term 'God.' There is no problem of divine au-

---

1. Unless I indicate otherwise, I will always read 'God is authoritative' as *de dicto* (i.e. *if* there is a being that is God, then that being is authoritative), in order to emphasize the broad agreement between theists and nontheists on this matter.

thority because the answers are so obvious: *of course* God is authoritative; it is part of the definition of 'God' that God has practical authority.

Suppose we accept that the task of defining terms takes as its starting point the gathering of platitudes in which those terms figure (cf. Smith 1994, pp. 29–32) and that it is a platitude that God is authoritative. It is nonetheless unwarranted to move from these claims to a dismissal of the problem of divine authority. It might be warranted if to define a term were simply to list, and to conjoin, the platitudes concerning that term. But in defining terms, one looks to see whether some platitudes are more central than others, either with respect to importance (some platitudes are more platitudinous than others) or with respect to explanatory power (some platitudes explain, or otherwise organize, others). Those platitudes that are more central have a better claim to serve as part of the *definiens* than those that are less central. One also can look to see whether certain salient coherence patterns emerge among the platitudes, even if there are no platitudes that are clearly more central than others; if certain sets of platitudes exhibit greater coherence than others, then they have a better claim to serve as the *definiens* than less coherent sets of platitudes do.

Consider, for example, one of Rachels's sample divine qualifications, that of being all-powerful. That God is all-powerful is indeed a platitude. But it would not do to proceed from this point to the conclusion that there is no problem of divine power, no reason to ask whether God is indeed all-powerful. There are important questions about the coherence of omnipotence with other alleged divine attributes. And there are important questions about whether omnipotence is an implication of 'master' platitudes about God—platitudes ascribing to God some general characteristic, appeal to which regulates our inclusion, or exclusion, of other properties in our descriptions of the divine nature—such as 'God is the first cause'[2] or 'God is a perfect being'[3] or 'God is that being that is worthy of wor-

---

2. Cf. Aquinas, *Summa Theologiae* Ia 2, 3: "It is necessary to admit a first efficient cause, to which everyone gives the name of God." Aquinas derives God's omnipotence from God's infinity (*Summa Theologiae* Ia 7, 1), and in turn derives God's infinity from God's status as first efficient cause (*Summa Theologiae* Ia 3, 4).

3. Cf. Anselm, *Proslogion*: "Now we believe that you are something than which nothing greater can be thought" (ch. 2); "you are . . . whatever it is better to be than not to be" (ch. 5). Anselm assumes that God's omnipotence is implied by this master platitude (ch. 6), though he takes it to be a key task to explain how this divine perfection is compatible with the perfections of incorruptibility and impeccability (ch. 7). See, for an example of this type of ap-

ship.'[4] One could sensibly claim that God is not all-powerful, justifying that claim on the basis that the denial of 'God is all-powerful' is necessary for coherence with other divine attributes and on the basis that 'God is all-powerful' is not an implication of any master platitude. It would *not* do to cut short investigation of the problem by declaring that since one platitude about God is that God is all-powerful, any investigation into whether God really is such is a waste of time. The same is true of the platitude concerning divine authority. It will not do to cut short the investigation into the presence and source of divine authority simply because it is platitudinous that God has such authority.

Even if it were allowed for the sake of argument that 'God is authoritative' is so central a platitude about God that no being that lacked such authority could count as God, we should keep in mind that there is more to the problem of divine authority than the question of whether God must be authoritative. There is also a question about the *explanation* of divine authority. Suppose, that is, that we grant that 'God is authoritative' is true by definition. We could still rightly wonder about the conditions under which such a being could exist. In keeping with philosophical convention, let us label 'Schmod' any being that has all of the properties required to merit the title 'God' *except* that of being authoritative. We might ask: Does meriting the title 'Schmod' *entail* meriting the title 'God'? Is it the case, that is, that the divine properties, aside from that of authority, guarantee that a being exemplifying those properties will be authoritative? Is authority just a further, brute property that in addition to Schmodhood makes for Godhood? Or are there, perhaps, other facts about the world that would have to obtain for Schmod to be God? Since the problem of divine authority is not just about *whether* God has authority, but about *why* God has authority, even an admission that 'God is authoritative' is true by definition would not trivialize the problem of divine authority.

Here is another way to think about it. Consider again the comparison between 'God is authoritative' and 'bachelors are unmarried.' One might think

---

proach that raises questions about omnipotence as a perfection and, as a result, about whether omnipotence should be ascribed to God, Schlesinger 1985.

4. Cf. Geach 1973. Geach rejects God's omnipotence in favor of the successor notion of almightiness, because omnipotence generates insoluble puzzles and almightiness is sufficient to satisfy the condition that God be worthy of worship. Geach is, I suppose all will agree, not to be counted an atheist on account of his denying God's omnipotence.

that if it were conceded that this comparison is an apt one, the problem of divine authority would be immediately reduced to triviality. But this is not so. Obviously, in *one* sense, the question 'Why are bachelors unmarried?' is uninteresting. For one to be a bachelor, one must be unmarried. But in another sense, 'Why are bachelors unmarried?' is an at least potentially interesting question, answered perhaps by 'some are afraid of commitment; others have aims they wish to accomplish before marriage; some are gay and live where homosexual marriage is not legally recognized . . . ' 'Why are bachelors unmarried?' is, in this sense, a *de re* question, a question about why *these people* are unmarried. Similarly, even if 'God is authoritative' were true by definition, there is an interesting sense of 'Why is God authoritative?': we can ask whether, if God exists, there is some further explanation for God's being authoritative, whether there are some other facts about God that account for God's being authoritative. We can ask, that is, the *de re* question about why *this* being, God, is authoritative. This is an interesting issue, even if we grant 'if *x* is God, then *x* is authoritative' to be a definitional truth.

It seems to me, then, that one reason that the problem of divine authority has gathered little attention is that the platitudinous character of 'God is authoritative' has led many to believe (falsely, I say) that this claim is trivially true and to conclude from that (again, falsely, I say) not in need of philosophical investigation. The second reason is precisely the opposite: that the notion that God is authoritative is false, and because it has been so thoroughly shown to be false, there is no need to spend more time fooling around with it. The idea is this: to hold that God has an extensive practical authority over all created rational beings is to espouse a *divine command* theory of morality; and since divine command theories of morality have been demolished, the notion that God is practically authoritative has been demolished. If theists are committed to the view that God is practically authoritative, then so much the worse for them: the refutation of divine command theories of morality shows that God, as theists tend to understand God, must not exist.

This dismissal of divine authority is based upon a dismissal of divine command theories of morality. In responding to this dismissal of divine authority, I will not rest my response on a defense of the viability of divine command theory. This is not because I agree with the assessment of divine command theory upon which the dismissal is based: I think that divine command theory remains a live option for ethics, and the place that various versions of divine command theory have in this book (see, for example, Chapter 4, as well as 5.6) testifies to the seriousness with which I take this view. But one does not need to think that divine command theory is at all viable in order to take seriously the problem of divine authority. For one can utterly reject divine command conceptions of ethics while still holding fast to the notion that God is authoritative. To think that if there is a God, then that being is authoritative does not commit one to the claim that divine command theory is true.

Here is why. Divine command theories of ethics can be divided into two types. *Metaethical* versions of divine command theory attempt to provide definitions of moral terms, or to lay bare the nature of moral properties, or to identify the properties on which moral properties supervene, or to give an informative causal story about the origin of moral properties; and they carry out these tasks by appealing to divine commands. (See 4.2 for a more complete account.) But there is no plausibility whatever to the claim that belief in God's authority ipso facto is belief in some metaethical version of divine command theory. It is abundantly clear that one can affirm the claim that God is authoritative without holding any particular view about the nature of moral properties. The thesis that God must be obeyed is a normative claim, not a metaethical claim: and so there would be no merit to the charge that affirmation of divine authority commits one to an untenable divine command metaethics.

The other type of divine command theory is normative. *Normative* versions of divine command theory assert that the supreme moral principle is that God's commands are to be obeyed. The principle that God is to be obeyed is, on normative versions of divine command theory, supreme due to its status as an independent moral principle that is the source of the correctness of all other moral principles. It is *independent*, lacking a source in any other moral principle: the principle that God is to be obeyed is fundamental. It is the *source* of all other moral principles: any moral principle that binds created rational beings is to be explained in terms of the principle of obedience to God. (For example: if we are bound not to murder each other, it is because God told us not to, and God's commands are to be obeyed.) Now, there is obviously a close connection between the view that God is authoritative and the normative version of divine command theory: the normative version of divine command theory entails that God is authoritative. But the thesis that God is authoritative does *not* entail the normative version of divine command theory. The normative version of divine command theory adds claims about the authority thesis that the defender of the authority thesis need not accept—that the authority thesis is independent of all other moral principles, not dependent upon them for its truth, and that it is the source of all other moral principles, so that all other moral principles are dependent upon it for their truth.

It is important that the claim that God is authoritative does not entail normative divine command theory: for one cannot immediately dismiss divine authority on the basis of a dismissal of normative divine command theory. But it is also important that what separates the assertion that God is authoritative from the assertions of normative divine command theory is, in particular, the added point about the status of God's authority as the supreme moral principle. The standard, allegedly devastating objections to normative divine command theory—that divine command theory makes morality arbitrary, that it eviscerates the notion that God is good, and that it leaves mysterious why we ought to obey God—target the notion that God's authority is supreme as a moral principle, not the notion as such that God is authoritative. By declaring that all other moral principles depend on God's commands, the objection goes, the divine command theorist commits him- or herself to the arbitrariness of morality. By making obedience to God the only fundamental moral principle, the divine command theorist must surrender any substantive sense in which God can be held to be morally good. And by asserting that all other moral principles are subordinate to the principle of obedience to God, the divine command theorist forfeits any argumentative resources to argue from some other moral principle to the conclusion that God is to be obeyed. I am not endorsing these objections. I am noting that these objections are leveled against features of normative divine command theory that are not shared by the thesis that God is authoritative. Thus, even if the reasons for rejecting divine command theory were good reasons, they would not in the least cast doubt on the claim that God has extensive practical authority.

So it is neither obviously true nor obviously false that God is authoritative over created rational beings. It is a live question whether, and to what extent, God is authoritative. The problem of divine authority is indeed a problem. I aim in this essay to solve it.

CHAPTER I

What Divine Authority Is

I.I REASONS AND PRACTICAL AUTHORITY

This essay is on divine authority: whether there is such a thing, and how it is to be explained. But we will not make much progress on these issues unless we can get a tolerably clear idea of what it is, in general, to be practically authoritative, and what divine authority is supposed to amount to.

Whatever else we should say about practical authority, it is a relationship that should be understood as a specific type of (positive) connection between one party's dictates and another party's reasons for action. While I do not aim to provide any in-depth account of reasons for action here, I need to say a few things about them that will be helpful in distinguishing genuine practical authority from other relationships that are in the vicinity of, but nonetheless are not instances of, such authority.

Following Raz (1975, pp. 16–19), I shall understand reasons for action to be *facts;* and I understand facts to be states of affairs that obtain, that are the case. In saying that reasons for action are facts, neither Raz nor I mean to suggest that reasons are facts *in contrast to* values. If there are genuine evaluative truths (*murder is wrong, knowledge is good,* etc.), then those truths state facts, facts that can be reasons for action.

Second, I shall understand reasons for action to be facts that make actions *worth performing;* the reason is that which constitutes the *choiceworthiness* of the action. (I offer here, however, no general account of the nature of choiceworthiness or of what makes acts choiceworthy.)[1] The notion of a reason is normative: a reason is what counts in favor of an act, or throws weight behind the performance of an act, or makes an act eligible.

Third, I shall understand reasons for action to be *complete* and *compact.* With respect to completeness: a fact must include within it all that makes an action choiceworthy in some way if that fact is to count as a reason to perform that action. While we may commonly say that the fact that one's hand is on a hot stove is a reason for one to move it, I will treat this common and perfectly intelligible way of speaking as shorthand for a more complex fact which includes the fact that one's hand is on the hot stove, the fact that one's hand's being on a hot stove causes one pain and damage, the fact that moving one's hand from a hot stove characteristically does not cause one pain and damage, and the fact that pain and damage are bad and to be avoided. A reason for action is a terminus in the explication of the choiceworthiness of an action, and it cannot serve as a terminus if it does not on its own render an action choiceworthy in some way. (See also Raz 1975, p. 24.)

Before explaining compactness, I want to register two clarifications concerning completeness. First, in saying that reasons must be *complete,* I am not saying that all reasons are *decisive.* A reason must on its own be enough to give point to acting a certain way; it need not be on its own enough to render that act the uniquely eligible choice in a situation of decision. And, second, I want to allow that a reason for action can be complete but susceptible to defeat. The idea is that a complete reason to ϕ[2] on its own account is enough to render ϕ-ing intelligible, but that even complete reasons can have their capacity to render an act intelligible blocked by defeating conditions. That I made a valid promise to you to ϕ is arguably a complete reason for me to ϕ. But this state of affairs can have its capacity to make my act intelligible undercut by defeating conditions, for example, your releasing me

---

1. I make an attempt at such an account in Murphy 2001a.
2. 'ϕ' is a variable that stands for an action verb—'run,' 'jump,' 'play,' etc. Because refrainings are acts as well, 'ϕ' can stand for such refrainings as well—'refrain from running,' 'refrain from jumping,' 'refrain from playing,' etc.

from my promise (cf. Raz 1975, p. 27, which calls such conditions "canceling conditions"; they are not canceling *reasons*, because they need not be, or
form any part of, a reason for action).

With respect to compactness: reasons for action include within them only
facts that are at least partially constitutive of the choiceworthiness of the action for which they are reasons. The fact that looking out when I cross the
road promotes my survival and my survival is a good is a reason for me to look
out when I cross the road. But the fact that looking out when I cross the road
promotes my survival, my survival is a good, and there are eight pens in my
desk at home is not a reason for me to look out when I cross the road. That
there are eight pens in my desk at home, even if true, is irrelevant to the
choiceworthiness of my looking out, and so is not part of a reason for me to
look out. As a general principle, if R is a reason for A to ϕ, then there is no
fact S included in R such that the choiceworthiness conferred on ϕ-ing by R
without S is identical to the choiceworthiness conferred on ϕ-ing by R.

‍‍Reasons are what make actions choiceworthy for agents. To be genuinely
practically authoritative is to be such that one's dictates are appropriately related to the reasons for action that others have, to the range of actions that
are choiceworthy for others, and to the degree to which those actions are
choiceworthy. What is this relation? Well, first of all, and fairly uncontro-
versially, the relation is one of *control*: one is practically authoritative over another in a certain domain only if one's dictates control to some extent the
reasons for action that others have in that domain. When one has practical
authority, one's dictates make a difference with respect to others' reasons for
action; they do not simply reflect the distribution of reasons for action that
others have prior to the dictates' being issued. If I have authority over my
child, then I am able through my commanding acts to alter what reasons for
action my child has, at least in some domains. Though she may have reason
to clean her room at some time or other, my dictate can give her further reason to clean her room now, or at some other specific time. If the state has
authority over its citizens, then it is able through its commanding acts to alter
what reasons for action its citizens have, at least in some domains. Though
citizens may have reason to adhere to some scheme of taxation or other, the
state's dictates can give its citizens reasons to adhere to some particular
scheme. A party whose dictates were unable to add to the choiceworthiness
of any action would be normatively impotent; but authority, whatever else
it is, is a kind of normative power (cf. Raz 1986, p. 24).

But what sort of control over reasons for action does an authority have? Note that in situations in which one party recognizes another as an authority, that party often cites the other's dictates as reasons for action. If we take to heart the idea that reasons for action must be complete, we may think that in many or even all such cases there is more to the reason than the dictate itself: there may be the fact that one consented to obey the ruler's dictates, or the like. But it is crucial that at least part of the reason is the authoritative dictate itself. That is what makes it understandable to cite the dictate as one's reason for action. What this suggests is that the control over reasons for action possessed by genuine practical authorities is *constitutive* rather than (say) merely *causal* control. I am not denying, of course, that authorities exhibit causal control over reasons by giving commands; I am denying that causal control over reasons by giving commands is *sufficient* for authority. It is not enough that the commands bring about reasons for action; the commands must at least partially constitute the reasons brought about. (See also Nowell-Smith 1976, p. 4.) In giving a command, a practical authority actualizes a state of affairs that is itself part of the reason for action for one subject to that authority.

Let me try to make the notion that constitutive control is essential to practical authority more precise. Say that *C* is a *reason-candidate* for *A* to *φ* if *C* is a possible state of affairs such that if it obtained, then it would be a reason for *A* to *φ*. If the state of affairs *its being good for Murphy to have $5 million and Murphy's winning $5 million if he buys a lottery ticket at precisely 11:03 A.M. on Friday, June 16, at the 7-Eleven on Crestview Drive* did in fact obtain, then that fact would be a reason for me to buy a lottery ticket under those conditions; and so it is a reason-candidate for me to buy a lottery ticket.

To be practically authoritative is to have some control over others' reason-candidates: the control is over which reason-candidates become reasons for action. Say that *A actualizes a reason* if and only if *A* performs some act such that a reason-candidate *C* that was not a reason for action prior to *A*'s performance of that act becomes a reason for action as a result of that act. The reason-candidate mentioned in the previous paragraph—*its being good for Murphy to have $5 million and Murphy's winning $5 million if he buys a lottery ticket at precisely 11:03 A.M. on Friday, June 16, at the 7-Eleven on Crestview Drive*—is, so far as we know, merely a reason-candidate. But suppose that you have the power to rig lotteries. You alter the workings of the ticket machines and the selection mechanisms so that the state of affairs *Murphy's win-*

ning $5 million if he buys a lottery ticket at precisely 11:03 A.M. on Friday, June 16, at the 7-Eleven on Crestview Drive now obtains. Assuming that the state of affairs *its being good for Murphy to have $5 million* obtained all along, you have actualized a reason: you have made it the case that what was prior to your action merely a reason-candidate is now a full-fledged reason for action.

But it is obvious that the power to actualize reasons is not sufficient to make for practical authority. You do not have authority over me in virtue of your ability to rig lotteries in my favor. Two further conditions must be met in order to capture the proper connection between one party's acts and another party's reasons for action.

The first of these two further conditions is that there must be an internal relation between the act that actualizes the reason and what the reason is a reason to do. Authority-bearing acts are content-bearing acts: they are speech-acts with propositional content. An authoritative act is always an act of one party telling another party to do something: A commands *that B ϕ*. When authoritative acts are performed, the reason for action that is actualized is a reason to perform the act that is the content of the command. If A has authority over B with respect to B's ϕ-ing, then if A commands B to ϕ, then A actualizes a reason for B to ϕ. This is part of the explanation for your ability to rig lotteries failing to install you as a practical authority over me. Rigging lottery mechanisms is not a speech-act; it does not bear content. Any capacity to alter my or others' reasons for action through the exercise of that lottery-rigging ability thus cannot of itself make you a practical authority over me.

The second further condition is that the agent's performing the act that actualizes the reason must be part of the reason-candidate that thereby becomes a reason. When an authority A issues a dictate that B ϕ, B typically cites the fact that A told B to ϕ as at least part of the resultant reason to ϕ that B has. It is *not* merely that A's dictating that B ϕ initiates a causal sequence which has at its outcome the full actualization of one or another of B's reason-candidates. This suggests that in genuine authority relationships, those under authority have a number of reason-candidates that include the authority's telling them to perform certain actions and that are fully actual save for the authority's telling them to perform those actions. The way that authorities actualize reasons through commanding is by actualizing a state of affairs that is the only nonactual element of a reason-candidate. I shall refer to this way of actualizing a reason as *constitutively actualizing* a reason.

For one to be authoritative over another, one's dictates must actualize reasons for the other; the content of the dictate and what the dictate actualizes a reason to do must be identical; and the dictates must be themselves parts of the reasons for action actualized. Let us put this analysis of practical authority to work in a simple illustration. Imagine a small political community bound by an explicit social contract, in which members have entered into a fair agreement to obey, with respect to public matters, the decisions of a representative body. According to the account offered so far, what makes it the case that this representative body is authoritative over members of that community is the following. Each of the members A of that political community has a stock of reason-candidates to ϕ of roughly the following form: *A's being bound to fulfill A's promises, A's having promised to obey the representative body in public matters, X's being a public matter, and the representative body's having told A, with respect to X, to ϕ.* Each member A has, for example, both of the following reason-candidates: *A's being bound to fulfill A's promises, A's having promised to obey the representative body in public matters, its being a public matter which side of the road to drive on, and the representative body's having told A, with respect to which side of the road to drive on, to drive on the left* and *A's being bound to fulfill A's promises, A's having promised to obey the representative body in public matters, its being a public matter which side of the road to drive on, and the representative body's having told A, with respect to which side of the road to drive on, to drive on the right.* What makes it the case that the representative body is authoritative over which side of the road members of the community drive on is that all of the elements of these reason-candidates, aside from the giving of the dictate laying down which side of the road to drive on, obtain; and so simply by issuing the dictate 'members of this community are to drive on the right (or the left) side of the road' the representative body can actualize a reason for all citizens to drive on the right (or the left) side of the road, a reason that includes the representative body's having issued that dictate.

Practical authorities constitutively actualize reasons for action by their commanding acts. Now, Raz says that the reasons for action at least partially constituted by authoritative dictates must be *protected* reasons: A's telling B to ϕ must be a first-order reason for B to ϕ and a second-order reason for B to disregard reasons not to ϕ (1979, p. 18). Authoritative reasons are not, according to Raz, simply first-order reasons that are to be thrown into the flow of one's deliberation along with the other first-order reasons for or against an action that one might have. Rather, in virtue of consisting in part of second-order reasons, they hold a privileged place, not only counting in favor of one course of action but also rendering reasons to perform incompatible actions irrelevant from the point of view of deliberation. Now, Raz is right to hold that authoritative reasons must be privileged, but it is wrong to think that authoritative reasons must always exhibit the structure of protected reasons. It could be that a person's dictate to another is so strong a first-order reason that all other first-order reasons pale in comparison with it. Consider the following case from Nagel: when one is rushing one's spouse to the hospital because the spouse has a life-threatening injury, the fact that a much longer route to the hospital is more scenic is absolutely squashed by the strength of the reasons to take the fastest way to medical help (1970, p. 51, n. 1). Suppose that a party's dictates were constituents of first-order reasons of sufficient weight that they, like the reason to get medical help in comparison with the reason to take in the view along the way, absolutely squash any competing reasons that might be offered as justification for violating those dictates. It would be very peculiar to say, of a dictate that possessed this level of first-order strength, that it nevertheless is not an authoritative dictate because there is no second-order reason protecting the first-order reason. This first-order reason does not *need* protection. It can take care of itself. Surely what is relevant is the decisive role played in proper deliberation by such a dictate, and not the particular characteristics of the reason (first-order yet powerful, protected, etc.) that gives the dictate that role in proper deliberation.

I will say, instead, that the reasons for action at least partially constituted by authoritative dictates are *decisive* ones. R is a decisive reason for A to ϕ just in case R is a reason that makes ϕ-ing *ultima facie* reasonable for A and not ϕ-ing *ultima facie* unreasonable for A. If one party is genuinely practically authoritative over another in a certain domain, then—in the absence of defeating conditions—that party's dictates provide that other with a decisive reason to perform the commanded act; in the absence of defeating conditions, the authoritative party's commands decisively determine what the other ought to do in that domain.

One might think that this attribution of decisiveness to authoritative reasons is a bit strong. But it does seem to be in keeping with the self-understanding of those who purport to wield practical authority. They take their dictates to determine, within a certain range, what those subject to them ought to do. That range is understood in terms of the scope of action over which they take themselves to be authoritative and in terms of the absence of those defeating conditions by which they take their capacity to generate authoritative reasons to be constrained. (When a state within a federal system lays down an authoritative dictate concerning how citizens of that state are to act, it takes itself to be acting within its power and to be operating in the absence of conflicting and superior statutes—for example, federal statutes—that would nullify its legislation.) So it is in keeping with the self-image of practical authorities that, within their limited domains, they generate decisive reasons in favor of some ways of acting to the exclusion of others. But I do not think that the privileging of *any particular sort* of decisive reason for action—protected reasons, extremely strong first-order reasons, or the like—is merited on the basis of the self-understanding of those that wield authority.

A is practically authoritative over B with respect to ϕ-ing if and only if A's telling B to ϕ constitutively actualizes a reason for A to ϕ such that if that reason is undefeated, then it will be decisive. Once it is noted that practical authority is a kind of control over reasons for action and that the species of control is constitutive, it becomes clear that certain sorts of relationship between an agent's dictates and another agent's reasons for action are, while in the neighborhood of practical authority, nonetheless not instances of it. Consider, for example, what Raz calls the recognitional conception of authority, on which commands merely reflect the preexistent order of reasons for action (1986, pp. 28–31). On this account, a successful exercise of authority is one on which a command for B to ϕ is issued only if B already has decisive reasons to ϕ. But this exhibits, as Raz notes, only a theoretical authority about practical matters, and not genuine practical authority: on this view, practical authority makes no difference to the reasons for action that agents have, and is thus at odds with the notion that authority is control of a certain sort over reasons for action. That another possesses theoretical authority over matters of one's practice does not give one further reasons for *action*, though it may well give one further reasons for *belief* about what reasons for action one has.

Neither does a merely causal relationship between dictates and reasons for action, however tight, make for authority. If you are a bully, and can bring down upon me or others unpleasant and undeserved consequences if I do not do what you tell me to do, you have a certain causal control over my reasons for action. You can associate unpleasant consequences with certain modes of behavior. But if you tell me to ϕ, and you will cause me or others to suffer if I do not ϕ, my reason for ϕ-ing is just that if I do not ϕ, then I or others will suffer, and suffering is bad. That you told me to ϕ is only a causal condition of the reason, assuming that you would not attach these negative consequences to not ϕ-ing if you had not told me to ϕ. (If those consequences were going to be present in any case, then your threat would be more like a passing along of information about the reasons for action that I already had yet of which I was not yet aware.) So neither theoretical authority about reasons for action nor merely causal control over reasons for action is sufficient for practical authority. One implication of these points, an implication that we will later consider at greater length, is that God's authority does not reside in God's having perfect knowledge of created rational beings' reasons for action (3.2) or in God's having causal control over created rational beings' reasons for action (3.4). In arguing for divine authority, one must argue that God has *constitutive* control over reasons for action, not merely knowledge of those reasons or power to determine which reasons are actual.

1.2 THESES ABOUT DIVINE AUTHORITY

We are now in a position to formulate the theses about divine authority that will be our main concern in this essay. Our main concern is to ask to what extent it is true that God has authority over created rational beings. Given the analysis of authority in the previous section, this is equivalent to asking to what extent it is true that God's commands that created rational beings ϕ constitutively actualize decisive reasons for created rational beings to ϕ.

The natural answer, as I noted in the Introduction, is the answer that magnifies the divine authority as far as is coherent. Motivated by the desire to magnify divine authority as far as possible, we might say that divine authority is over *all* created rational beings, ranges over *all* of the actions that created rational beings might perform, and is insusceptible to *any* defeating conditions. But the latter two of these are in need of qualification for the sake of plausibility and coherence, and the first is subject to more than one understanding.

First, it is not entirely clear whether it is plausible to hold that divine authority ranges over all actions that a created rational being might perform. Some might want to say that there are some actions that are so inherently unreasonable that they could not be made reasonable options, even by divine commands. One might think that, say, torturing an innocent child is an act of this sort. Whether there are indeed acts of this sort is not an issue that looms large in this book—though I need on some occasions to advert to it (see, for example, 3.4)—so I would prefer a description of the acts that fall within the range of divine authority that remains neutral on this issue. I will interpret the familiar, robust view on divine authority to hold, then, that divine authority ranges over all of those acts that, in the context of the addressed agent's situation, are not otherwise excluded by moral or more generally practical considerations.[3]

Second, it is unclear to what extent we want to say that, on the common view of divine authority, God's commands are subject to defeating conditions that prevent them from constituting decisive reasons for action. One might want to say that no such conditions are allowable. This seems a bit too strong, though: it appears plausible enough to allow the possibility that God could *revoke* one of God's commands, and this revocation would count as a defeating condition that prevents a prior divine command from making an act rationally required. But it does seem plausible to ascribe to the traditional view the claim that there are no *external* defeating conditions, that is, that there are no defeating conditions on divine commands that do not proceed from God's own choices to cancel God's commands. On the traditional view of divine authority, there cannot be, for example, other authorities that can nullify the normative force of exercises of divine authority. I will take this 'no external defeaters' condition on divine authority for granted in the sequel: on the traditional view, God's commands constitute decisive reasons for action, and they are revocable only at God's pleasure.

Third, while it is clear that the traditional view of divine authority holds that God is authoritative over all created rational beings, it is unclear what modality that thesis is supposed to have. We can offer the following array of theses about divine authority, from the modally weakest to the modally strongest.

---

3. One could say that divine authority ranges over all acts but that running contrary to practical reasonableness constitutes a defeater that prevents divine commands from constituting decisive reasons to perform them. Since the decisiveness of the reason would be, ex hypothesi, invariably blocked by such defeaters, it seems plainer to simply allow that the range of divine authority might be restricted to potentially reasonable acts.

Strong. If *A* is a created rational being, then God has authority over *A*. (Or: If *A* is a created rational being and ϕ-ing is an action not otherwise excluded, then God's command that *A* ϕ constitutively actualizes a decisive reason for *A* to ϕ.)

Stronger. If *A* is a created rational being, then, necessarily, God has authority over *A*. (Or: If *A* is a created rational being and ϕ-ing is an action not otherwise excluded, then, necessarily God's command that *A* ϕ constitutively actualizes a decisive reason for *A* to ϕ.)

Strongest. Necessarily, if *A* is a created rational being, then God has authority over *A*. (Or: Necessarily, if *A* is a created rational being and ϕ-ing is an action not otherwise excluded, then God's command that *A* ϕ constitutively actualizes a decisive reason for *A* to ϕ.)

(I assume that *being a created rational being* is a property that created rational beings have essentially: if *A* is a created rational being, then necessarily, if *A* exists, then *A* is a created rational being. Only on this assumption can these theses be straightforwardly ranked by modal strength.) Suppose that the only created rational beings that exist are humans and angels. The Strong thesis holds that every human and every angel that actually exists is under divine authority. The Stronger thesis holds that every human and every angel that actually exists is necessarily under divine authority: those humans and those angels could not exist without being under divine authority; every human and every angel exemplifies essentially the property *being under God's authority*. And the Strongest thesis holds that any rational being that God could create would, if created, be under divine authority.

The bulk of this work is devoted to a critical examination of the Strong, Stronger, and Strongest authority theses; and the majority of this critical attention is paid to the Strongest of these authority theses. (When I speak simply of 'the divine authority thesis' or 'the authority thesis,' it will be the Strongest version of this thesis that I have in mind.) My main reason for focusing my attention on the Strongest version is that most people are inclined to believe the Strong and Stronger theses just because they are inclined to believe the Strongest thesis: it is commonly supposed that any being that would count as God would have the sort of authority ascribed to God by the Strongest of the authority theses. For such persons, the rejection of the Strongest thesis would likely bring in its wake not simply a retreat to the Stronger or the Strong thesis but a withholding of belief in, or a rejection of, the Stronger and the Strong theses, for they take as the warrant for their affirming the weaker two of the three theses the fact that the Strongest is true. So it seems to me justified to devote what might seem to be a disproportionately high share of attention to the Strongest of these claims about divine authority.

In the next chapter I argue for the truth of a thesis about a connection between God's commands and created rational beings' reasons for action that approaches, but falls short of, the Strongest authority thesis. The establishment of this thesis—I call it the 'compliance thesis'—places pressure on one who wants to affirm some version or other of the authority thesis: given the existence of a well-established claim that is so close to, yet which is not quite, the Strongest authority thesis, is there reason to go beyond the affirmation of that thesis to the affirmation of the authority thesis? I turn to that question in Chapters 3 through 6. It is only after I offer grounds for rejecting all of the strong authority theses that I consider reasons to affirm a more modest account of divine authority. This more modest account of divine authority is presented in Chapter 7.

CHAPTER 2

The Compliance Thesis

According to the Strongest authority thesis, necessarily, if A is a created rational being, then God's commanding A to ϕ constitutively actualizes a decisive reason for A to ϕ (1.2; for the idea of 'constitutively actualizing' a reason, see 1.1). Consider, by contrast, the Strongest *compliance thesis*: necessarily, if A is a created rational being, then if God commands A to ϕ, then there are decisive reasons for A to ϕ.

The authority thesis entails the compliance thesis, but not vice versa. (When I say simply 'authority thesis' or 'compliance thesis,' I am referring to the Strongest versions of these theses.) That the entailment runs in only one direction is the result of the compliance thesis's remaining silent on the character of the decisive reason to act in accordance with God's command: all that it says is that one commanded by God to ϕ has some reason, or set of reasons, that decisively renders ϕ-ing reasonable for A, and not ϕ-ing unreasonable for A. But it does not say what that reason is: in particular, it does not say that the reason is, or is partly constituted by, God's command. So far as the compliance thesis goes, the reason *could* implicate God's command in this way; or it could be a prudential reason, or an independent moral reason, or any combination of these reasons. Practical authority exists, though, only when one party's dictate at least partly constitutes for another a reason for action, and is not merely a signal of the presence of reasons for action (1.1). And so the authority thesis is distinct from, and not entailed by, the compliance thesis.

The compliance thesis plays a key role in my argument against the authority thesis. What makes the compliance thesis an effective means to call the authority thesis into question is, paradoxically enough, its nearness to the authority thesis. We can, I shall argue, provide a compelling argument for the truth of the compliance thesis. Because the compliance thesis is quite similar to the authority thesis, differing from it only on account of its silence on the type of reasons for action that mandate compliance with God's commands, it is capable of doing the work that one might think the authority thesis must do. But the authority thesis contrasts unfavorably with the compliance thesis with respect to the warrant for affirming it: we lack anything like a similarly compelling argument for the authority thesis. And I say that if the compliance thesis does the work that the authority thesis is supposed to do yet does not suffer from the drawbacks of the authority thesis, then we have reason to affirm the compliance thesis while declining to affirm the authority thesis.

2.2 THE ARGUMENT FOR THE COMPLIANCE THESIS

According to the compliance thesis, it is a necessary truth that if God commands a rational creature to ϕ, then that creature has decisive reasons to ϕ. My argument for this thesis relies on four premises, two of which concern speech-acts and two of which concern the divine nature.

(1) Necessarily, if in performing speech-act SA one necessarily implies that p, then if one sincerely performs SA, then one believes that p [premise].
(2) Necessarily, one who performs an act of commanding A to ϕ necessarily implies that there are decisive reasons for A to ϕ [premise].
(3) Necessarily, if God sincerely commands A to ϕ, then God believes that there are decisive reasons for A to ϕ [(1), (2)].
(4) Necessarily, if God commands A to ϕ, then God sincerely commands A to ϕ [premise].

(5) Necessarily, if God commands A to ϕ, then God believes that there are decisive reasons for A to ϕ [(3), (4)].

(6) Necessarily, if God believes that p, then p [premise].

(7) Necessarily, if God commands A to ϕ, then there are decisive reasons for A to ϕ [(5), (6)].

I will say nothing more about (6) other than this: it is as entrenched as a thesis of perfect-being theology can be. It expresses no more than that God is inerrant, and even those theists who would want to endorse some nonstandard specification of God's omniscience—that, for example, God does not know some propositions about the future, for the future is in some ways "open" (see, for example, Hasker 1989, p. 186)—would want to say, at least, that with respect to those propositions that God does believe, God makes no errors. But the claims about speech-acts and the claim that God is necessarily sincere all require some discussion.

2.3 IMPLICATIONS OF SPEECH-ACTS AND SINCERITY

Premise (1) requires little defense, I think, once I make clear what I mean for one who performs a speech-act necessarily to *imply* some proposition and what I mean for one to be *sincere* in performing a speech-act. (In using the term 'implication' here I follow Austin, who helpfully contrasts this notion with that of entailment and that of presupposition [1962, pp. 47–52].)

First, with respect to implication: when I say that one who performs a certain speech-act implies that p, I am *not* saying that if one performs that speech-act, then it is true that p. For example: I would say that the one who asserts that p implies that p; yet one may assert that p and just be wrong about it. Nor do I mean that if one performs that speech-act, then one believes that p. Again, one can assert that p, but be lying, and it is an essential condition of a lie that what one asserts is believed by him or her to be false. Rather, if it is an implication of a speech-act that p, then the speaker that performs that speech-act puts him- or herself forward as accepting that the proposition is true: in asserting that p, one puts him- or herself forward as believing that p.

Now, speech-acts can possess their implications in modally stronger or weaker ways. Some implications are *merely conversational*: in holding that a given speech-act has a conversational implication that p, we need be saying no more than that one who performs that speech-act *normally* puts him- or herself forward as believing that p. In cases of mere conversational implication, it is possible for the speaker explicitly to cancel that implication without thereby undercutting the successful performance of that speech-act. (See Grice 1989b, p. 39.) To take a common example: in standard contexts it is conversationally implied by the asking of a question that the speaker does not know the answer to the question; that is, one who asks a question normally puts him- or herself forward as taking him- or herself to be unaware of the question's answer. But one might make it clear that one takes him- or herself to know the answer—perhaps he or she wishes to test the listener—without undercutting the successful asking of the question.

Some implications of speech-acts are, however, *necessary*: not only does one who performs a speech-act of a given type normally put him- or herself forward as believing some proposition, but this implication cannot be canceled without undercutting the successful performance of the speech-act. One who performs a speech-act with the necessary implication that p is committed to affirming that p and committed to refraining from denying that p; and to perform a speech-act with the necessary implication that p and then to deny that p is to perform a paradoxical act, to do something that is performatively inconsistent. Thus, one can test whether a proposition is a necessary implication of a given class of speech-acts by seeing whether it is invariably paradoxical to perform that speech-act while denying that proposition. (See also Alston 1999, pp. 77–78.) If, for example, one asserts that p, one cannot cancel the implication that one believes that p without rendering the assertive act paradoxical, unintelligible.

A necessary implication of a speech-act is a proposition that one performing that speech-act invariably puts him- or herself forward as believing. For one to be *sincere*, though, is just for one to be what he or she puts him- or herself forward as being, and so to be sincere in performing a speech-act is, in part, just to believe what one puts him- or herself forward as believing. So: if a given speech-act necessarily implies that p, then anyone who sincerely performs that speech-act must take it to be true that p. (See also Austin 1962, p. 50.)

I think that the meanings of 'implication' and 'sincerity' that I employ in holding that (1) is analytic are recognizable and at least fairly standard. But this is not an issue on which I would put any weight. For the sake of the argument we may, if we wish, treat the meanings of 'implication' and 'sincerity' that I employ here as stipulated. The only effect of this admission of stipulation would be to focus our attention on premises (2) and (4), premises that make substantive claims about the implications of commanding (in the case of [2]) and about God's necessary sincerity (in the case of [4]). And this is, it seems, where our attention should be.

2.4 COMMANDS AND DECISIVE REASONS FOR ACTION

According to (2), when a commander issues a command, he or she implies that the commanded has decisive reasons to perform the act commanded. This premise is subject to more than one interpretation: it might be interpreted as the claim that the commander implies that there are decisive reasons for compliance independent of the command, or it might be interpreted as the claim that the commander implies that once the command is given there are decisive reasons for the commanded to comply, reasons that may or may not be thus independent. It is the latter of these interpretations that I have in mind. If the former were the case, then it would be paradoxical for anyone to attempt to make a nonrequired act required by virtue of his or her authority: for the compliance thesis thus interpreted entails that every commander puts him- or herself forward as believing that there are independent reasons to do as he or she commands. Only the latter thesis is at all plausible. According to it, when one issues a command, one puts him- or herself forward as holding that upon being given the command, the commanded has decisive reasons for compliance: *either* reasons that are independent of that commanding act *or* reasons that are generated by the commanding act *or* a combination of independent reasons and reasons generated by the command.

Premise (2) carries the heaviest burden in this argument, establishing the crucial link between commands and decisive reasons for action. We may first consider why we should think that one giving a command implies that the commanded has any reasons for action at all, and then turn to the question of why the reasons for action implied must be decisive ones.

Commanding that p is an attempt to do something with language, to realize some state of affairs by the performance of a speech-act. It is, in particular, a *directive* act: the aim internal to a commanding act is that of having the addressee or addressees carry out the action represented in the proposition that is the object of the command. Now, in performing a directive act one invariably implies that the party addressed has a reason to perform the directed act. (Note well: to say that in performing a directive act one invariably implies that the party addressed has a reason to perform the directed act is not to affirm that if one directs another to ϕ, then that other has a reason to ϕ. It is only to say that if one directs another to ϕ, then one puts him- or herself forward as believing that the other has a reason to ϕ; see 2.3.) Why should we think this true? After all, directive acts are of all sorts—requests, supplications, pleas, demands, orders, etc. Why think that common to all of these is the implication that the addressee of a directive act has reason to act in the manner directed?

Most straightforwardly, it is clear from the paradox test that whenever a directive act is performed the speaker is committed to the proposition that there are such reasons. It is paradoxical for a speaker to perform a directive act yet to deny that the addressee has any reason to go along. Imagine being given the following demand to do push-ups: "There is nothing in the world, and nothing that I could say, that would give you any reason at all to do ten push-ups. Now: do ten push-ups!" The paradox is apparent. Even the most mild of directives, cases of mere requests, include this implication of reasons for compliance. When one says "I know that you have no reason to do me a favor, but please grant this request," what is meant is that apart from the fact of the request, the addressee has no reason to perform the requested action; the reason for action implied in such contexts of utterance is only the directive itself.

Even if the paradox test confirms this connection between the performance of directive acts and the commitment to the existence of reasons for the addressees to comply, one might take this to be merely a constituent feature of particular species of directive act and not a necessary feature of directive acts generally. But even apart from the fact that a survey of types of directive acts seems to indicate that there is an implied connection between directive acts and reasons for compliance, there is a plausible argument that there is a necessary connection between directive speech-acts and this implication. In communicative acts there is the presumption that one is speaking as a rational being to other rational beings. In assertive acts, this presumption is manifested in its being implied that one's assertions are justified: "I assert that p, but have no justification for holding it to be true that p" is performatively inconsistent. (I use 'justification' here just as convenient shorthand for 'positive epistemic status'; I do not mean by this remark to make any substantive claims about justification as a privileged sort of epistemic status with respect to assertion.) In performing a directive act, one is trying not simply to move the other to act, but instead intending that the other act on the propositional content of the directive. But rational beings can guide their conduct by the propositional contents of directives only if there is reason to do so. And so all directives imply the existence of reasons for compliance, and the inconsistency involved in denying such reasons while giving such a directive shows that the giver of directives is committed to the existence of these reasons.

In performing directive acts, and a fortiori commanding acts, one implies that there are reasons for the addressed party to act as directed: one who directs an agent to ϕ implies that the agent has reasons to ϕ. Now, this does not show that the reasons to whose existence one is committed by the giving of a command are decisive reasons. To show this we need to note a component of commanding acts that does not hold of all directive acts. Some directive acts allow the addressee the option of noncompliance; others do not allow such an option.[1] A request, for example, is a directive act that allows the one to whom the request is addressed to opt out of compliance. An order, by contrast, does not allow such an option. Note: the recognition that some directive acts permit the addressee to opt out does not involve in any way a withdrawal of the claim that directive acts imply reasons for action on the addressee's part. That a request allows the addressee to refuse does not mean that a requester can nonparadoxically allow that the one requested has no reason at all to comply with the request: all it allows is that one may act against that reason on this particular occasion.

Now, it is clear that in this broad division of directives, commanding acts clearly fall on the side of the nonoptional. One can nonparadoxically say "I request that you do this, though you may refrain if you choose"; one cannot nonparadoxically say "I command that you do this, though you may refrain if you choose." But in tandem the facts that (a) commanding acts display a nonoptionality feature and (b) all directive acts, including commanding acts, imply the existence of reasons for action on the part of those addressed give us grounds to believe that the reasons for action implied by commanding acts are of a specific sort, that is, decisive ones.

To see why this is so, consider a contrast between requests and com-

---

1. See the discussion of this feature of directive acts in Searle and Vanderveken 1985, pp. 198–199. I am indebted to this work for its lucid account of illocutionary acts, though I do not think that any of my claims are tied to the particulars of their view.

mands. In the case of requests, one can nonparadoxically request that another ϕ while allowing that the other not ϕ. How can this be squared with the implication that requested acts are backed by reasons? If the request does not imply that the reasons for action are decisive, then the recipient of a request might be reasonable in refusing the request as well as in granting it; and thus there is no paradox in one's requesting that another ϕ while allowing that the other not ϕ. But in the case of commands, one cannot nonparadoxically command that another ϕ while allowing that the other not ϕ. Unlike in the case of requests, then, commanding implies not only that there is reason to follow the course of action that is the content of the imperative but that courses of action incompatible with it are not adequately supported by reasons. One can nonparadoxically say "I hereby request that you ϕ, while recognizing that you can reasonably, all things considered, refrain from ϕ-ing"; one cannot nonparadoxically say "I hereby command that you ϕ, while recognizing that you can reasonably, all things considered, refrain from ϕ-ing." The reasons for action implied in all directive acts and the strength of the directive force partially constitutive of commanding acts together entail that in commanding one implies the existence of decisive reasons for compliance. (See also MacIntyre 1971b, p. 131.)

In commanding, one implies that the commanded has reason to comply; and in commanding, one implies that the reasons for compliance are decisive. Does the commander also imply that his or her command is at least partially constitutive of that decisive reason? It certainly is not a feature of every directive act that one who performs that act implies that the act is part of the reason for the addressee to perform the directed action. Advising someone to ϕ is a directive act, but advising does not seem at all to imply that the advising act is itself a reason to ϕ—as opposed to, say, a reason to *believe* that there are reasons to ϕ.[2] But there is a more plausible suggestion to be made, that is, that even if directive acts do not all imply that the act itself is or is part of a reason for compliance, *some* of them do, and among these are commanding acts. It might be thought that one cannot sincerely command

2. There may be special cases in which advice can count as a reason for action. If, for example, I solicit your advice, and you give it to me, I may have reason to do what you suggest even apart from the intrinsic merit of your proposal: it may be an expression of respect for you, whose views I have solicited, to do what you suggest. But this does not call into question the claim that advising does not of itself imply that the act of advising is a reason for another to act.

someone to perform an action unless one takes him- or herself to be an authority over the commanded. (See Searle and Vanderveken 1985, p. 201, and Alston 1999, p. 71.)

But sincere commanding requires not belief in one's authority but, at most, belief that one possesses some superiority relevant to the modification of reasons for action through the speech-act. A bully can, without possessing practical authority, give commands, in part because he or she has, through physical strength or other means of making others' lives unpleasant, the capacity to modify the reasons for action others have by his or her commands. The commander does not as such imply that he or she is an authority over the commanded.

Now, one might say that this is nevertheless an important result. If we know that the commander believes him- or herself to be modifying reasons for action in commanding, we know that the reasons for action necessitating compliance with God's commands are the result of God's modifying those reasons through commanding.[3] But I doubt that commanding requires even the position of superiority with respect to modifying reasons for action that I granted for the sake of argument in my initial response to the objection. The *superiority* part seems right, but satisfiable outside of the condition that the reasons for action be modified by the command. It would not be particularly paradoxical for a being with, say, perfect moral knowledge to issue commands to me about how to act in cases where morality dictates a unique solution, even while that being disclaims the status of a practical authority over me (as opposed to, say, the status of a theoretical authority about practical matters). Or, more mundanely, we sometimes command others not to do what is morally wrong in cases in which others either do not see that the act is morally wrong or are strongly tempted to perform the wrong act even in their awareness of its wrongness.

Here is an example of what I have in mind. If I am tempted to act badly, you may advise me not to, or suggest that I refrain from doing so, or argue that what I am up to is vicious. But you may eventually command me: "Don't; I'm telling you not to." This does suggest that you are taking up some sort of posture of superiority to me. But it may well be a posture of superiority with respect to recognizing what there is reason to do, not a posture of superiority with respect to modifying my reasons for action. One

---

3. I leave to the side here worries about overdetermination.

might think that since in this case your commanding aims at modifying how I act, you must, in commanding, aspire to modify what reasons for action I have. But your commanding can modify how I act on reasons other than by modifying what reasons for action I have. You can make those reasons more vivid to me. You can stir up my willpower. And so forth.

We might note that even if it *were* an implication of commanding acts that the reasons for action of the commanded be modified by the command, it would not follow that we should think that all of God's nonoptional directives have this feature: it could be that not all of God's nonoptional directives are commands. Call a 'demand' a nonoptional directive act that lacks this modification implication. There is nothing incoherent about the idea of a demand, and it could be that all, or some, of God's nonoptional directives are demands rather than commands. In the absence of an independent proof that God's nonoptional directives are commands, even the concession that commanding implies that the listener's reasons for action are modified by the command does nothing to move us closer to the claim that all of God's nonoptional directives imply that our reasons for action are modified by those directives.

2.5 GOD'S NECESSARY SINCERITY

One who commands another to ϕ implies that the other has decisive reasons to ϕ. If, then, one is sincere in issuing a command, one actually believes that there are decisive reasons for the commanded party to comply. So if one is always sincere in giving commands, one always believes there to be decisive reasons for the addressee to perform the acts that one has commanded; and if the sincere commander is also inerrant, then his or her beliefs in the existence of such decisive reasons are correct. As I noted earlier in this chapter (2.2), inerrancy is as firmly rooted among the divine perfections as a property can be, and I will offer no further defense of divine inerrancy here. But the claim that God is necessarily sincere is, while common enough, sometimes denied, either explicitly or by implication.[4] So I will provide two arguments for God's necessary sincerity: one moral, one epistemological.

Begin with the moral argument. Lying, and other insincere communica-

---

4. One example of committing oneself to divine insincerity is a common response to the story of God's command that Abraham sacrifice Isaac, that is, that God was *merely testing* Abraham. This looks to me like the claim that God was giving an insincere command. I discuss this case later in this section.

tive acts, are prima facie deeply morally evil. Consider the lie, the paradigm of insincerity in communication. One thing that is bad about lying is that lying is characteristically intended to deceive, that is, to cause another to believe something that is false; and it is bad to have false views. What is *especially* evil about lying is that it is not merely intended to cause false belief, but also that the false belief is produced in a particularly objectionable way.[5] Lies are betrayals, acts of treachery. (I owe this understanding of the wrongfulness of lying to MacIntyre 1995 and Garcia 1998.) Why is this?

For *A* to lie to *B* is for *A* to assert something to *B* that *A* believes to be false with the intention to deceive *B*. Assertions count as lies, as I understand them, only if they are addressed to the parties who are the targets of the intentional deception. This is a real qualification because it is clearly possible for one to make a false assertion that is intended to deceive another but that is not addressed to the party whom one wishes to deceive. Suppose, for example, that I am in my office with a student, having a conversation with her; there is a student listening outside my closed door, who does not believe that I know that he is there, though in fact I am aware of his presence. I assert something false—say, that a colleague has done something scandalous—with the intention of deceiving both of them. I have clearly lied to the student in my office; but I do not think that I have lied to the student outside my office. I do not doubt that I have wronged the student outside my office by attempting to produce in him a false belief. But lies are told to those whom one is addressing; and I am not addressing the student outside my door, even though I know that he is there and intend that he hear my words.

One morally relevant difference between the wrong that I do to the student in my office and the wrong that I do to the student outside my office—a difference that makes what I do to the student inside worse than what I do to the student outside—is that I have, through interacting conversationally with the student inside, *invited* her to believe that I am communicating what I in fact believe, *invited* her to trust in the veracity of my words. Meanwhile, I am acting in a way that is contrary to that invited trust. The student outside my office is tricked by the fact that people, even college professors, usually tell the truth. But I have not invited him to heed my words, have not

---

5. My earlier treatment of the evil of lying ignores this feature of lies, much to its detriment. See Murphy 1996; an abbreviated version of this account appears in Murphy 2001a, pp. 234–236.

through my assertion assured him that what I say I take to be the truth. That is why I say that lies, because they essentially involve this sort of duplicity, are betrayals. Since treachery is morally repugnant, and lying is treachery, lying is the sort of act that one has extraordinarily strong reasons not to perform.

Now, one might say that even if it is true that lying is characteristically an act of betrayal, and thus an act that one has strong reasons not to perform, that does not mean that a morally good being would never perform such an act. One might note the near-consensus, both inside and outside of academic moral philosophy, that lying is in some cases morally permissible. The most problematic cases for those that hold that lying is exceptionlessly prohibited are cases of forced communication, cases in which one is forced to answer an evildoer's questions. (Donagan 1977, which is generally strict on lying, takes this to be the only exception to the rule that one may not lie to mature adults who are of sound mind; see pp. 88–90.) In such cases, one might say, either the invitation to trust that is characteristically present in assertion is absent (so that the lie is not an act of betrayal), or the betrayal, though present, is (because of the forced nature of the relationship) morally justifiable.

While I have my doubts about the merits of these responses, it is pretty clear that even if they constituted successful defenses of some lies by us finite rational beings, they would not constitute successful accounts of why we should believe that a morally perfect being like God would tell lies. What makes us think that we humans might be free to lie in such cases is that we often lack the ready practical intelligence to think of a nondeceptive plan to respond to the coercive threat or the ability to carry out such plans that come to mind. But these human infirmities are not divine infirmities, and thus God is never forced by anyone to say anything; God's communication is entirely free. We could not plausibly say, of a divine lie, that God was forced to perform that act. So the most troubling worries for those that assert an absolute moral prohibition on lying are not relevant with respect to God, and cannot be employed to show that God may have adequate reason to lie.

One might offer instead an a fortiori argument for the possible rightness of divine insincerity. It is sometimes argued against absolute moral prohibitions on lying that since there are other, generally harmful forms of conduct that we take to be morally justifiable in some cases, and the harms produced by such conduct are typically worse than the harm produced by lying, it would be unreasonable to declare lying exceptionlessly prohibited. So, one might say, if there is an exception to the rule that lethal force should not be inflicted on others in cases in which lethal force is the only way to prevent evildoers from doing grave harm to innocents, surely there is a fortiori an exception to the rule that lies should not be told in cases in which lying is the only way to prevent evildoers from doing grave harm to innocents. Jerome Gellman writes, for example, that theists are committed to the view that God allows horrible suffering to occur. And surely the suffering that God allows to occur is worse for those that experience it than might be the false beliefs occasioned by divine lies. So, since we grant that God must have sufficiently good reasons to allow suffering, we should grant a fortiori that God may well have sufficiently good reasons to tell lies (Gellman 1997, pp. 97–98).

This sort of reasoning is flawed in two ways. The first is that, unless we are simply consequentialists about morality, we should distinguish (as Garcia does; see his 1998, pp. 529–530) between the *depth* of a moral wrong and the *size* of the harm that results. Even if we grant that the relevant harms to be compared are the particularly egregious harms to innocent sufferers allowed by God and the harms of false belief occasioned by divine lies, it is a relevant difference that in the latter case the harm results because a believer trusted God, responded to the invitation to accept God's word. It is not only a harm that God aimed at rather than simply allowed; it is a harm that occurs contrary to the assurance present in each act of assertion that this particular harm is not taking place. (Imagine how much worse the problem of evil would be if God had assured us that our present life would be free of suffering.) The second thing to note is that it is wrong to take the harm resultant from God's lie to be simply the false belief itself. The harm is also the rupture of community between God and human beings. It is very hard to believe, given the sacrificial love that God has displayed in trying to bring humans into community with God, that God would take the sort of treachery present in all lying to be an acceptable way to achieve divine purposes. (For a helpful account of the wrongfulness of lying that emphasizes the rupture of community involved, see Grisez 1993, pp. 390–412.)

But if lying is not the sort of act that God would perform, it seems also that God would lack adequate reason to perform any sort of insincere communicative act. The morally objectionable feature of the lie upon which I have focused is its character as a treacherous act, in which one is invited to hold a certain view as true but in which one is being told what is false. It is the duplicity that makes the lie vicious. But this duplicity is present in any insincere speech-act: one puts oneself forward as believing what one takes to be false; indeed, one invites the addressed party to believe what he or she takes to be false. If this sort of treachery is present in insincere speech-acts generally, we can conclude from the fact that God will not lie that God will not perform any insincere speech-act, including acts of insincere commanding. Gellman's claim that "God could reveal a falsehood or give a command He does not mean to have carried out" (1997, p. 98) is therefore false.

According to this first line of argument, speaking insincerely is an act of the sort that God would not perform. The second line of argument aims at a conclusion that is, while short of the claim that God would never communicate insincerely to a created rational being, nonetheless sufficient for my argumentative purpose: one is warranted in taking a divine speech-act to be sincere only if one takes all divine speech-acts to be sincere. This claim does not entail the premise as it is employed in the argument for the compliance thesis, for, first, the sincerity premise of the argument for the compliance thesis is nonepistemic in its formulation while the present proposition is epistemic; and, second, the sincerity premise affirms that all divine speech-acts are sincere while the present proposition affirms that we can be warranted in accepting the sincerity of all divine speech-acts *or* not accepting the sincerity of any of them. To be entirely precise, then, since I am offering an argument for this epistemic proposition, and in its 'all-or-nothing' form, I should recast the argument for the compliance thesis, and the compliance thesis itself, accordingly. In part to save words and avoid clutter, I will not recast the argument for the compliance thesis, but will instead reconfigure the audience to whom the argument for the compliance thesis is addressed: it is addressed to those who think that it is possible for one to be warranted in accepting the sincerity of a divine speech-act. (It is hard to see why one who did not accept this possibility would be interested in the question of divine authority.) Those who accept this claim should hold, I say, that all divine speech-acts are sincere.

This argument is an elaboration of an argument of Peter Geach's. Geach is a defender of a divine command conception of ethics, but he also thinks that there must be some moral knowledge available to humans apart from, and independent of, their knowledge of God's revealed will. An example of this moral knowledge is that lying is generally morally objectionable.

Now it is logically impossible that our knowledge that lying is bad should depend on revelation. For obviously a revelation from a deity whose 'goodness' did not include any objection to lying would be worthless; and indeed, so far from getting our knowledge that lying is bad from revelation, we may use this knowledge to test alleged revelations. . . . It is not that it would be too dreadful to believe in mendacious deities; a revelation destroys its own credibility if it is admitted to come from deities . . . who may lie. (Geach 1969b, pp. 119–120)

As an argument that humans are under a prima facie obligation not to lie, this argument is unsuccessful: it moves from the claim that there is something incoherent about accepting the revelation of a God who is thought to tell lies on occasion to the conclusion that humans must see themselves as therefore under a moral obligation not to tell lies. Yet that there is something self-defeating about God's being mendacious does not show that humans are under a prima facie obligation not to lie, especially if one accepts the sort of divine command view that Geach champions. God could be unwilling to lie yet place humans under no obligations at all with respect to lying.[6] But Geach's point that a revelation destroys its own credibility if it comes from deities who may lie is, I think, correct, at least when applied to a deity like God.

As I understand Geach's point, it is this. We may suppose that an agent's testimony that p is a reason for one to believe that $p;$ and, a fortiori, we may suppose that an omniscient agent's testimony that p is the case is a reason to believe that p. But if one allows the possibility that one of God's testimonies might be deceptive, that fact constitutes a defeater for the warrant-conferring character of God's testimony. (Following Pollock, mutatis mutandis, we may say that if its being true that p confers warrant on S's believing that q,

6. It may be claimed that other commands of God could not be followed if one lies, and therefore there is bound to be at least a derivative obligation not to lie. But I think that these derivative obligations are not really obligations at all. For suppose that God gives a command to ϕ that cannot be satisfied if we tell lies but does not command us not to tell lies. If we lie and therefore preclude our ϕ-ing, all of the wrongness comes from our not ϕ-ing and none of it from the lie. Our not ϕ-ing isn't made *worse* by its being brought about by a lie. Now, I say that there really is no moral obligation not to ϕ unless there are some cases in which ϕ-ing makes an otherwise permissible act wrongful or makes an otherwise wrongful act worse. But if lying were merely an act the performance of which precluded the satisfaction of our other moral obligations, then it would not make otherwise permissible acts wrongful or make wrongful acts worse.

then its being true that r is a defeater for this reason if and only if r is logically consistent with p and its being true that $p\&r$ does not confer warrant on S's believing that $q;$ see Pollock 1986, p. 38.) One who takes it to be possible for God's testimony to confer warrant on one's belief in the propositions to which God testifies, then, must reject the possibility that on any occasion God would engage in deception.

Why, though, would the mere possibility that God might perform a deceptive act constitute a defeater for the warrant-conferring status of divine testimony? The suggestion has an immediate air of implausibility about it: after all, we know full well that other human beings sometimes testify falsely, yet that they sometimes do so does not constitute a defeater for the warrant that would otherwise be conferred on our beliefs through their support by testimony. So why would we think that the concession that God might speak deceptively would undercut the warrant offered by divine testimony?

My argument that the concession that God might speak deceptively would undercut the warrant offered by divine testimony proceeds in two steps. In the first step, I argue that we would have no adequate basis to trust the assertions made to us by R. M. Hare's 'Archangel' (1981, p. 44); in the second step, I show that by allowing that God might perform deceptive speech-acts, we are committed to the view that God's assertions are in the same boat as the Archangel's. Since the Archangel's testimony that p provides us with no warrant in believing that p, neither would God's, on the assumption that God might communicate insincerely.

Hare's Archangel has the following three interesting features. (1) The Archangel lacks a characteristic feature of human action that I will call 'practical inertia.' An agent A has practical inertia toward ϕ-ing if and only if A tends to ϕ unless A recognizes that there is a reason not to ϕ. (A fortiori, it lacks the characteristic feature of human action that I will call 'strong practical inertia': A has strong practical inertia toward ϕ-ing if and only if A has practical inertia toward ϕ-ing and there are reasons not to ϕ of such a strength that even if A recognizes those reasons A still tends to ϕ.) The Archangel, lacking practical inertia, does not act when it does not judge that there is reason to do so. (2) The Archangel is perfectly rational, acting on the principle that there is most reason to act on: and that principle turns out to be act-utilitarianism. The Archangel, possessing perfect rationality, acts when it judges that there is reason to do so. (3) The Archangel has perfect knowledge by which it can forecast the results of

different available courses of action. This perfect knowledge is not only extensive in its detail; it is also temporally limitless. Thus the Archangel can
engage in perfect utilitarian calculation, and is a perfect act-utilitarian agent
(R. Hare 1981, pp. 44–45).

Now, I say that none of us has any basis to trust any of the Archangel's
assertions: the Archangel's telling one that p utterly fails to confer warrant
on one's believing that p. The reason that this is so is that certain back-
ground conditions are absent, conditions the obtaining of which is crucial
to the warrant-conferring character of testimony. It is commonly remarked
that humans display what I have called practical inertia, indeed strong practical inertia, toward truth-telling. We humans tend to tell the truth unless
we see a reason to the contrary, and indeed we tend to tell the truth unless
we see reasons to the contrary of sufficient strength. But the Archangel
lacks this quality: it is thus not true that ceteris paribus, the Archangel
speaks the truth. Further, while it is true that the lack of malevolence that
is a precondition for the trustworthiness of communication is realized, the
sort of benevolence that the Archangel practices is nearly as bad with respect to the trustworthiness of the communication. For the Archangel's
principle of action with respect to lying is: lie when, and only when, lying
maximizes preference-satisfaction. But given the immense knowledge that
the Archangel has—knowledge of all future outcomes of various proposals
for action—we limited humans have pretty much no idea when, and with
what frequency, the Archangel will take this principle to be satisfied and
when, and with what frequency, the Archangel will take it to be unsatisfied.
From our point of view, the Archangel is a black box out of which assertions emerge, and it is highly implausible that one could be warranted in
believing that p on the basis that such a black box produces the assertion
that p.

One might say: at least we should allow that we have *pragmatic* reasons to
believe the Archangel's assertions to us. For we can be confident that, since
it is a perfect act-utilitarian agent that is making this assertion, it will be for
the greatest good to believe it. But even this does not follow. That the
Archangel makes the assertion shows only that it maximizes utility for the
Archangel to *make* that assertion; it does not show that any particular response to it maximizes utility. Since the Archangel knows all future outcomes, the Archangel must think that the reaction that it will produce in us
by making a certain assertion is part of the outcome of the best action avail-

able to the Archangel. But we lack a basis for thinking that this reaction to the Archangel's assertion is one of belief.

I say, then, that even though, generally speaking, testimony that *p* provides a rational basis for believing that *p*, the Archangel's testimony that *p* does not provide a rational basis for believing that *p*. But if we allow that God might speak insincerely, then we thereby commit ourselves to the view that God's testimony provides as little warrant for our belief as that which is provided by the Archangel's testimony. For what is relevant in undercutting the warrant-conferring character of the Archangel's testimony is not that the Archangel is, specifically, an act-utilitarian, but that the Archangel has no inertia toward truth-telling and that the Archangel's decision-procedure concerning when to tell lies is such that we have absolutely no access to when it is satisfied and when it is not. Now, God is not inertial: it is not as if God has habits of action that God needs to overcome in order to act on the divine reason's judgment of what God should do; God, as a perfectly rational being, is perfectly reasons-responsive (see also Swinburne 1977, pp. 141–148). And if we grant that God might tell lies, then we are committed to holding that God acts on some such principle of the following form: it is within reason to tell lies under such-and-such circumstances. But, just as in the case of the Archangel, we have nothing like the complete knowledge that God has in acting on such principles; and, even worse, in the case of God we have only the most meager information about the circumstances under which God would take it to be permissible to lie. I am not saying that if God is ever willing to lie, then we must take God to be, like the Archangel, a utilitarian about lying. Rather, I am saying that if we open the door to God's employing the option of lying, we must view God's assertions as *in relevant respects* like the assertions of the Archangel—that is, we have no idea when and how often the circumstances in which God is willing to lie arise—and thus take them not to confer warrant on any beliefs that the propositions asserted are true.

Now, one might respond: there are real, live, human act-utilitarians; and it is not as if we cannot take their testimony as reasons for belief in the propositions that they assert. So surely the fact that the Archangel is an act-utilitarian, and that a lying God must be acting on some view relevantly similar to act-utilitarianism, would not be enough to defeat the warrant-conferring character of the Archangel's or God's testimony. The first point to be made in response is that we should not have much trust in sincere, self-aware, and committed act-utilitarians. If they are devoted act-utilitarians, then we must think of their decisions to assert the truth to us as subordinate to their calculations as to the overall consequences of so doing; and those who make decisions about truth-telling on the basis of such considerations are not much to be trusted.

The second point to be made is that to the meager extent that such persons' assertions are to be trusted, they are to be trusted because of features that humans do *not* share with God and the Archangel. Humans tend to truth-telling inertially; it is a fact about humans that we tend to tell the truth unless we find some reason to do otherwise. Indeed, this inertia is, in most cases, strong inertia: we have to be pulled out of tendency to truth-telling by more than negligible reasons. Further, even if act-utilitarians are willing to tell lies when it is for the overall good to do so, the limitedness of their knowledge of future consequences makes it relatively rare that they clearly see a promise of extra good in the telling of lies. The short-term negative effects of lying are clear to see—often such lies have detrimental effects on the deceived, and on the deceiver as well—but the benefits are in the vast run of cases far more contingent, remote, and hazy. So the fact that humans exhibit strong practical inertia toward truth-telling and that humans' knowledge of the consequences of their actions is extremely limited makes it possible in some cases to trust the assertions of even an act-utilitarian. But since these features of human act-utilitarians are not shared by God and the Archangel, the fact that the testimony of human act-utilitarians can confer warrant on belief does not give any grounds to suppose that the testimony of God and the Archangel can as well.

The epistemological argument offers an additional route to the necessary sincerity premise, or at least, a premise close enough to it to do the work that we want that premise to do. The epistemological argument proves the following conditional claim: if we are to hold ourselves warranted ever in believing that p on the basis of God's testimony that p, then we must take God to be completely truthful on all occasions on which God offers such testimony. We must take God's assertions to be absolutely truthful or have no trust in those assertions at all.[7] This argument is, of course, about God's assertive acts. But it also holds, I think, in cases of other speech-acts as well.

---

7. Gellman assumes that so long as God does not lie to us too often, trusting God would not be a problem. He does not consider an argument of the sort considered here, and he does not note difficulties about knowing how often God has in fact lied to us (1997, p. 98 n. 9).

The pattern of argument displayed in the case of assertive acts is: God's assertive acts provide a basis for those to believe what is asserted; but if God's assertive acts might be insincere, then this possibility rules out reasonable reliance on God's assertive acts with respect to one's beliefs. In the case of directive acts, a similar pattern is displayed: God's directive acts provide a basis by which an agent may guide his or her conduct; but if God's directive acts might be insincere, then this possibility rules out reasonable reliance on God's directive acts with respect to one's conduct. In order for one to understand him- or herself as being commanded to do something, one must understand the commander as intending him or her to act as the command directs. Sometimes humans give to each other insincere commands, but that does not preclude our taking commands as guides for our own conduct, for there is little reason to suppose, in most cases, that the command being given to one is insincere. But if it were allowed that God might give insincere commands, then, again, given our limited knowledge, it seems just as likely as not that on any given occasion God's commands are not sincere. And so if we are to take ourselves ever to warranted in believing some one of God's commands to be sincere, we must take all of God's commands to be sincere.

As far as I can tell, we have extremely strong reasons to think that God would find insincerity in communication to be morally repugnant and that we must, upon pain of having to give up all trust in divine communication, take all of God's communications to be sincere. It is important to note that to endorse this conclusion is not to endorse any particular view about how we determine, from an act of divine communication, what God has in fact asserted, or commanded.[8] I have offered here no theory of interpretation of divine speech-acts, no account of how we should move from our acknowledgment that a certain event or events occurred to the conclusion that God has performed a particular speech-act with a particular content. The conclusion about sincerity is, instead, that whatever speech-act we take God to have performed, we must take God to believe all of the necessary implications of that speech-act.

---

8. The thesis that God is necessarily sincere, in conjunction with divine inerrancy, does provide one interpretive guideline, though: if we know that it is false that p, then in determining what speech-act God is performing we can rule out any speech-act that has the necessary implication that p. (Of course, other evidence that God has indeed performed that speech-act may lead us to reconsider our view that it is false that p.)

In particular, I am not committed at all to the view that God's utterances should always be understood literally or strictly. When I say that God is necessarily sincere, I am not committed to, and would deny, the claim that God's communications must always be understood literally. For speaking figuratively is not ipso facto speaking insincerely. If I say "It is raining cats and dogs," this utterance does not show that I am either confused or insincere. I am using the expression figuratively, and so while I say "it is raining cats and dogs," I am not asserting that it is raining cats and dogs; rather, I am asserting that it is raining very heavily. And when I say that God is necessarily sincere, I am not committed to, and would deny, the claim that God's communications must always be understood strictly. For speaking loosely is not ipso facto speaking insincerely. If my daughter asks me at what temperature water freezes, and I say "water freezes at thirty-two degrees" (we are still a Fahrenheit household), what I say is, if interpreted strictly as being quantified universally under the modality of physical necessity, false, and I know it to be false. But my statement "water freezes at thirty-two degrees" is ambiguous: I could mean it strictly, or I could mean it more loosely, as what is usual or typical or good enough for our purposes. When I say in this context "water freezes at thirty-two degrees," I do not assert that necessarily, if water reaches thirty-two degrees, then it will freeze. The charge that I speak insincerely to my daughter in answering would therefore be baseless. Because one can speak figuratively or loosely without thereby speaking insincerely, it does not follow from the view that God is necessarily sincere that we should interpret God's utterances literally or strictly.[9] (See, for an account of the intelligibility and interpretation of divine communication, Wolterstorff 1995.)

In challenging the thesis that God is necessarily sincere, one cannot simply point to cases of divine utterances that, if understood literally or strictly, have false implications. One will have to produce an instance of a divine communication that, given the most plausible interpretation of that communication, has a false implication. I know of only one especially hard case: that of Abraham and Isaac (Genesis 22:1–18). God commands Abraham to

---

9. It thus does not follow from my view about divine sincerity that the fact that God uttered "Thou shalt not bear false witness" means that God commanded us to refrain, under all circumstances, from bearing false witness. We would need to ask whether the context of God's making this utterance, and other facts that we know about God, make a stricter or looser interpretation more plausible.

take Isaac to Moriah and make of him there a burnt offering. Abraham takes Isaac to Moriah, binds him, and lifts the knife to slay his son. Yet God sends an angel to tell Abraham not to harm the child. So if we affirm the substantial truth (or possible truth) of the story, and we interpret God's speech-act—as Abraham interpreted it—as a command to kill Isaac, there must be an error in the arguments for the conclusion that we should affirm the sincerity of all divine speech-acts. For it appears that God was not, after all, sincere in giving the initial command that Abraham slay Isaac.

Now, a response that one often hears with respect to the Abraham and Isaac case that there really is no trouble here, because God was simply testing Abraham. And it is obvious that the description of this event as a test is right, given the characterization of that event in the biblical narrative, for it is stated at the outset that what God was doing was testing Abraham. But the invocation of the fact that God was testing Abraham helps not at all with respect to questions about sincerity. For we do not test people generically, but set before them particular tests. And if the particular test that is set before someone concerns the following of a command—and surely it was a command that God gave Abraham; if Abraham had thought that God was not giving him a command, Abraham would have been confused about his situation—then we can raise the question of whether the command was a sincere one or not. If I test a student by commanding her to complete a proof for a proposition that I know to be false, I may learn all sorts of things about her ingenuity, about her ability to deal with stressful situations, and so forth. But to demand that she perform a task that I know that she cannot perform is to be duplicitous, to command insincerely, for commands invariably imply the possibility of compliance by the addressee. Now, one might say: surely to give insincere commands might be justified in light of the benefits that can be gained by testing people in this way. While I have my doubts about this, it is not the point at issue. So long as it is admitted that what is being given in such cases are insincere commands, we lack a solution to the difficulty that faces the view that I am defending, that is, the view that we must take God to be sincere on all occasions.

I cannot hope to dispel the puzzles surrounding the Abraham and Isaac case, but I do hope not to add any more to the books. So the question is whether we can square the claims about God's necessary sincerity with a plausible view of what God intended with respect to Abraham and Isaac. As I see it, there are at least two difficulties in squaring God's necessary sincerity with the Abraham and Isaac case. The first is that in any commanding act the commander implies that he or she intends the commanded to carry out the required act: but it seems that God did not intend that Isaac be killed. The second is that in any commanding act the commander implies that it is possible for the commanded act to be carried out: but it looks as though God meant to ensure that Abraham not kill Isaac.

First: with respect to God's alleged lack of intention that Isaac be killed. I think that without too much strain we can see that it is consistent with God's sincerity and the command that God gave to Abraham that God lacked the intention that Isaac be killed. It is, so far as I can tell, a general truth about intentions that one can intend that $A \phi B$ without intending that B be ϕ-ed by A. Here is an example. Bob and Doris had one child, Jane, during their marriage; but now Bob and Doris are divorced and entirely hostile to one another. They love Jane, though, and want her to be a good person. Because Bob and Doris believe that children should act respectfully toward their parents, Bob directs Jane to respect Doris, and Doris directs Jane to respect Bob. But, nonetheless, Bob and Doris can't stand each other, and do not wish each other well: Bob doesn't want Doris to be a person who is respected by her child, and Doris doesn't want Bob to be a person who is respected by his child. It seems to me that Doris can intend that Jane respect Bob without intending that Bob be respected by Jane, and Bob can intend that Jane respect Doris without intending that Doris be respected by Jane.

If there is a temptation to suppose that one cannot intend that $A \phi B$ without intending that B be ϕ-ed by A, it is likely that the source is that view that what one intends is a state of affairs, and the state of affairs A's ϕ-ing B is indistinguishable, even conceptually, from B's being ϕ-ed by A. But if we want to say that these states of affairs are one and the same, then we will need some other device to pick out what is intended in them—say, *aspects* of these states of affairs. For, even if *Jane's respecting Doris* and *Doris's being respected by Jane* are allowed to be identical, clearly Bob is interested in different things with respect to that state of affairs. And so even on this supposition of identity Bob's will is thus differently inclined toward distinct aspects of this state of affairs, and it is likely that whatever terms one uses to mark out this difference should suffice to explain how it is that God might intend *Abraham's killing Isaac* but not intend *Isaac's being killed by Abraham*.

One might claim that even if it is possible to intend that $A \phi B$ while failing to intend that B be ϕ-ed by A, that does not show that it can ever be *ra*-

tional to intend that $A \phi B$ while failing to intend that B be ϕ-ed by A. Since my argument requires that I say not only that God intends that Abraham kill Isaac yet that God does not intend that Isaac be killed by Abraham, but also that God's perfect rationality is thereby left intact, if it were true that such intentions were inevitably irrational my argument would be in danger. But the claim that it can never be rational to intend that $A \phi B$ while failing to intend that B be ϕ-ed by A is false. It is surely the rankest irrationality to intend incompatible things: to intend both that $A \phi B$ and that B not be ϕ-ed by A would be irrational, for one is thereby setting oneself to achieve the impossible. But what we have here is not two incompatible intentions, but an intention and the absence of an intention. Where, then, is the irrationality?

Consider, for example, someone who takes an interest in the aesthetic features of equiangular figures, and collects various paper cutouts that exhibit equiangularity.[10] She may intend to produce various three-sided equiangular cutouts without intending to produce various three-sided equilateral cutouts. After all, she is interested in the equality of the angles, not the equality of the lengths of the sides. Surely there is no irrationality here. There would be irrationality only if she set herself both to producing equiangular figures and to refraining from producing any equilateral figures. But she has not done that: she intends to produce the equiangular figures while failing to intend to produce the equilateral figures. If there is no necessary irrationality in this case, I cannot see why there must be in the case of God's intending that Abraham kill Isaac without intending that Isaac be killed by Abraham.

One might respond, though, that even if we grant all this it is nonetheless obvious that God did *not* intend for Abraham to kill Isaac. To kill is not just to perform an act that aims at a living thing's death, and thus has as its successful completion the death of that thing, but it is also to perform that act successfully. I do not kill you if I aim at taking your life yet do not take your life. So if God intended that Abraham kill Isaac, he intended not only that Abraham aim at taking Isaac's life—which Abraham surely did—but also that Abraham be successful. It seems, though, that God did not intend for Abraham to be successful in killing Isaac.

But it is not an implication of commanding acts that the commander in-

10. This example is indebted to the discussions in Sober 1982 and Jackson 1998, pp. 126–127.

tends their successful outcome, even if the verb employed in the command is characteristically a success term. There is nothing paradoxical (although the cases are admittedly unusual) about a commander directing an agent to ϕ while also voicing the hope, the wish, etc. that the agent fail to be successful in ϕ-ing. Consider a drill sergeant who routinely makes the recruits scrub the latrine floor and who, having taken a particular dislike to this group of recruits, hopes that they are unable to do the job adequately, thus justifying the infliction of discipline: "I order you to scrub that floor so hard it sparkles! Let me tell you, though: I hope I come back and find a spot, you worms!" The recruits find themselves in receipt of an unusual, though not paradoxical, combination of speech-acts; and there need not be the least *insincerity* in the drill sergeant, no matter what other desirable qualities he or she lacks. Presumably, the recruits knows what they have been directed to do, and have plenty of reason to do it. But it is also perfectly intelligible to the recruits why the drill sergeant hopes a spot will remain: so that he or she can use their failure as a pretext for severely punishing them.

It is not clear to me why commands are like this, why in a command that A ϕ the commander's intention need not extend beyond what A does in ϕ-ing to the state of affairs that is the result of a successful act of ϕ-ing. Perhaps it is just that commands work by directing conduct, and so the sincerity conditions on such speech-acts extend only to intentions concerning the conduct of the directed agent and not necessarily to the states of affairs realized through the directed agent's performances. At any rate, if I am right about this feature of commanding acts, then we can offer an interpretation of God's intentions with respect to Abraham's act: God intended that Abraham do everything that an agent does in an act of killing, but God did not want the act to achieve a successful end. God did not want Isaac killed by Abraham, though God wanted Abraham to do what was necessary to kill Isaac. Once Abraham did this, God sent the angel to tell Abraham that the killing of Isaac might be averted, for God's intention in ordering Abraham to do the killing had been satisfied.

One might say, though, that since God intended to prevent Abraham from killing Isaac, one of the sincerity conditions on commands had been violated. It is paradoxical to command one to ϕ while declaring that it is impossible for one to ϕ; and if it was impossible for Abraham to complete the mission, then God was in fact insincere in issuing the command. But we should reject the argument's assumption that it was impossible for Abraham successfully to kill Isaac, for we have no basis from the biblical story to think that Abraham could not have completed the act. God sent an angel to tell Abraham not to complete the act: God did not immobilize Abraham's arm, or put up a force field around Isaac, or turn the knife into a fluffy pillow at the moment of contact.[11] Abraham, so far as we know, could have ignored the angel, even supposing the angel to be a demon rather than God's messenger, on a mission to distract Abraham from what God asked of him.[12] (There are, of course, problems about divine foreknowledge and human freedom in the vicinity, but my point is only that the case of Abraham and Isaac presents no special problem. If there is an unsolvable problem with divine foreknowledge and freedom, then we can throw in the towel now, because God knew from eternity that God's commands would be disobeyed.)

We must take God's commands to be backed by decisive reasons for action; if God tells a rational creature to ϕ, then that rational creature has decisive reasons to ϕ. But this is short of the authority thesis. The compliance thesis tells us that we rational beings cannot act reasonably while failing to comply with God's dictates. But it does not tell us that God's dictates themselves constitute reasons for compliance. Do we have grounds to move beyond the compliance thesis to the authority thesis? The next several chapters are devoted to considering, and rejecting, grounds that might be put forward for this move.

---

11. All of these are possibilities raised by students in my introductory ethics classes to explain how Abraham could have aimed the knife at his son's chest while remaining a morally decent person: according to my students, Abraham could have gone through the motions of the command while trusting that God would miraculously prevent the killing act from being efficacious.

12. For a recent illuminating discussion of Abraham and Isaac that notes this point, see Goodman 1995, pp. 21–31.

CHAPTER 3

Divine Authority and
Divine Perfection

3.1 DIVINE AUTHORITY AND PERFECT-BEING THEOLOGY

It is tempting to suppose that any being worthy of the title 'God' must possess the authority ascribed to that being by the Strongest of the authority theses. This idea is readily translated into the language of perfect-being theology: since practical authority is a perfection, or a logical implication of a perfection, then God, as an absolutely perfect being, of necessity possesses practical authority over all rational beings. I will argue that appeals to several standardly ascribed divine perfections—omniscience (3.2), moral goodness (3.3), omnipotence (3.4)—do not provide us with reasons to affirm the authority thesis. I will also consider, and reject, the suggestion that practical authority is on its own a perfection, so that we should ascribe it to God even in the absence of an argument from some other standardly affirmed divine perfection (3.5). The conclusion to be drawn from this chapter is, then, that perfect-being theology does not offer an adequate basis to affirm the authority thesis.

3.2 OMNISCIENCE

That God is omniscient gives us no reason to suppose that God is a practical authority over rational beings. Since God is omniscient, God knows all truths. Now suppose that there is, in every situation of choice in which a created rational being might find itself, a fact of the matter about which available act there is decisive reason for that rational creature to perform. Even if this supposition were true, God's passing along that information to rational creatures could provide those rational creatures with nothing more than decisive reasons to *believe* that there is decisive reason to perform that act. But theoretical authority, even theoretical authority about matters of action, is not practical authority. That a being is a theoretical authority about what is to be done provides us with no basis for thinking that the being has *control* over what reasons for action there are, let alone *constitutive control* over what reasons for action there are. But such control over reasons for action is essential to authority (1.1).

Suppose, on the other hand, that there are some situations in which, abstracting from God's dictates concerning those situations, there is more than one course of action that a rational being might reasonably follow. In such cases, God's omniscience would give us no reason to suppose that God's dictates could actualize reasons to act in one of these ways rather than another. For God's omniscience guarantees only that God knows what reasons for action agents have; it does not guarantee that God will be able to add to that stock of reasons by issuing commands. (See also McLeod 2000, pp. 26–28.)

3.3 MORAL GOODNESS

Perhaps God's moral goodness, or God's moral goodness in conjunction with God's omniscience, lends credence to the notion that God is necessarily practically authoritative over all rational creatures. When we are less than certain about what to do, we often look to morally good people to guide us. God is absolutely morally good, and God's omniscience guarantees that God will be prone to no mistakes of fact that sometimes contaminate even the advice of eminently virtuous human agents. So if God tells us what to do, then we have decisive reason to do it.

Nothing in this argument need be denied, unless it is taken to establish God's practical authority over humans. For the conclusion of the argument is not the authority thesis, but the compliance thesis. The compliance thesis just is the claim that if God tells us to ϕ, then there are decisive reasons for us to ϕ, and this is the conclusion of the argument from perfect moral goodness. To return to the analogy with those virtuous fellow humans from whom we seek guidance: nothing like practical authority is found there; when we make decisions on the basis of a virtuous person's say-so, we treat that say-so as advice, perhaps even *conclusive* advice—for the virtuous person has better access to independently existing practical reasons. The reasons for action involved do not extend to the virtuous person's directives themselves.

Now, one might respond: to criticize the argument from the perfection of moral goodness this way presupposes our seeing it simply as a version of the argument from omniscience: the relevance of God's moral goodness is that God has an adequate grasp of our reasons for acting. But we might understand the argument from moral goodness in a slightly different way. The idea is that the relevance of God's moral goodness is not that it gives God perfect access to a realm of practical truth—access to this realm is given entirely by God's omniscience—but rather that it regulates God's commanding activity. A morally good being would not command agents to do what they lack adequate reason to do, for it would be disrespectful to them as rational beings to subject them to a demand that they do what they lack adequate reason to do. Such an argument would, if successful, establish a connection between God's commands and agents' reasons for action distinct from that which the argument from omniscience is able to provide.

We may grant the claims about moral goodness requiring respect for rational agents and about respect for rational agents requiring that one not command a rational agent to do what he or she lacks adequate reason to do. But such an argument does not prove the authority thesis. What it proves is, at most, the compliance thesis: that God's commands are always backed by decisive reasons for agents to comply with them. Since the compliance thesis does not entail the authority thesis, though (2.1), this appeal to God's moral goodness does not help to establish God's practical authority over rational beings.

3.4 OMNIPOTENCE

If we are looking for an argument for the authority thesis from a traditionally affirmed divine perfection, omnipotence appears to be the most promising candidate. Omniscience and moral goodness may ensure God's theoretical authority regarding practical matters, but they cannot deliver genuine practical authority. By contrast: if we think of practical authority, as Raz does, as a kind of normative power (1986, p. 24), it may seem that to deny practical authority to God is to deny God certain powers, which is tantamount to denying divine omnipotence. And, after all, it does seem that, if God lacks authority over some rational beings, then there are some acts that God cannot perform—such as acts of giving binding commands to those rational beings.

But unless we have some other ground for holding that the authority thesis is true, we can construct an argument that the *rejection* of the authority thesis is essential to preserving the doctrine of omnipotence that is just as plausible as the argument that the *affirmation* of the authority thesis is essential to preserving the doctrine of omnipotence. God's omnipotence includes, in part, God's freedom and capacity to create whatever it is broadly logically possible to create. But the *affirmation* of the authority thesis entails that either God lacks this creative freedom or it is broadly logically impossible to create a rational being such that God's commands would not be decisive reasons for action for it. Now, we would have to reject the former of these options to preserve God's omnipotence, holding instead that there could not be a rational being for whom God's commands are not decisive reasons for action. But the impossibility of such a being goes beyond what can be gathered from the concept of a *rational being*, and even beyond what can be gathered from the concept of a *created rational being*. It *seems* possible to describe coherently a rational being that is not subject to God's authority in this way.

Here is a brief attempt to describe coherently such a rational being. God, it seems, might have created beings for whom various different sorts of states of affairs were goods and thus reasons for action: life, knowledge, friendship, even being in harmony with God's will could be reasons for action for such beings. (Being in harmony with God's will would not, however, be for such a being a *decisive* reason for action.) God has arranged things, though, such that all of these beings are bound in reason to submit themselves to the divine will and thus make God authoritative over them. Such beings would be unreasonable to fail to place themselves under divine authority, but would nonetheless not be under divine authority until they submitted themselves to God's rule.[1] Why would God create rational beings directed toward divine authority by reason but not naturally under it? Perhaps there is a great good in free and reasonable submission to divine authority, a good that could not be realized in a world in which God is naturally authoritative over all rational beings. Here is an analogy: in marriage one has special reasons to heed another's wishes that one does not have with respect to the population at large; and (at least according to the faith to which I belong) God has displayed a pretty clear view about the goodness of our entering a condition where we have such reasons for action with respect to particular others. But the others with respect to whom we have such reasons for action are not given by nature. These special relationships are, rather, results of decisions, with respect to which we can decide well or badly, followed by commitments, which commitments generate reasons for action. If there is a good involved in the making of a choice to commit oneself to a particular other person in marriage, perhaps there is also a good in submitting oneself to God, in making oneself subject to divine authority. At any rate, we probably should not have too much confidence that a world of rational beings naturally subject to God is the only creative possibility.

Now, one might reply: even if the appeal to divine creative freedom raises questions about the authority thesis, this sort of criticism cannot be employed by one who would also defend the compliance thesis. For a similar argument might be leveled against the compliance thesis, that is, that it too endangers God's creative freedom. After all, if the compliance thesis is true, then God cannot create beings for whom God's commands are not always backed by decisive reasons. And this may seem to cause as much trouble for God's creative freedom as the notion that God cannot create beings for whom God's commands are not themselves decisive reasons for action.

But this is wrong. God's creative freedom is not endangered by the compliance thesis. God's creative freedom is not the capacity to realize any state of affairs, but the capacity to realize any state of affairs that is broadly logically possible to realize. But I think that it is not broadly logically possible for God to create rational beings with respect to whom the compliance thesis is false. The implication of commanding acts that they be backed by decisive reasons has its truth simply from its being the case that commands are

---

1. This is, in very rough outline, the conception of divine authority the truth of which I defend in Chapter 7.

speech-acts addressed to rational beings, where rational beings are, unsurprisingly, just beings that act on reasons. No constraint is suggested by the compliance thesis about the *kind*, the *content*, of the reasons involved. By contrast, the authority thesis specifies the content of the reasons for action that created rational beings must have. It is this mandate concerning content that does not follow from the concept of created rational beings, and so leaves open the question of why we should take that constraint to be a broadly logically necessary one.

There is no doubt that our intuitions about what is possible with respect to creation are not much to be relied upon, no matter how vivid (or pallid) the stories we can tell; and so my telling a quick story about a possible world in which a created rational being is not subject to divine authority should carry little weight in an argument for the genuine possibility of that state of affairs. (For a skeptical view of our capacities to judge reliably in modal matters outside of the range of our everyday lives—a view with which I have a great deal of sympathy—see van Inwagen 1995b, pp. 11–14, 19–21.) But the point of the story is not to establish that the authority thesis is false but only to make clear that we can summon up intuitions that suggest that divine omnipotence threatens the authority thesis just as easily as we can summon up intuitions that suggest that divine omnipotence underwrites the authority thesis. There is, I allow, a nonrigorous way to suggest that God's omnipotence implies the truth of the authority thesis; but there is also, I say, a nonrigorous way to suggest that God's omnipotence implies the falsity of the authority thesis. So far as these arguments go, with respect to the preservation of the omnipotence thesis, the defender and critic of the authority thesis are on an argumentative par.

One way to address the argument from omnipotence for the authority thesis is to construct an equally plausible argument from omnipotence against the authority thesis. But the rejection of any argumentative route from omnipotence to authority would be more convincing if we could identify precisely what precludes such an argumentative route. The key to seeing the error in the argument from omnipotence to divine authority is recognizing that the control that authorities have over reasons for action is *constitutive* control: authorities actualize reasons for action through actualizing a state of affairs that is a constituent of that reason (1.1). But it is a general truth that whether or not one can bring about an x that wholly or partially constitutes a y can depend on whether or not other states of affairs obtain, states of affairs that make possible x's constituting y's. For example: even God could not bring into existence a stop sign that is constituted by a red octagonal object in a world that does not also contain a certain social practice, that of treating red octagonal objects placed in certain locations as signals to stop. Again: even God could not bring into existence a heart that is constituted by a heart-shaped lump of tissue in a world that does not contain animals. God's inability to produce a stop sign in one world by producing a red octagonal object and God's inability to produce a heart in another world by producing a lump of heart-shaped tissue are only conditional—conditional on God's having chosen not to actualize (in one world) the social practice of treating red octagonal objects as signals to stop and (in the other world) the existence of animals. Similarly, it is plausible that states of affairs that are reason-candidates (1.1) have their status as such only given certain features of the world—features such as the nature of the created rational beings in those worlds, the forms of action available to those beings, the characteristics of those beings' environments, and so forth. So there is no basis to suppose that God's inability in some worlds to give a command that constitutively actualizes a reason for action for the beings in that world would be an instance of divine impotence; rather, God's inability to give a command that constitutes a reason for action in those worlds may well be conditional on God's having chosen to actualize a world with created rational beings of a certain kind, the structural features of whose action is of a specific variety, and whose environments exhibit a particular set of characteristics. The fact that, given certain choices about the world that God has made, God cannot give commands that constitutively actualize reasons for action no more threatens God's omnipotence than the fact that, given certain choices about the world that God has made, God cannot make brown cows that constitute stop signs.

The defender of the view that affirmation of the omnipotence thesis commits one to the affirmation of the authority thesis may hold, however, that affirmation of the omnipotence thesis and denial of the authority thesis nonetheless continue to seem paradoxical. It may be helpful, then, to look at more particular arguments from the omnipotence thesis to the authority thesis, in order to diagnose the failures of such arguments. These more particular arguments attempt to identify states of affairs that an omnipotent being would be able to bring about but which God could not bring about if the authority thesis were false.

Let us employ the following rough test[2] for omnipotence: a being B is omnipotent if and only if for every logically coherent state of affairs S such that S does not entail that S is not brought about by B, necessarily B's willing that S obtain brings about S's obtaining. Given this test for omnipotence, to show that the authority thesis follows from God's omnipotence it needs to be shown that the denial of the authority thesis commits one to the existence of a state of affairs that meets the following *omnipotence-threatening* conditions: that state of affairs (a) is logically coherent, (b) does not entail that God did not bring it about, and (c) were it willed by God, would fail to obtain. (These conditions follow, roughly, Swinburne 1977, p. 152.)

But is one who asserts the falsity of the authority thesis committed to the possibility of any state of affairs meeting these conditions? The authority thesis holds that, necessarily, for any rational being A, God's command that $A \phi$ constitutively actualizes a decisive reason for A to ϕ. To deny the authority thesis is to hold that it is possible that, for some rational being A, God's command that $A \phi$ would not constitutively actualize a decisive reason for A to ϕ; it is possible that the state of affairs *God's commands that $A \phi$ constitutively actualizing decisive reasons for A to ϕ*—call this state of affairs *DA*—fails to obtain. We may suppose, for the sake of argument, that *DA* is logically coherent, and that it does not entail that God did not bring it about. But we have no reason to suppose, from the denial of the authority thesis, that there is any world in which *DA* would fail to obtain even if God were to will that *DA* obtain. The denial of the authority thesis provides no support for the view that there is *any* possible world in which God wills that God's commands constitutively actualize decisive reasons for action for some rational being, yet in that world God's commands do not constitutively actualize decisive reasons for action for that rational being.

---

2. What is offered here is a rough test, not a definition, of omnipotence. It does not handle a perennial difficulty with conditional analyses of omnipotence: generally, that beings that are obviously not omnipotent but that necessarily will only what is within their limited powers turn out to count as omnipotent. (So stones, which necessarily will nothing, turn out to be omnipotent; and the fabled McEar, who has only the power to scratch his left ear but who serendipitously can will only to scratch his left ear, turns out to count as omnipotent as well. See La Croix 1977, p. 183, and Plantinga 1967, p. 170.) But this test will do for our purposes: none of my arguments for a lack of entailment from omnipotence to authority turns on the quirky features of this approximation, and I do not see that my arguments would be significantly altered if I were to adopt a test for omnipotence based on any of the other contending notions of omnipotence extant.

DA's possibly failing to obtain does not of itself call into question God's omnipotence. Since all that is involved in the denial of the authority thesis is the assertion that *DA* possibly fails to obtain, the omnipotence thesis could be threatened by the denial of the authority thesis only if *DA*'s failure to obtain entails that some other logically coherent state of affairs might fail to obtain even if God were to will its obtaining. In the absence of an exhibition of this entailment from *DA*'s failure to obtain to a state of affairs that meets omnipotence-threatening conditions (a) through (c), we have no reason to suppose that the rejection of the authority thesis commits one to a rejection of the omnipotence thesis.

That the burden of proof rests on those who would assert such an entailment is perfectly obvious. Suppose that you assert, and I agree with you, that the possible failure to obtain of *there being at least one red object* does not of itself call into question God's omnipotence, because the possibility of a world in which it does not obtain does not give any reason to suppose that there is a world with no red things in which God nevertheless wills that there be red things. It would be very strange if I went on to say, though, that the burden of proof was on you to show that the fact that the state of affairs *there being at least one red object* possibly fails to obtain does not entail the truth of some other proposition that calls into question God's omnipotence. Rather, if I want to appeal to the truth of *possibly, there are no red objects* to call into question God's omnipotence, the burden is on me to show that the truth of this proposition entails that there is a state of affairs that meets the omnipotence-threatening conditions.

Are there, then, any states of affairs to whose possibility one is committed by denying the authority thesis and which satisfy the omnipotence-threatening conditions? Perhaps one who denies the authority thesis is committed to God's being unable to actualize the following state of affairs: *God's commanding rational beings to ϕ in the absence of independent decisive reasons for them to ϕ*, where a reason for action is independent if and only if it is a reason not at least partially constituted by God's command. For suppose that in some possible world God does not have practical authority. Then in those worlds in which God lacks authority God could not give certain commands—that is, commands to perform acts for which there do not exist independent decisive reasons for adherence—since God cannot give commands to ϕ unless the agents would have decisive reasons to ϕ. Since there is in these worlds an act that God cannot perform—to wit, commanding rational beings to ϕ in the absence of independent decisive reasons for them to ϕ—then the rejection of the authority thesis would compromise the divine omnipotence.

A first point to be made is that this argument cannot be relied upon by those who would hold that the divine authority has any limits whatever. I have understood the divine authority thesis to include within its scope all actions not otherwise excluded by morality, or practical reasonableness generally (1.2). But one who allows that this is a real limitation—that there are some actions that are excluded in such a way that not even a divine command could provide decisive reason to perform them—cannot simultaneously affirm this argument from omnipotence to divine authority. For if we were to affirm any real limits to the scope of divine authority, then it would follow that there are at least some acts of commanding that God cannot perform, that is, commanding acts that are already excluded by practical reasonableness, because there could not be decisive reason to perform such actions. The only persons who could rely on this argument linking omnipotence and the divine authority thesis would be those who hold that God can, by commanding, actualize decisive reasons to perform any action whatsoever.

But there is a deeper reason why this challenge must be unsuccessful. The alleged difficulty concerning God's omnipotence that can be avoided only by affirming the authority thesis is not a problem that arises from the denial of that thesis; it is a perfectly general, and well-known, problem that is generated by the view that God's actions are subject to moral assessment and that God is perfectly morally good. If we take there to be morally better or worse options available to God in every possible world, then in every possible world there will be some actions that God necessarily does not perform because of God's optimal moral goodness. Granting for the sake of argument the possibility of rational beings not under divine authority, in worlds in which such beings exist God will have to decide whether to give such beings commands in the absence of independent reasons for them to comply; the fact that God cannot give them such commands is simply a result of God's perfect moral goodness, on account of which God never can give a command not adequately backed by reasons for compliance (2.5, 3.3).

There are a number of ways to deal with this tension between moral goodness and omnipotence, and I will not choose among them here. One can allow that God's power is limited by God's moral goodness, while holding that since this makes God no less worthy of worship the limitation is acceptable (Swinburne 1977, pp. 160–161; and also, in the same spirit, Geach 1973): one could say, then, that while God cannot give certain commands, God's inability to do so makes God no less worthy of worship, and so the denial of the authority thesis entails no unacceptable limitation of the divine power. One can deny the problem's assumption that the mere fact that there is a state of affairs that God necessarily never actualizes entails that God lacks the power to actualize that state of affairs: this maneuver involves the making of a strong distinction between the possession of a power and the possible obtaining of those conditions under which the power is exercised (see Morris 1987b and Wielenberg 2000, pp. 37–44). Or one can offer a revisionary conception of God's perfect moral goodness, on which it is not true that God is *necessarily* morally good but rather that God *in fact* has never acted, and *in fact* never will act, in a morally suboptimal way (see Howsepian 1991 and Guleserian 1985).

With respect to these alternative views, the first thing to note is that the argument from omnipotence to the authority thesis is blocked on any of these three solutions. We can say that *God's commanding rational beings to φ in the absence of independent decisive reasons for them to φ* cannot be actualized by God in some cases, but that this does not constitute a threat to the divine omnipotence, for it makes God no less worthy of worship that God cannot command beings to do what they lack decisive reason to do. Or we can say that while God has the power to actualize this state of affairs even in worlds in which there is incomplete divine authority, God necessarily never exercises that power in any such world. Or we can say that while there are possible worlds in which God does actualize that state of affairs in a world of incomplete divine authority, the actual world is one in which God has complete divine authority or one in which God does not actualize that state of affairs on account of God's free choice not to act in a morally suboptimal way. Now, I am not affirming that any of these three views is free from difficulties. My point is simply that the most reasonable attempts to deal with the tension between God's omnipotence and God's moral goodness all defuse this argument from omnipotence to the authority thesis. And so we can see that there is no *new* problem about omnipotence brought on by the denial of the authority thesis. The absence of divine authority would be just one more contingent fact, relevant to the moral assessment of God's actions, that would play a role in specifying what sorts of morally suboptimal acts

God could not or would not perform in the worlds in which that fact obtains.

In the line of argument just considered, the state of affairs that God is unable to actualize in incomplete-divine-authority worlds is an act of commanding. One might, however, argue that the state of affairs that God is unable to actualize in such worlds is that of giving reasons for action by way of commands. In those allegedly possible worlds in which some rational being is not under divine authority, there are instances in which God cannot constitutively actualize reasons for action for those beings by God's commands. Since there is an act of constitutively actualizing reasons for action that God cannot perform in such worlds, even if God were to will to actualize reasons in that way, God's power does not hold to the logical limit.

But this argument fails as well. For God to constitutively actualize a reason for action for a rational being by a divine command, two things must be the case: God must have given that being a command and God's commands must at least partially constitute reasons for action for that being. We have already seen that *God's giving rational beings commands not adequately backed by reasons* is, while a state of affairs whose actualization is precluded by God's moral goodness, not a state of affairs whose necessary failure to obtain threatens God's omnipotence—or, at the very least, not a state of affairs whose failure to obtain adds to the threat to God's omnipotence already posed by God's perfect moral goodness. And while in some worlds there are some beings for whom God's commands are not decisive reasons for action, it does not follow that God cannot give those beings decisive reasons for action by God's commands; only that in those worlds God has not willed it to be the case that God's commands partially constitute reasons for those beings. It is of course true that if there is a possible world α in which God does not possess complete practical authority over all rational beings, it follows that

necessarily, if α obtains, then there are logically coherent states of affairs (for example, *God's commands constitutively actualizing decisive reasons for action*), which states of affairs do not entail God's not actualizing them, that God does not actualize.

But it would be the least subtle of fallacies to draw the further conclusion from the denial of the authority thesis that if α obtains, then necessarily, there are some logically coherent states of affairs (for example, *God's commands constitutively actualizing decisive reasons for action*), which states of affairs do not entail God's not actualizing them, that God does not actualize.

If this were not fallacious, it would follow that God lacks the power to actualize *any* state of affairs that is not actual in α. Indeed, an argument of this form could be employed to show that God lacks the power to actualize any contingent state of affairs. Since this is obviously absurd, no argument of this form can be a successful argument from the omnipotence thesis to the authority thesis.

3.5 PRACTICAL AUTHORITY AS A DIVINE PERFECTION

If the authority thesis is an implication of perfect-being theology, it is not because an appeal to God's omniscience, omnipotence, or optimal moral goodness can show that God has practical authority over all rational beings in every possible world. Nor does it seem to me that any other attribute that is plausibly alleged to be a divine perfection—any other attribute distinct from authority itself, that is—offers an argumentative route to the authority thesis. If we are to hold, then, that the authority thesis is a truth of perfect-being theology, it must be that practical authority is itself among the divine perfections.

A prima facie case for authority as a divine perfection may be stated as follows. Just as there is a good in rational self-direction, to formulate, settle upon, and carry out plans of action concerning one's own conduct, there is a good in rational other-direction, to formulate, settle upon, and have carried out plans of action concerning the conduct of other rational beings. But one's plans of action cannot be carried out by other rational beings unless those other rational beings have sufficient reason to act on those plans. Other rational beings may act in accordance with those plans of action without having reason to do so, but the good of adherence to reasonably formulated plans of action is not that of simple conformity to a plan but rather that of acting on it, of taking it as one's guide. Nor is the good of adherence to reasonably formulated plans of action realized fully by one's acting on what one believes, wrongly, to be adequate reasons to act on the plan. Rather, the good of adherence to reasonably formulated plans of action involves acting on a correct assessment of the reasons for following a reasonably formulated plan. But for God to exhibit fully the perfection not only of self-direction but of direction of other rational agents, God must have the practical authority of the Strongest authority thesis: for only that practical authority would ensure that God exhibits the perfection of direction of rational agents to the fullest extent.

Now, one might attack this argument on the basis of its proving too much: the perfection involved in the fulfillment of reasonably formed plans of action would push not only to God's giving reasons for action to all rational agents by God's commands, but further to all rational agents' adhering to those plans. But to ensure this is contrary to the good involved, which concerns free adherence to plans of action. Hence God's making plans of action concerning free beings is bound to make God in some sense vulnerable to God's plans, at some level, being frustrated. Even if there is a clear sense in which all that God wills is actualized, there is also a clear sense in which not all that God wills is actualized: if there is sin, and sin is thought or deed contrary to divine will, we cannot deny that there is a sense of divine willing on which God does not get all that God wills.

Here is what we should grant to the argument. There is a deficiency involved in one making plans for rational beings to act on when those rational beings may act contrary to that plan while remaining within the limits of practical reasonableness. But this deficiency may be avoided if one never forms, and perhaps cannot ever form, a plan of action for rational beings to act on who lack decisive reasons to act on that plan. If, then, authority is a perfection, it must be due to the *range* of possible plans of action available for the making: if not all rational beings are subject to divine authority, there are some plans that God cannot make, for some of the rational beings mentioned in those plans would not have decisive reason to act on them. But the mere limitation on the range of possible plans of action cannot count as a deficiency in God. God chose to create nonrational animals; and God's plans of action cannot be for nonrational animals to act on. This limitation on God, if we may call it such, does not count as a divine deficiency; it is due to God's own choice, to God's decision to create nonrational along with rational animals. Now: if there are some possible *rational* beings whose reasons for action do not necessarily include reasons of divine authority, neither could this count as a limitation on God's plans of action. God's not being able to propose certain plans of action upon which such beings are to act is a result of the nature of that kind of being; it is no more than a reflection of God's choice to create beings not under divine authority rather than beings under divine authority.

The only plausible argument that I can think of for the notion that authority is a perfection appeals to the good of formulating and choosing plans of action and the good of those plans of action being implemented by rational beings as rational beings; and this argument is ultimately unsuccessful. But that the only plausible argument that I know of for the notion that authority is a divine perfection fails may be a result of my lack of argumentative imagination rather than the result of there being no good arguments for that notion. Further: one might claim simply that, *obviously*, it is better to be authoritative than not to be authoritative; it is just *intuitively clear* that practical authority is a perfection. If we think of two beings, arrayed in the traditional divine perfections, yet one of these beings possesses authority while the other lacks it, we may suppose that the latter being falls short with respect to perfection. Given the possibility of alternative arguments for practical authority as a divine perfection of which I am not aware, and the possibility that one might take it to be reasonable to rest on the brute intuition that necessary practical authority is a divine perfection, I want to offer two, more direct arguments against the idea that authority is among the divine perfections. The arguments against practical authority as a divine perfection that I have in mind both appeal to features that divine perfections exhibit but which practical authority does not exhibit.

The first of these arguments is the *argument from no intrinsic maximum*. It has two premises: first, that all divine perfections possess an intrinsic maximum; and second, that practical authority lacks an intrinsic maximum. The conclusion to be drawn is that practical authority is not a divine perfection.

Why must divine perfections have intrinsic maxima? (See also Broad 1953b, pp. 179–180, and Mann 1975, p. 151.) For A to be maximally great is for A to be maximally excellent in every possible world with respect to every perfection. For A to be maximally excellent in a world with respect to a perfection P is for A to exhibit P to an extent such that no being in any world exhibits P to a greater extent. Now, suppose P is a perfection that lacks an intrinsic maximum. Then for every extent n to which A exhibits P in some world, there exists another world in which a being exhibits P to an extent greater than n. It follows, then, that no being is maximally excellent with re-spect to P, and thus there is no maximally great being. If there is a maximally great being, then divine perfections must have intrinsic maxima.

But practical authority lacks an intrinsic maximum; there is no upper limit to how practically authoritative a being can be. The extent to which one is practically authoritative depends on two factors: first, on the number of rational beings over whom one is authoritative (call this the *person-scope* of authority); and second, on the scope of the actions with respect to which one's dictates constitute reasons for action (call this the *action-scope* of au-thority). Now, we may assume that the action-scope of practical authority possesses an upper limit: the extent to which one can be authoritative is, we may suppose, either just the range of all actions open to a rational agent in any given situation, or perhaps the range of all actions open to a rational agent in a given situation that are not otherwise excluded by practical rea-sonableness. But the person-scope of authority does not possess an intrinsic upper limit: there could always be one more rational being over whom one might be authoritative. (And even if there were some very interesting modal truth about the upper limit of the number of created rational beings, it is nonetheless pretty clear that that world isn't this world.)

Why can one define a plausible intrinsic maximum for, say, knowledge, power, and goodness, but not a plausible intrinsic maximum for practical au-thority? From a slightly different angle: is it not true that we can exhibit dif-ficulties for the notion that knowledge has an intrinsic maximum, or that power does, or that goodness does, just as easily as we can show that the no-tion that authority has an intrinsic maximum is plagued by such difficulties? No. For omniscience, omnipotence, and goodness are plausibly character-ized in terms of God's standing in a specific relationship to a certain class of necessary existents: the totality of this class of existents defines the intrinsic maximum with respect to which one can exhibit that property. The class of existents with respect to which God has knowledge is the class of proposi-tions: God knows the truth-value of every proposition. The class of exis-tents with respect to which God has power is the class of possible states of affairs (actually, some subclass of the class of possible states of affairs, to avoid the paradoxes of omnipotence): God has the power to actualize every mem-ber of that class. The class of existents with respect to which God is good is the class of truths of appropriate valuing: God wills and acts in accordance with those truths of appropriate valuing.[3] These classes can set an upper bound of knowledge, power, and goodness, and thus can define an intrinsic maximum for the respective perfections.

But: there is no such class of necessary existents to set the upper bound for divine authority. There is no set of created rational beings existing in all possible worlds such that God could have authority over all of those beings.[4] Divine authority thus lacks an intrinsic maximum, and as a result cannot be a divine perfection.

Now, one might say: look, it is not at all obvious that we can so straightforwardly define the traditional divine perfections with reference to sets of necessary existents that mark the upper bounds to the perfections in question. Some might think, for example, that singular propositions—*Socrates is mortal*, say—would not exist unless the objects that they are about existed. If that is the case, then a world that possesses one more individual than the actual world contains would also contain some extra propositions, propositions about that individual. Because there might always be one more individual being, it would immediately become unclear, on this view, how we are to define the intrinsic maximum of omniscience. But I do not think that the argument from no intrinsic maximum depends on my considering and offering decisive reasons against every conception of propositions, states of affairs, and truths of appropriate valuing that is on its own individually plausible and which would, if accepted, make trouble for our understanding of some divine perfection as possessing an intrinsic maximum. Rather, my only claim here is that we have ready to hand some plausible ways to interpret the traditional divine perfections; the defender of practical authority as a divine perfection cannot truly say that even if there is trouble seeing how practical

3. The phrase 'truths of appropriate valuing' is cumbersome, but I want to avoid both the suggestion that God's relation to evaluative truths is like our relation to imperatives and the suggestion that the range of God's goodness is restricted to any particular form of value.

4. What about the *haecceities* of created rational beings? If the individual essences of created rational beings are necessary existents, can't God's tremendous practical authority be defined relative to that set? The obvious immediate response is that authority is not over *haecceities*, but over *persons*: haecceities do not do anything, and a fortiori do not do anything for reasons, and thus are not the sort of thing over which one can be authoritative. Any definition of maximal practical authority by appeal to haecceities would have to be a conditionalized one: God is so related to every haecceity that if that haecceity were instantiated, then God would be authoritative over the being that instantiates that haecceity. I consider, and give reasons for rejecting, the conditionalized notion of the perfection of practical authority later in this section.

authority could have an intrinsic maximum, there is just as much trouble seeing how omniscience, omnipotence, and moral goodness could have intrinsic maxima. This just is not so. There is *some* plausibility to the notion that the entities by reference to which omniscience, omnipotence, and moral goodness can be understood form sets of necessary existents; there is *no* plausibility to the notion that the entities by reference to which maximal practical authority must be understood—that is, created rational beings— form sets of necessary existents.

Rather than look to another divine perfection as a 'partner in crime' with respect to the intrinsic maximum issue, one might instead try to rescue the notion that practical authority has an intrinsic maximum. One might either reject the method for measuring practical authority that I have offered or put forward a distinct understanding of that in which the perfection of practical authority consists in order to accomplish this task. But since both of these approaches can serve double duty, responding both to the argument from no intrinsic maximum and to my second argument against practical authority as a divine perfection, I will develop that second argument before I turn to these lines of response.

The second objection to the notion that authority is a divine perfection is the *argument from contingency*. As a first approximation, the argument is as follows. God is necessarily perfect, and so all divine perfections are possessed by God necessarily. But God's practical authority is had in relation to contingent objects, that is, created rational beings. If there had been no created rational beings, God would have lacked practical authority. Since God might have lacked practical authority, practical authority cannot be a divine perfection.

The notion that divine perfections cannot entail the existence of contingent objects cannot be denied by anyone who thinks that God is necessarily perfect but only contingently a creator. But one might claim that even if it is obviously true that any particular created, contingent object might have failed to exist, nevertheless God necessarily creates, and indeed necessarily creates rational beings. No created rational being exists in every possible world, but there is in every possible world some created rational being. And if this claim is true, then the fact that practical authority requires the existence of a created rational being does not call into question the notion that practical authority is a divine perfection.

While I find the view that God necessarily creates implausible, and a fortiori I find the view that God necessarily creates rational beings implausible, I do not want to make this argument against the status of practical authority as a divine perfection turn on this dispute. Rather, I want to say that even if it were true that God necessarily creates, the sort of argument that is offered for that thesis bars us from affirming that practical authority is among the divine perfections. For those that want to say that God necessarily creates base their argument on the divine perfection: a perfect being is the sort of thing that necessarily creates; God is not made to create by something external to the divine being but rather the plenitude of the divine perfection is self-diffusive and thus is certain to express itself in a creative act (see, for example, Kretzmann 1991, p. 223). But if this is the sort of argument that must be offered for the claim that God necessarily creates, we are precluded from holding that practical authority is among the divine perfections. For God's possessing practical authority over created rational beings is logically posterior to there being created rational beings; and there being created rational beings is logically posterior, given the self-diffusiveness argument for God's necessary creativity, to God's being absolutely perfect. God's possessing practical authority, then, is logically posterior to God's perfection, and so God's possessing practical authority cannot itself be among the divine perfections.

As I mentioned earlier, the arguments from no intrinsic maximum and contingency can be attacked both by attacking my method for measuring practical authority and by offering a reconception of the perfection of practical authority. First, with respect to the measurement issue: one might deny that if action-scope is held constant, the cardinality of the person-scope determines the extent of practical authority. One might put forward as a competing account the notion that the extent of practical authority is not an additive notion but a *completeness* notion—one has greater authority to the extent that one's authority over a given set of rational beings is more complete. This competing conception would indeed defuse the argument from no intrinsic maximum, for we could say that in every world God has authority over every rational being in that world, and so God has an equal, maximal amount of practical authority in every world. And this competing notion would defuse the argument from contingency, for one's authority over a set of created rational beings that is null would be complete, and thus maximal: it turns out, then, that the possession of maximal authority in a possible world does not depend on the existence of any contingent object.

The difficulty with this view, though, is that the completeness criterion is an extremely implausible one. First, isn't it obvious that a person who is practically authoritative over two out of two people has less practical authority than one who has practical authority over 4.99999 billion out of 5 billion people? And second, isn't it obvious that someone who has authority over all 5 billion people in a world has more authority than someone who has authority over no one at all? The completeness criterion also implies that the extent of one's authority varies with population changes: you can undergo a reduction in your overall level of authority as a result of population growth (you can lose your level of authority simply by the emergence of rational life on the other side of the universe) and you can achieve a higher overall level of authority as a result of population loss (you can increase your level of authority by killing those not under your authority).

It is more plausible to allow the criterion for measuring practical authority that I have offered but to reject the understanding of the perfection of practical authority upon which I have relied.[5] On the view that I have suggested, to say that A has the perfection of practical authority is to say that A is authoritative to such an extent that there is no being B in any possible world such that B has a greater amount of authority than A has. One might reject this understanding of the perfection of practical authority, offering in its place an account on which we *relativize* the notion of maximum practical authority to each possible world, and then define the perfection of practical authority in terms of this relativized notion. To say that A has the perfection of practical authority is, on this alternative view, to say that for every possible world w, A has the maximum practical authority possible in w.

The gist of the idea is clear enough, I hope, but there is a minor technical wrinkle to be ironed out. Following Plantinga (1974b, p. 44), I take possible worlds to be maximal states of affairs, and so there is a straightforward sense in which the maximum practical authority possible in w is just the amount of practical authority possessed by the most authoritative being in w. This would not yield the conclusion sought by the defender of the au-

---

5. One might also reject cross-world comparisons of practical authority. This strikes me as a scorched-earth policy. Why would one deny a comparison between a person's level of authority in one possible world and a person's level of authority in a different possible world, even if there is no created rational being that exists in both worlds? Why would that be any more plausible than the deeply implausible claim that the level of authority enjoyed by leaders of two distinct nations in the actual world cannot be compared?

thority thesis, that is, that since God possesses the perfection of practical authority, it follows that in every world God has practical authority over every created rational being in that world. (Unless, of course, we were to add the ad hoc premise that in each world the being with more authority than any other being in that world has authority over every created rational being in that world.) So we need to specify some other way of stating what the maximum practical authority possible in a world is. The maximum authority possible in a world is determined, on this view, by the same considerations to which we appealed in laying out the arguments from no intrinsic maximum: the number of created rational beings and the size of the range of actions not otherwise excluded for each of those agents. The maximum authority possible in a world is just: authority over all created rational beings in that world, and with respect to all actions not otherwise excluded for those agents.

This understanding of the perfection of practical authority would enable the defender of the authority thesis to avoid the arguments from no intrinsic maximum and contingency. Given this revised understanding, the perfection of practical authority possesses an intrinsic maximum: since the perfection of practical authority is defined in terms of the relation between a being and a world—that of having the most practical authority possible in that world—the intrinsic maximum of the perfection of divine authority is that of having maximum practical authority possible in a world in *every* world. And, further, it is clear that thus understood the perfection of practical authority does not presuppose the existence of any contingent objects. For this formulation of the perfection of practical authority does not require that any contingent object actually exist for God to possess that perfection: it requires only that *if* a created rational being should come into existence, *then* God will have complete practical authority over that created rational being.

But this revised view, though it offers the most promising available line of response to the arguments from no intrinsic maximum and contingency, is nonetheless unacceptable. It is an extremely unhappy implication of this position that God can have the perfection of practical authority without actually having any authority. At first glance, this is about as strange as holding that God can have the perfection of omniscience without having knowledge, or that God can have the perfection of omnipotence without having power. One would think that if there is something intrinsically nifty about

God's having practical authority, then the perfection of practical authority would involve God's necessarily having some of it. But the defender of the revised conception must embrace this unhappy implication in order to satisfy the desiderata that practical authority possesses an intrinsic maximum and that it does not presuppose the existence of contingent objects.

Here is a second unhappy implication, closely connected to the first. For any finite amount of practical authority that God possesses in a possible world, if that world were actual, we could say truly that God could have had a hundred times as much authority as God actually has, while asserting in the same breath that nevertheless God fully possesses the perfection of practical authority. Again, at first glance this is as peculiar as to say that God could have been a hundred times more knowledgeable than God in fact is, yet God is perfectly knowledgeable, and at first glance it is as peculiar as to say that God could have been a hundred times more powerful than God in fact is, yet God is perfectly powerful.

Further: What motivation is there to adopt the view that divine authority is a perfection once we embrace this revised conception of authority as a perfection? On the proposed view, God's actually having authority depends on the existence of created rational beings, though God's having the *perfection* of practical authority does not depend on the existence of created rational beings. If God chooses to create rational beings, then God will be actually authoritative. But if we are willing to say that God's being actually authoritative depends on God's choice to create rational beings, why would we not be willing to make the claim that God's being actually authoritative depends on God's choice to create rational beings *of a certain kind*? In either case, we are making God's authoritative character depend on nothing other than a divine choice. What motivation is there for holding that it is more in line with the divine perfection that the choice on which God's authority depends is a choice to create rational beings rather than a choice to create rational beings of a certain kind?

The defender of the revised view of divine authority as a perfection owes an answer to this question. Only if the dependence of actual divine authority on the former choice is more fitting to the divine perfection than the dependence of actual divine authority on the latter choice can one make a successful appeal to the perfection of divine authority on behalf of the authority thesis. But once God's status as actually authoritative depends on God's own choice, I don't see why it is more fitting to the divine perfection for God's authoritative character to depend on God's choice to create rational beings than for it to depend on God's choice to create rational beings under divine authority.

Here is another difficulty for the relativized account of the perfection of practical authority. On this account, that perfection consists in a kind of disposition. It consists in God's tending to be authoritative in the presence of created rational beings. But how are we to explain the presence of this tendency? Surely we do not want to understand it as simply a brute conditional, as a basic, inexplicable truth that if a created rational being comes into existence, then God will be authoritative over it. But if it is conceded that this conditional requires explanation, the idea that the perfection of practical authority consists in a disposition to be authoritative is in trouble.

For to what sort of facts can a proper explanation of this conditional authority appeal? The conditional concerns God's tendency to be related to created rational beings in a certain way. A satisfying explanation of this tendency must, then, appeal either to facts about God, or to facts about created rational beings, or facts about both. But we cannot appeal simply to facts about created rational beings to explain a divine perfection: how could any truth that is explained simply by facts about creatures be a truth that expresses a divine perfection?

Any explanation of this conditional will have to appeal, then, to facts about God. But what would these facts be? Again, consider two possibilities. Either the facts to which we appeal to explain this conditional include facts about divine perfections, or they do not. Consider the former: we will explain the conditional by appeal to facts about God that include facts about divine perfections. But we have seen that this is not an option. For any explanation from facts about the divine perfections to the truth of this conditional would be, in effect, an argument that some divine perfection or other (apart from practical authority), alone or together with facts that hold in all possible worlds, implies the truth of the authority thesis; but, as we have seen, there is no argument from the divine perfections (other than practical authority) to the authority thesis (3.2–3.4). Consider, then, the latter: we will explain the conditional by appeal to facts about God that do not include the divine perfections. But this proposal is unpromising. For, first, I doubt that there is any property essential to God God's instantiation of which is not itself a divine perfection or explained by a divine perfection. But only a property essential to God would be sufficient to explain an entailment between the existence of created rational beings and God's being authoritative over those beings. And, second, even if there were such properties, it strikes me as prima facie implausible that we could explain the presence of some perfection exhibited by God by appeal to some property exhibited by God that is not a divine perfection.[6]

Practical authority neither is itself a divine perfection nor is an implication of any other divine perfection. Perfect-being theology thus gives us no reason to suppose that God is necessarily practically authoritative. To deny that the authority thesis is an implication of perfect-being theology is not to deny, though, that there are a number of divine perfections in the vicinity of practical authority. God is omniscient, knowing all practical truths; and so God is a perfect theoretical authority about practical matters. God's omni-science and God's perfect moral goodness make God entirely worthy to hold practical authority. God's omniscience and perfect moral goodness ensure that God's exercise of whatever authority God does possess will be entirely excellent. God's omnipotence and creative freedom give God control over what kinds of rational beings there are, and thus over the content of the reasons for action that the rational beings in the actual world have. God's omnipotence, within the scope of the necessities of nature and the freedom of self-determining rational agents, controls the circumstances under which created agents act, and thus gives God power over the set of actions toward which agents' reasons will direct them. But, as we have seen with the compliance thesis, the nearness to practical authority established by all of these divine perfections in tandem does not make the idea that authority is a divine perfection easier to establish; it makes it rather harder. For we can see why one might, naturally but mistakenly, conclude from them that practical authority is an implication of perfect-being theology; yet we lack a plausible argument that practical authority is an implication of perfect-being theology.

6. Surely we can rig up some properties that God has that are not perfections yet whose presence entails divine perfections. God is either purple or perfect and God is not purple. I will allow that *being purple or perfect* and *being not purple* are not divine perfections; and of course God exemplifies them; and of course they entail God's being perfect. But no one would count God's being purple-or-perfect and God's not being purple as together *explaining* God's being perfect.

CHAPTER 4

Divine Command Metaethics and the Authority Thesis

4.1 MORAL PHILOSOPHY AS A ROUTE TO THE AUTHORITY THESIS
Authority is, paradigmatically, a relation between persons. Divine authority is a relation between God and created rational beings. To appeal to perfect-being theology as a route to the authority thesis, as we did in the previous chapter, is to approach the topic of divine authority from the side of the commanding God. As we have seen, though, considerations raised within perfect-being theology provide us with no basis to affirm that thesis. We can approach the question of divine authority from the other side of the relation, from the side of rational creatures, by considering whether there are good arguments within moral philosophy—I understand moral philosophy broadly as the systematic study of rational action—for the idea that God's commands are, for such beings, necessarily decisive reasons for action.

The moral view that bears most closely on the authority thesis, as I noted in the Introduction, is divine command theory. There I distinguished between metaethical and normative versions of divine command theory. The normative version is, as I understand it, simply the Strongest of the authority theses conjoined with two further claims: first, that the truth of the authority thesis does not result from the truth of any other practical principle; and second, that the authority thesis is that practical principle from whose truth the truth of all other moral principles results. We will consider the normative version of divine command theory in the next chapter (5.6). What will concern us in this chapter is whether a *metaethical* version of divine command theory—a divine command theory that aims to provide an analysis of, reduction of, supervenience basis for, or causal story about normative properties or states of affairs—can provide us with a viable route to the authority thesis.

4.2 DIVINE COMMAND METAETHICS (DCM)

Metaethical views aim to lay bare the nature of normative properties (for example, goodness, rightness, virtue) and states of affairs (for example, *peace on earth's being good, lying to the axe-murderer's being right,* and *Mother Teresa's being virtuous*). Such views attempt to lay bare the nature of such properties and states of affairs in a number of ways. *Conceptual analyses* aim to provide analyses of our normative concepts. *Reductions* aim to identify these normative properties or states of affairs with other properties or states of affairs. *Supervenience* views offer an account of those properties or states of affairs on which these normative properties or states of affairs supervene. *Causal* theories attempt to describe the causal origin of those properties (or those properties' exemplification) or those states of affairs (or those states' actualization). (One could also present an informative metaethical position *denying* the possibility of a correct view of one of these sorts: one might deny that such analyses are possible, or that any nontrivial identification is sensible, or that any informative characterization of the supervenience base is possible, or that there is any distinctive causal story about normative properties or states of affairs.) For a view to be a version of *divine command* metaethics—hereafter 'DCM'—is just for it to be an attempt to explicate normative properties or states of affairs in terms of God's commands.[1] So those versions of DCM that offer an analysis of normative concepts analyze those concepts in terms of what

---

1. Some divine command theorists prefer to appeal to God's will rather than to God's commands. Whether divine command theorists should appeal to divine command or divine will is treated at some length in Murphy 1998; for a response, see Adams 1999, pp. 258–262.

God has commanded; those that offer a reduction identify certain normative properties with the property of being commanded by God; and so forth.

Now, a variety of DCM might be more or less ambitious with respect to its attempt to explicate normative properties or states of affairs. A wide-ranging version of DCM might attempt to provide an account for all normative properties—*being good, being right, being a reason for, being virtuous, being valuable,* etc.—in terms of God's commands. A less wide-ranging view would focus on some proper subset of these normative concepts. One might hold, for example, that while notions of virtue are best understood in non-theistic ways, notions of rightness are best captured within a version of DCM. It would be tedious to run through all of the permutations that DCM might take and it is, fortunately, unnecessary. While I will need to survey all four of the different sorts of connection between divine commands and normative properties and states of affairs that the defender of DCM might endorse, we can, without prejudicing the issue, fix on a certain account of the range of normative properties and states of affairs with which DCM will be concerned. I will assume only that DCM wants to provide an account of those normative properties and states of affairs that are within what Robert Adams has called "the obligation family"—right, wrong, ought, duty, etc. (Adams 1987, p. 262, and 1999, pp. 250–252; see also Alston 1990, p. 324).

I assume here that DCM's aspirations are limited to offering an account of the obligation family because all we need to make a case in favor of a DCM argument for divine authority is a version of DCM that accounts for obligation. That ϕ-ing is obligatory, that one ought to ϕ, that one must ϕ, that it is right to ϕ—all of these are commonly thought to be overriding requirements, requirements of the sort that constitute decisive reasons for action.[2] Since we are interested in whether divine commands are connected to decisive reasons for action in a way that would account for God's status as a practical authority, it is sufficient for our purposes to ask whether God's commands should figure in a metaethics of obligation, and whether the way that God's commands would figure in such a metaethics would make for divine authority. My assumption that DCM is concerned only with obligation

---

2. Some deny that obligations are properly understood as overriding; see, for example, Simmons 1979, p. 9. I will assume that they are in order to present the most charitable case possible for the authority thesis on the basis of versions of DCM.

is not, then, because there are no defenders of DCM who offer more ambitious accounts—that is surely false (see, for example, P. Quinn 1978)—but because I do not want us to become distracted by objections that might apply to the more ambitious versions of DCM but not to this less ambitious version.

I will consider, then, four versions of DCM in order to assess their plausibility as bases for affirming the Strongest authority thesis. According to *analysis* DCM, the best conceptual analysis of 'it is obligatory for A to ϕ' is 'God has commanded A to ϕ.' On *reduction* DCM, the property *being obligatory* is identical to the property *being commanded by God*. On *supervenience* DCM, *its being obligatory for A to ϕ* has as its supervenience base *God's commanding A to ϕ*. On *causal* DCM, necessarily, if God commands A to ϕ, then that commanding act causes it to be obligatory for A to ϕ, and necessarily, it is obligatory for A to ϕ only if God's commanding A to ϕ has caused it to be obligatory for A to ϕ.

I will not go into the merits of any of these positions at this point. Since I am interested in them here only to the extent that they bear on the authority thesis, I will not consider the substantive merits of any of these views unless we can first see that there is a valid argument from that view to the authority thesis. But we may note here the initial case for taking all of these views seriously as potential routes to the authority thesis. The initial case for taking them seriously is that, given the assumption that obligations constitute decisive reasons for action, all of them imply the compliance thesis (2.1). Each of them entails that whenever God commands A to ϕ, it is obligatory for A to ϕ. If obligations constitute decisive reasons for action, then the truth of any one of these versions of DCM would support the compliance thesis. What we need to see, then, is whether any of these views takes the step beyond the compliance thesis to the authority thesis by implying that God's commands not only are always backed by decisive reasons for action but are themselves at least partially constitutive of such reasons.

4.3 CAUSAL AND SUPERVENIENCE DCM ARGUMENTS FOR THE AUTHORITY THESIS: INVALID

Neither the causal nor the supervenience versions of DCM support the authority thesis. Consider first the causal view. On this view, necessarily, if God commands A to ϕ, then that commanding act causes it to be obligatory for A to ϕ, and necessarily, it is obligatory for A to ϕ only if God's commanding A to ϕ has caused it to be obligatory for A to ϕ. God's commanding is, on this view, causally sufficient to bring about obligations, and obligations exist only as results of efficacious acts of divine commanding. (See, for an instance of such a view, P. Quinn 1979.) One might hold a weaker version of the causal view, on which some obligations exist even apart from acts of divine command. But even the initial, stronger version, on which the relationship between God's commands and the existence of obligations is incredibly tight, is not sufficient to make for authority.

Recall that an authority relationship exists between A and B only if A's commanding B to ϕ constitutively actualizes a decisive reason for B to ϕ. A's commanding B to ϕ constitutively actualizes a reason for B to ϕ only if A's commanding B to ϕ is itself part of the reason for B to ϕ that is actualized by A's command. But the presence of an invariant causal relationship between A's commanding B to ϕ and B's having a reason to ϕ would give us no grounds to suppose that A's commanding B to ϕ is part of the reason for B to ϕ. Causal DCM entails that God's commands actualize obligations, and causal DCM entails that all obligations are actualized by God's commands. But it does not entail that God's commands *constitutively* actualize such reasons.

Think about it this way. If God's commands to ϕ have merely causal power to bring about obligations to ϕ, then the resultant state of affairs that is the reason for action is *its being obligatory to ϕ*—a state of affairs that need not be in any way constituted by God's issuing any commands. If God were to issue a set of commands to rational beings, that they ϕ, that they ψ, etc., then it would be as if an intuitional morality—a morality of a plurality of fundamental duties—were in place. If such a morality were in force, then we would have a variety of reasons of the form 'it is obligatory to ϕ,' 'it is obligatory to ψ,' and so forth. But none of these reasons for action need include God's commanding anything. If one were providing an *etiological* account of (for example) why one should keep promises, that account would, on this version of DCM, have to include God's commanding that all beings keep their promises. But the complete *normative* account of why one ought to keep promises would be simply that it is obligatory to keep promises. It would be no more appropriate for one to talk about God's command in one's normative account of why one ought to keep promises than it would be for one to talk about the complete evolutionary history of the pain mechanism in providing a normative account of why one ought not to inflict needless pain.[3] No version of DCM that is built simply around God's causal role in actualizing reasons for action can generate an account of divine authority.

One might be prone to miss the fact that the causal view falls short of providing an account of divine authority just because the causal version of DCM and the normative version of divine command theory are easily confused (see also Murphy 1998, p. 11). On the normative version of divine command theory, the state of affairs *its being obligatory to obey God* obtains, and every specific type of act (distinct from obeying God) that one is obligated to perform is made obligatory by God's commanding the performance of acts of that type. Thus, on the normative view, it is straightforwardly true that God causes these specific acts to be obligatory by God's commands, and that the reasons for performing these acts are partly constituted by divine command: no formulation of any decisive reason to ϕ is complete unless that formulation includes that God commanded ϕ-ing. But on the metaethical causal view, there is no prior normative state of affairs *its being obligatory to obey God* that obtains; *all* states of affairs of the form *its being obligatory to ϕ* obtain only by God's commanding agents to ϕ. On the basis of such a metaethics alone, we have no basis to suppose that all of God's commands will constitutively actualize, rather than merely actualize, reasons for action.

Similarly, supervenience DCM fails to entail the constitutive relation between God's commands and obligation. A defender of supervenience DCM would surely say that the relationship between obligation and divine command is that which Kim labels "strong" supervenience. Let A and B each be sets of properties. A strongly supervenes on B if and only if

Necessarily, for any object x and any property F in A, if x has F, then there exists a property G in B such that x has G, and necessarily if any y has G, it has F. (Kim 1993b, p. 64)

If we specify that set A contains only the property *being obligatory*, that set B contains only the property *being commanded by God*, and that the range of rel-

3. A statement of what constitutes the choiceworthiness of refraining from inflicting needless pain that included a complete history of the evolution of the pain mechanism would not be compact (1.1), and thus would not be an accurate characterization of the reason not to inflict needless pain.

evant objects includes only act-types, then we have the claim made by the defender of supervenience DCM:

> Necessarily, for any act of ϕ-ing, if ϕ-ing is obligatory, then ϕ-ing is commanded by God, and necessarily if any act of ψ-ing is commanded by God, then it is obligatory.

(We are able to dispense with the "any property F in A" and "a property G in B" locutions that appear in the definition of strong supervenience because supervenience DCM, as I interpret it, holds that there is only one property in the supervenient family A and only one property in the supervenience base B.)[4] As is clear, the result of these substitutions is that supervenience DCM asserts simply the mutual entailment of divine commands and obligations: necessarily, an act of ϕ-ing is obligatory if and only if ϕ-ing is commanded by God.[5]

If the argument that causal DCM does not entail the authority thesis was successful, then a fortiori supervenience DCM does not entail the authority thesis. For causal DCM entails supervenience DCM: causal DCM is the thesis that obligations and divine commands are mutually entailed plus the thesis that there is a relationship of causal dependence between them. If causal DCM cannot support the authority thesis, then, neither can supervenience DCM. The fact that obligations exist only in the presence of divine commands, and always exist in the presence of divine commands, gives in itself

---

4. Just as causal DCM might affirm a weaker view, on which it is claimed only that divine commands are sufficient to produce obligations, one might present a weaker supervenience view, on which the supervenience base includes other properties in addition to divine command: it could be that obligations could be realized in a number of ways, including divine command. But, as I am about to show, supervenience DCM even in its full-blooded formulation fails to entail the authority thesis.

5. It is worth noting that this position could be affirmed by people who are not plausibly thought of as divine command theorists. One might hold both that it is a necessary truth whether a state of affairs is obligatory and that it is a necessary truth that God commands all and only those acts that are obligatory. It would be strange to count a certain sort of intuitionist about morality who also holds a strong view about the relationship between God's commanding acts and our necessary duties as a divine command metaethicist. This may simply count against Kim's particular account of supervenience, since it does little to capture the asymmetry of the supervenience relationship. Quinn, in elaborating upon his view that deontic properties depend on divine commands, considers the possibility that the relationship between divine command and obligation is one of supervenience, interpreting supervenience relationships to be asymmetrical. See P. Quinn 1999, p. 54.

no basis to think that God's commands themselves constitute reasons to perform any act. Neither relationships of supervenience nor those of causation are as such sufficiently intimate to make for divine authority.

4.4 THE ANALYSIS DCM ARGUMENT FOR THE AUTHORITY THESIS: VALID BUT UNSOUND

According to analysis DCM, the concept of *being obligatory* is identical to the concept *being commanded by God*. Because of this identity between concepts, A is obligated to ϕ if and only if God has commanded A to ϕ; indeed, *its being obligatory for A to ϕ* and *God's having commanded A to ϕ* are one and the same fact. Now suppose that obligations are, as I have so far assumed, decisive reasons for action. Given this supposition, the Strongest authority thesis follows from analysis DCM. The Strongest authority thesis is true if and only if God's commanding A to ϕ constitutively actualizes a decisive reason for A to ϕ (1.2). But analysis DCM entails that *God's commanding A to ϕ just is A's being obligated to ϕ*. So analysis DCM entails that when God commands A to ϕ, God makes it true that A has a decisive reason to ϕ, and that decisive reason just is God's commanding A to ϕ. Analysis DCM entails the authority thesis.

We can take Quinn's response as our entry into the discussion of this position (P. Quinn 1979). Quinn supposes that it is a criterion for the identity of propositions that if the proposition that p is identical to the proposition that q, then one who believes that p also believes that q. But an atheist certainly can believe that refraining from lying is obligatory without believing that refraining from lying is commanded by God. So the proposition that refraining from lying is obligatory cannot be the same proposition as the proposition that refraining from lying is commanded by God. But if analysis DCM were true, Quinn says, the proposition that refraining from lying is commanded by God and the proposition that refraining from lying is obligatory would be the same proposition. The defender of analysis DCM must go contrary to common usage in offering his or her analysis of 'obligatory,' with philosophically untoward results:

To be sure, nothing forces the divine command theorist [who defends analysis DCM] to stick to normal usage; he is free to use his sentences in a deviant fashion if he pleases. But if [analysis DCM] merely registers his decision to use 'Lying is ethically wrong' to express the proposition that lying is contrary to the commands of a loving God, then it is of little philosophical significance. Presumably [analysis DCM] would be philosophically important only if it were offered as an analysis of standard meaning rather than a stipulative definition. . . . I conclude that [versions of analysis DCM] are either incorrect or uninteresting specimens of trivial semantic conventionalism. (P. Quinn 1979, p. 308)

Now, the way that Quinn formulates this argument is unsatisfactory: it simply ignores the paradox of analysis. For example: while it is a massive understatement to say that there are difficulties involved in providing an adequate analysis of knowledge, it would be a bit too quick to say that because there might be one who judges an instance of belief to be justified and true without judging it to be an instance of knowledge, any defender of the analysis of knowledge as justified true belief would offer an incorrect analysis or an uninteresting specimen of trivial semantic conventionalism. It is true that it counts as evidence against the analysis of knowledge as justified true belief that one can take a case to be an instance of justified true belief while denying that it is an instance of knowledge. But it is conclusive evidence against that analysis only if we add that the person who so judges is an expert in the use of that concept, that is, that he or she masterfully employs it in judging and believing. If one understands the task of analyzing a particular concept as the task of making explicit and systematizing the platitudes implicitly held by those who masterfully employ that concept (see, for example, Smith 1994, pp. 36–39), then Quinn's argument as formulated is unsatisfactory. For the fact that one might believe that refraining from lying is obligatory while failing to believe that it is commanded by God would show no more than that the defender of analysis DCM is committed to the view that those who believe that refraining from lying is obligatory while not believing that refraining from lying is commanded by God lack mastery of the concept of obligation.

We can restate Quinn's objection, though, in a way that does not depend on a questionable conception of analysis. Quinn's point, mutatis mutandis, is just this. One can stipulate a concept of obligation the masterful use of which entails treating 'that act is obligatory' and 'that act is commanded by God' as synonymous. This would be an instance of trivial semantic conventionalism about 'obligation.' But if one were to defend the notion that our concept of obligation includes that of being commanded by God, one would be defending a very implausible claim indeed: for it seems just false to say that, as a class, atheists, who would not allow that an act is obligatory only if they allow that that act has been commanded by God, invariably fail to be masterful users of deontic concepts.

Quinn's argument assumes that the only options for analysis DCM are that it is put forward as an account of the meaning of 'obligation' for all speakers of English or that it is a stipulative definition. But in the best-developed version of analysis DCM, that suggested by Adams (1973), the analysis is put forward as the meaning of 'obligation' only within the moral discourse of those *within the Judeo-Christian tradition*. So, on Adams's (former)[6] view, analysis DCM is not supposed to capture the meaning of 'obligation' as used by all English speakers, nor is it merely stipulated: it captures the meaning of 'obligation' within a natural, distinctive community of moral discourse.

A key difficulty for this sort of position, and the difficulty with which Adams most struggled in light of the restriction of the analysis to the Judeo-Christian tradition of discourse, is the fact that those within the Judeo-Christian tradition seem able to engage with those outside that tradition in substantive argument about what is morally obligatory, but substantive argument about what is morally obligatory would be impossible between those inside and those outside that tradition if they lacked a common concept of obligation. Adams's ultimate suggestion was that what explains the possibility of substantive discourse is that, while different, the Judeo-Christian concept of wrongness and the atheist's concept of wrongness do share a number of features. The orthodox theist and the atheist have a great deal of agreement on those actions to which their respective concepts of wrongness apply, and they have similar attitudinal and volitional responses to what they affirm to be wrong. Thus, although the concepts are different, the patterns of inference and action into which these concepts enter is sufficiently similar that substantive moral discourse can proceed.

But this is, after all, a simulacrum of substantive moral discourse, not substantive moral discourse itself, and thus Adams does not extricate this position from this objection. First, we should note that the success of Adams's account of how discussion between those inside and those outside the

6. Adams's version of analysis DCM was superseded, however, by his defense of reduction DCM. We will consider the latter in the next section.

Judeo-Christian tradition is possible is dependent on analysis DCM being a covert doctrine, one not widely known. The form of interaction between those inside and those outside the tradition could not go on as it does if it were widely known that the parties have meant different things by a central term employed in their debates. When I say to you 'so-and-so is such-and-such,' I do so in the expectation that we share a common use of 'so-and-so' and 'such-and-such'; but analysis DCM would, if known, preclude this expectation with respect to discourse about the morally obligatory. So it appears that Adams's response accounts for the possibility of common discourse employing the terms 'wrong' and 'obligatory' only insofar as analysis DCM is not a public doctrine.

Second, even if the affirmation of common platitudes about obligation makes it possible for those inside and those outside the Judeo-Christian tradition to reason in common in truth-preserving ways about what is obligatory, Adams's response helps not a whit to rid analysis DCM of the most unhappy implication that no one inside the Judeo-Christian tradition and no one outside the Judeo-Christian tradition have ever disagreed when the former made a claim of the form 'ϕ-ing is not obligatory' and the latter made a claim of the form 'ϕ-ing is obligatory' (or vice versa), and no one inside the Judeo-Christian tradition and no one outside the Judeo-Christian tradition have ever agreed when both made claims of the form 'ϕ-ing is obligatory' or 'ϕ-ing is not obligatory.' It is certainly true that by making these claims, adherents of these different traditions can commit themselves to inconsistent propositions, or to one and the same proposition. But that does not relieve the burden on analysis DCM that every single instance of what appeared to be agreement on sentences employing the term 'obligatory' among those inside the Judeo-Christian tradition and those outside was only apparent, and every single instance of what appeared to be disagreement on sentences employing the term 'obligatory' among those inside the Judeo-Christian tradition and those outside was only apparent.

So Quinn's argument does not make contact with the best-defended version of analysis DCM extant, though the maneuver that Adams suggests in order to avoid criticisms like Quinn's leaves it vulnerable to other deep difficulties. Quinn's criticism has greater force when explicitly aimed at the thesis that *within* the moral discourse of the Judeo-Christian tradition 'wrong' is correctly analyzed as 'forbidden by God.' For defenders of analysis DCM will have to deal with Quinn's problem without recourse to a further subdividing of the discourse community, upon pain of falling into mere stipulative definition. What shall we say about those theists who have wondered whether God's commands cover every obligatory act, have wondered whether God might have seen fit not to command of us everything that is morally obligatory? What shall we say about those theists who have wondered whether there are acts that we should perform, not merely because God commanded them, but because they are otherwise morally obligatory? Do we say that by virtue of seriously considering these questions, they have shown themselves not to be masterful users of the concept of obligation? The coherent formulation of these questions by capable users of the concept requires a conceptual distinction between the obligatory and the commanded; the charge that these are, within the moral discourse of the Judeo-Christian tradition, incoherent ramblings would smack of persuasive definition. Or: consider questions about the authority thesis itself. To raise the authority thesis seriously is to assume a conceptual difference between the obligatory and that which is commanded by God. And again the defender of analysis DCM will have to say either that one who raises such questions is outside of the Judeo-Christian discourse community or deeply conceptually confused.

In his early paper defending analysis DCM, Adams makes much of the fact that believers characteristically move freely between claims of the form 'ϕ-ing is commanded by God' and 'ϕ-ing is obligatory' (Adams 1973, p. 89). But to support the claim that 'commanded by God' correctly analyzes 'obligatory' within Judeo-Christian discourse communities, evidence of the presence of this free movement would need to be supplemented with evidence about the responses of those within such communities to those who do not move freely between such claims—those who refuse to move between them or those who raise questions about that movement. Surely those within the Judeo-Christian community who would raise the question of whether God's commands should, after all, be obeyed would be treated as making claims that are tragically, horribly wrongheaded. Those who raise the question of whether everything that is obligatory is the object of a divine command may be treated with a bit more puzzlement, as (I hope!) less obviously wrongheaded, even if deeply suspicious in some way. But in looking at the responses of the community of discourse to those that raise such questions, it is highly implausible that the wrongheadedness of these questioners would be treated as *conceptual*. Their wrongheadedness would be treated, I would think, as a straightforwardly *moral* matter: by raising such questions, one shows that one's relationship to God has in some way gone awry. One does not need lessons in conceptual analysis but rather moral education or spiritual guidance. One needs to be told of God's greatness, or given reminders of God's sovereignty, or made more vividly aware of God's gracious benevolence; or one needs to spend more time praying and reading the Bible. This makes very implausible the idea that the *meaning* of 'obligation' when employed by a member of the Judeo-Christian discourse community is definable in terms of God's commands.

4.5 THE REDUCTION DCM ARGUMENT FOR THE AUTHORITY THESIS: VALID BUT UNSOUND

The most plausible route to the authority thesis from DCM is from reduction DCM. On this view, it is not claimed that the concept of obligation is to be analyzed in terms of God's commands. Rather, the idea is that the property instantiated in the world that best answers to the concept of the obligatory—a concept shared by those inside and outside traditional theistic communities—is the property *being commanded by God*.

This view shares the strength (for the purposes of this essay) of the analysis view: there is a valid argument from reduction DCM to the authority thesis. Reduction DCM claims that while the meaning of 'obligatory' is distinct from the meaning of 'commanded by God,' the property *being obligatory* just is the property *being commanded by God*. So when God actualizes the state of affairs *God's commanding A to φ,* God is also actualizing the state of affairs *its being obligatory for A to φ*. (An analogy: when by emptying the contents of a pitcher into a glass I actualize the state of affairs *there being water in this glass*, I also actualize the state of affairs *there being H_2O in this glass*.) If *its being obligatory for A to φ* is a decisive reason for A to φ, the identity view entails that God's commands are themselves decisive reasons for action, and thus that the authority thesis is true.

Further, reduction DCM avoids the most troublesome implications of analysis DCM. It allows that there is a common concept of obligation, so that those within the Judeo-Christian tradition and those outside it can engage in moral debate and can have substantive agreements and disagreements with each other, and so that those within the Judeo-Christian tradition can raise substantive questions about the relationship between God and obligation without ipso facto excluding themselves from the class of masterful users of the moral concepts of that community. Reduction DCM claims that while the concept of obligation is on its face nontheistic, the property that best fills the role assigned to it by that concept is a theistic one.

Adams's case for reduction DCM is as follows. Following the now standard Kripke–Putnam line, Adams affirms that there are necessary a posteriori truths, among which are included property identifications. He holds that the property of *being wrong* is identical to the property of *being contrary to the commands of (a loving) God* because the property *being contrary to the commands of (a loving) God* best fills the role assigned by the concept of wrongness (Adams 1979, p. 74; see also Adams 1999, pp. 252–258). By conceptual analysis alone we can know only that wrongness is a property of actions (and perhaps intentions and attitudes); that people are generally opposed to what they regard as wrong; that wrongness is a reason, perhaps a conclusive reason, for opposing an act; and that there are certain acts (e.g., torture for fun) that are wrong. But given traditional theistic beliefs, the best candidate property to fill the role set by the concept of wrongness is that of *being contrary to (a loving) God's commands*. For that property is an objective property of actions. Further, given Christian views about the content of God's commands, this reduction fits well with widespread pre-theoretical intuitions about wrongness; and given Christian views about human receptivity to divine communication and God's willingness to communicate both naturally and supernaturally, God's commands have a causal role in our acquisition of moral knowledge (Adams 1979, p. 76; see also Adams 1999, pp. 257).

Nonetheless reduction DCM must be false, for it, in conjunction with a very weak and plausible claim about God's freedom in commanding, entails that the moral does not supervene on the nonmoral. And if reduction DCM entails that the moral does not supervene on the nonmoral, then reduction DCM fails its own test of adequacy: for the property *being commanded by God* does not adequately fill the role set by the concept of the obligatory.

God is a free being. On most views, God could have refrained from creating anything at all; on all views, God could have created a world different in some ways from the world that God actually created. Not only is God's action in creating a world free; God's action within the created world is free as well. God has intervened miraculously in the world, but God could have failed to intervene miraculously, or could have intervened miraculously in different ways than God in fact did.

Among God's free acts are acts of commanding: at least some divine commands are free. What I mean by saying that God has at least some freedom in commanding is that even if the world were in relevant respects otherwise the same, God might have given slightly different commands: God could have given at least a slightly smaller or larger number of such commands, or could have given commands at least slightly different in content, or could have given commands to an at least slightly different group of people. What God commands is not entirely fixed by the way the world otherwise is.

Now, one might say: there is nothing objectionable about holding that God's commands are wholly fixed by the way the world otherwise is. For the way that the world otherwise is is determined by other free choices that God has made. Consider the following analogy. God is truthful. So God's assertions are wholly fixed by the way the world otherwise is. But that is no restriction on God's freedom, because the way the world otherwise is is determined by God's own free choices.

The objection does not succeed. First, to assert is to perform a speech-act with a mind-to-world direction of fit: in successful acts of assertion, one has to describe the world the way it is, so it is not surprising that the content of God's assertions would be fixed by the way the world is. But to command is to perform a speech-act with a world-to-mind direction of fit: commanding is thus not (wholly)[7] constrained by the way the world is. So the fact that it is unsurprising that God's assertions are fixed by the way the world is would not make it less surprising that God's commands are fixed by the way the world is.

Second, God's truthfulness in assertion constrains God, if at all, only in the following way: *if* God chooses to assert something to somebody on some occasion, *then* what God asserts will be true. It does not, of itself, entail that God must assert anything, or to any specific person, or on any specific occasion. But to say that God's commands are wholly fixed by the other features of the world is to say that every relevant detail of God's commanding—not just the content, but whether, to whom, and on what occasions—is determined by those other features.

---

7. It is true that commands characteristically have some presuppositions that are truth-valuable (for example, that the person commanded exists, that the act commanded is possible, etc.), and which therefore have a mind-to-world direction of fit. These presuppositions do not constitute anything like the absolute constraint on the content of commanding acts that the alleged analogy with assertive acts would suggest, though.

Third, there are other reasons to suppose that God's commands are not entirely determined by other features of the world besides that it would constitute a real constraint on God's freedom. For it just is massively implausible that other features of the world could entirely fix God's commands. Think about it this way: how would we explain how it could be that the other features of the world entirely determine every last detail of God's commanding—whether God commands, on what occasions, to whom, and with what precise content? We would have to say something like the following: given the features of a world other than what God in fact commands in that world, it is either the case that God lacks power to command other than God does in that world, or that God simply will not so command, perhaps on the basis of there being decisive reasons for God to command just as God does. It is hard to imagine that the former could be true: how could other features of the world limit God's power, so that God can give only that particular set of commands, on just the occasions that God gives them, and to just the people to whom God gives them? It is also hard to imagine how the latter could be true: how could it be simply impossible, true in no possible world whatever, that the reasons that God has for giving commands leave God indifferent between one of two slightly different commands, so that God might choose to give either one? That God lacks any discretion in commanding in light of the other features of a world appears to be a highly implausible claim. (It must appear especially implausible for someone who is concerned to argue that moral obligation is determined entirely by God through God's commanding acts.)

So we have every reason to believe that God has some discretion in commanding. We also have every reason to believe that moral properties supervene on nonmoral properties. There is some confusion over why this is so, and what modal strength this supervenience is supposed to have, and what the ultimate philosophical significance of supervenience is, but there is no doubt whatever that it is a fixed constraint on any adequate accounts of the concept of the moral and of what properties are identified as moral properties that they recognize this truth. Here is Michael Smith:

> Everyone agrees that moral features of things supervene on their natural features. That is, everyone agrees that two possible worlds that are alike in all of their natural features must also be alike in their moral features; that the moral features of things cannot float free of their natural fea-

tures. Moreover, everyone agrees that this is a platitude; that is an a priori truth. For recognition of the way in which the moral supervenes on the natural is a constraint on the proper use of moral concepts. (Smith 1994, pp. 21–22)

The supervenience relationship between moral and nonmoral properties is susceptible to more than one interpretation: it can be interpreted as either weak or strong supervenience. We have already run across strong supervenience in our discussion of supervenience DCM. Recall that set of properties A strongly supervenes on set of properties B if and only if necessarily for any object x and any property F in A, if x has F, then there is a property G in B that x has, and necessarily any y that has G has F. Again following Kim, we can say that a set of properties A (the supervenient family) *weakly supervenes* on a set of properties B (the supervenience base) if and only if

necessarily for any property F in A, if an object x has F, then there exists a property G in B such that x has G, and if any y has G it has F. (Kim 1993b, p. 64)

If the supervenience relationship between moral and nonmoral properties is that of strong supervenience, then it is an a priori truth that for any item[8] i and any moral property M, if i has a moral property M, then there is a set of nonmoral properties N that i exemplifies such that necessarily any item that exemplifies the properties in N will exemplify M. On the other hand, if the supervenience relationship is that of weak supervenience, then it is an a priori truth that for any item i and any moral property M, if an item i has moral property M, then there is a set of nonmoral properties N that i has such that any item that has N will have M. The difference between the claims that the moral strongly supervenes on the nonmoral and that the moral weakly supervenes on the nonmoral consists simply in the modal strength of the condition that there be no difference in moral properties without some difference in nonmoral properties. On strong supervenience, if an item has a certain moral property due to its having a certain set of nonmoral properties, then any item *in any possible world* that has that set of nonmoral properties in that world will have that moral property in that world. On weak su-

---

8. I apologize for 'item' here, but what better term is there to capture the range of x's (persons, character traits, mental states, actions, states of affairs, events) that exemplify moral properties?

pervenience, if an item has a certain moral property due to its having a certain set of nonmoral properties in some possible world, then any item *in that possible world* that has that set of nonmoral properties will have that moral property.

God's commanding acts are not entirely fixed by the other features of the world. Any adequate account of the moral must accommodate the supervenience of the moral on the nonmoral. But if reduction DCM is true, this view of God's freedom in commanding is false or the moral does not supervene on the nonmoral. Of these three theses—reduction DCM, the doctrine of moral supervenience, and God's freedom in commanding—at least one must be false.

There is no consensus in favor of construing moral supervenience as strong rather than merely weak supervenience, or vice versa; we will therefore consider both possible readings, beginning with strong supervenience. Assume that reduction DCM is true and that the moral strongly supervenes on the nonmoral. *Being obligatory* thus strongly supervenes on the nonmoral. Necessarily, then, whether an act is obligatory is wholly fixed by a set of properties that does not include *being obligatory*. Now, if reduction DCM is true, then *being obligatory* just is *being commanded by God*. And so, by substitution, necessarily, whether an act is commanded by God is wholly fixed by a set of properties that does not include *being commanded by God*. It thus follows from the conjunction of reduction DCM and the supervenience of the moral on the nonmoral that God's commands are wholly fixed by features of the world other than those commands themselves. But to accept this last claim is to reject God's freedom in commanding.

This, then, is a trilemma with respect to reduction DCM: one must reject either reduction DCM, the notion that the moral strongly supervenes on the nonmoral, or God's freedom in commanding. Now, one might say: all that this shows is that the defender of reduction DCM ought not allow that the supervenience of the moral on the nonmoral is to be interpreted as strong supervenience. Some philosophers have held that moral supervenience is weak supervenience (see, for example, R. Hare 1952, p. 145, and Blackburn 1988, p. 63), and if moral supervenience is weak supervenience, then all that is entailed by the conjunction of DCM and the doctrine of moral supervenience is that *being commanded by God* weakly supervenes on other features of the world. But the notion that *being commanded by God* weakly supervenes on other features of the world is not, the defender of

DCM might insist, objectionable at all. For while God's commands are *free*, are not fixed by other features of the world, God's commands are also *rational*, for God is a rational commander. To be a rational commander is, at least in part, to exhibit consistency in commanding. So if in a world God commands ϕ-ing, then any act in that world that displays the relevant properties that ϕ-ing displays would also be commanded by God, on account of God's consistency. To command ϕ-ing but to fail to command an act identical to ϕ-ing in all relevant properties is to command inconsistently. But God is surely a consistent commander, and so the weak supervenience of God's commands on other features of the world is guaranteed by God's rationality in commanding.

But the appeal to weak supervenience is unpersuasive for two reasons. The first is that there are good reasons to move beyond weak to strong supervenience as an account of moral supervenience. By weak supervenience alone, one who says that ϕ-ing is obligatory commits him- or herself to the view that there is a set of nonmoral properties that ϕ-ing exemplifies, and any act of ψ-ing in this world that has that set of nonmoral properties will also be obligatory. But when asked why having that set of nonmoral properties guarantees that ψ-ing will be obligatory in this world, but having that set of nonmoral properties would *not* guarantee that an act of ξ-ing would be obligatory in some other world, surely there must be some answer: it will not be a brute fact.[9] But there are only two possibilities. Either the explanation is wholly in terms of nonmoral properties—ψ-ing exhibits some nonmoral property that ξ-ing does not, or vice versa—in which case the presence or absence of that nonmoral property would be part of a base for strong supervenience.[10] Or the explanation is at least partly in terms of moral properties, which would have to be grounded in nonmoral properties, leading us

9. See Blackburn's discussion in his 1988, pp. 61–63. Blackburn resists the line of argument that follows.

10. For example: suppose that stabbing's being prima facie wrong supervenes on stabbing's tending to cause bodily damage. Weak supervenience entails that any act that causes bodily damage in our world will be prima facie wrong. But why would we not go for strong supervenience here? Not because there is some other world in which it is just brutely the case that what tends to cause bodily damage is not prima facie wrong. Perhaps in this other possible world what tends to cause bodily damage is immediately compensated by increase in vigor. But if that were the case, we should say that stabbing's being prima facie wrong strongly supervenes on stabbing's causing bodily damage that is not immediately compensated. In this way any claim that a moral property only weakly supervenes on the nonmoral can be transformed into a claim that a moral property strongly supervenes on the nonmoral.

back to the first possibility. So it is hard to escape the impression that a re-treat from strong to weak moral supervenience would constitute a conces-sion that reduction DCM cannot adequately accommodate the formal fea-tures of moral concepts.

A second, entirely independent reason that the move to weak superve-nience does not save the defender of reduction DCM is that it is very plau-sibly part of the concept of the moral that it supervene not on individual but only on *general* properties. Earlier I quoted Michael Smith's description of the consensus about the supervenience of the moral on the nonmoral. In re-stating his point, he continues:

> If two possible worlds are alike in the kinds of individuals who occupy
> them, the motivations and aspirations they have, the extent to which the
> world lives up to their aspirations, their relative levels of well-being, and
> if the worlds are otherwise identical in natural respects as well, if they
> differ only in which particular individuals and objects have these various
> natural features, then there is a conceptual confusion involved in suppos-
> ing that these worlds could differ in their moral standing. (Smith 1994,
> p. 22)

R. M. Hare's view, the locus classicus for treatments of supervenience in moral philosophy, is also the locus classicus for this view (see his 1952; also his 1963, pp. 38–40).

The relevance of this point is that even if we allow the propriety of the move to weak moral supervenience, the fact that the supervenience base in-cludes only general properties makes trouble for the defender of reduction DCM. For while it is part of the concept of the moral that the moral weakly supervenes on nonmoral general properties, it is not a plausible thesis about God's commanding activity that God's commands must weakly supervene on nonmoral general properties. For the only argument that God's com-mands must weakly supervene on nonmoral properties is that it is a con-stituent of rationality in commanding that such commands display consis-tency. But it is not a constituent of rationality in commanding that such commands exhibit consistency *with respect to general properties*. It can be per-fectly rational to issue a command to one party and to fail to issue that com-mand to another party, even though those parties, and the acts commanded of them, differ in no relevant *general* property.

Here is a case that illustrates this point. Suppose that I see a small child drowning, but I am a poor swimmer and would botch the rescue. There are nearby two stronger swimmers, Jane and Tom, each of whom could surely save the child; but if both attempt to jump in, the attempt will be less likely to succeed: each will get in the other's way. So, I give a command: "Jane, jump in and save the child! Tom, stay on the bank!" This is a reasonable act of commanding: I had a reason to command one and only one of them to save the child; but there was no relevant general property to distinguish Tom and Jane; so I gave a command that was not determined by their general properties. It was random; I just picked. There is no basis to think that *God's* commands, even though God is a supremely rational commander, would always have reasons determined by general properties for issuing one command rather than another; we have no basis to think that God never just picks.

If the supervenience basis for moral properties contains only nonmoral general properties, then the weak supervenience of the moral on the nonmoral requires that an act be obligatory only if every other act that has the same relevant general nonmoral properties is obligatory as well. But we have no basis to believe, and some basis to doubt, that the fact that an act is commanded by God entails that every other act that has the same relevant general properties is commanded by God as well. And so, in addition to the worries raised above about weak supervenience as an adequate account of the supervenience of the moral on the nonmoral, reduction DCM is unable to accommodate even the weak supervenience of the moral on the nonmoral.

One might, of course, consider tinkering with the doctrine of moral supervenience in order to produce a modified formulation of that doctrine that would enable the defender of reduction DCM to avoid the objection. Consider, for example, the version of reduction DCM defended by Adams. Adams allows that God might have given commands that differ from those that God in fact gave: God might have forbidden or permitted euthanasia, and might have required or failed to require certain religious rituals (1999, pp. 255–256). If we ascribe to Adams an affirmation of the doctrine of moral supervenience, then Adams's views are subject to the objection. But one might note that while Adams explicitly endorses the view that an object's axiological properties—its goodness, its value, etc.—supervene on its non-axiological properties (1999, p. 61), he does not explicitly endorse the view that an act's deontic properties—its rightness, its obligatoriness, etc.—supervene on its nondeontic properties. Since reduction DCM as I have understood it is a view about the identity of deontic properties, not axiological properties, if a defender of reduction DCM refrains from endorsing the view that deontic properties supervene on nondeontic properties, then he or she will not be open to the objection.[11]

It would be a very bad idea, though, for the defender of reduction DCM to avoid the trilemma by modifying the doctrine of supervenience so that it excludes deontic properties from the supervenient family. The presumption against tinkering in this way with the doctrine of supervenience is extremely high, because the overwhelming intuitive support for the notion that axiological properties supervene on nonaxiological properties extends just as readily to the notion that deontic properties supervene on nondeontic properties. Just as it appears straightforwardly obvious that one lacks a grip on the concept of goodness if one allows that two objects are alike in all nonaxiological features yet holds that one is good but the other is not, it appears just as straightforwardly obvious that one lacks a grip on the concept of obligation if one allows that two acts are alike in all nondeontic features yet holds that one of those acts is obligatory but the other is not. In the absence of a genuinely compelling reason to alter the standard formulation of the doctrine of moral supervenience, it would be simply an ad hoc maneuver, constituting special pleading on the part of the defender of reduction DCM, to adjust the doctrine of moral supervenience to allow reduction DCM to avoid the objection.

How could one think that there could be compelling reason to adjust the doctrine of moral supervenience so that it does not apply to deontic properties? Perhaps what might tempt one in this direction is that we want to allow that God's commanding is free, and that what God commands us to do, we are obligated to do. In one possible world, God commands us to perform religious ritual R_1, and we are thus obligated to perform it; in another possible world, God commands us to perform a distinct ritual R_2—though R_2, in itself, differs from R_1 in no morally relevant way—and we are thus obligated to perform R_2. Our being obligated to perform one of these rituals or the other does not supervene, then, on the intrinsic features of the rituals. But this is obviously no basis to adjust our views on the supervenience

---

11. Note that I am not ascribing this view to Adams. I mean only to say that it is a possibility for avoiding the trilemma that is left logically open by Adams's text.

of deontic properties on nondeontic properties; we want to say here that the property that distinguishes the required ritual from the nonrequired ritual in each world is *being commanded by God*. But that appeal is precisely what the defender of reduction DCM is barred from making. By *identifying* the property *being obligatory* with the property *being commanded by God*, defenders of reduction DCM remove the property *being commanded by God* from that set of nonmoral properties on which the property *being obligatory* can supervene.

Reduction DCM appears to be pretty much a disaster as far as the supervenience of the moral on the nonmoral goes. God's having a free, albeit rational, will guarantees that the supervenience relationships that partially define the moral cannot hold on reduction DCM: the connections between a rational agent's commands and the nonmoral truths about the world just are not closely aligned with the connections between moral obligations and the nonmoral truths about the world. Since the case for reduction DCM is that *being commanded by God* fills well the role set by the concept of *being obligatory*, that the commands of God fail the supervenience test is a serious difficulty indeed.

I have argued in this chapter that two versions of DCM—causal and supervenience versions—do not entail the authority thesis, and that two versions of DCM—analysis and reduction versions—entail the authority thesis but are too implausible to serve as a reasonable basis for affirming that thesis. If moral philosophy is to provide help in establishing the authority thesis, it will be not through metaethical accounts of the source and nature of moral properties, but through a direct appeal to moral principles themselves. We will consider the possibility of a route to the Strongest authority thesis through normative ethics in the next chapter.

CHAPTER 5

Moral Arguments for the Authority Thesis

5.1 MORAL PRINCIPLES AND DIVINE AUTHORITY

When arguments are offered for the authority of the state over citizens, or of parents over children, these arguments characteristically proceed by formulating clearly a particular moral principle, giving some reasons to think that moral principle true, and then appealing to certain facts that allegedly trigger the application of that moral principle and entail that a state's citizens, or a parent's children, are bound to obey its, or his or her, dictates. Following this model, moral arguments for the authority thesis would proceed by appealing to certain moral principles, binding on all created rational beings, which alone, or in conjunction with truths that hold in all possible worlds in which there are created rational beings, imply that all created rational beings have decisive reason to obey God's commands.

There are likely to be questions concerning moral arguments for the authority thesis provoked by the requirement that such arguments appeal to moral principles binding on created rational beings in every possible world. *Pace* Kant, we may wonder whether our grasp of moral principles is a grasp of what binds us simply in virtue of our rationality, or whether we are bound in virtue of more particular features of our human condition, and indeed whether we have any way to tell the difference. I am going to bypass this worry by giving the defender of moral arguments for the authority thesis plenty of slack here: unless we can point to a feature of human existence possibly not shared by other rational beings and on which the truth of a moral principle seems clearly to depend, I will grant that the principle applies to created rational beings as such and not simply some subclass of such beings.

5.2 JUSTICE

It is sometimes said that obedience to God is due from created rational beings as a matter of justice, and so the authority thesis is true. But this argument is uninformative unless we are able to articulate precisely what it is about the relationship between God and created rational beings that makes it the case that such obedience is due. In the absence of such an articulated rationale, the appeal to justice is not itself an argument for divine authority but rather a way of emphasizing that God has such authority and so created rational beings should render obedience in recognition of it.

5.3 PROPERTY

One way to articulate the feature of the relationship between God and created rational beings that is relevant to justice is through the idea of *property*. As Locke writes,

> For Men being all the Workmanship of one Omnipotent, and infinitely wise Maker; All the Servants of one Sovereign Master, sent into the World by his order and about his business, they are his Property, whose workmanship they are, made to last during his, not one another's pleasure. (Locke, *Second Treatise*, § 6)

The conclusion Locke is striving for here is that no human has the right to destroy another human. But earlier in the passage Locke notes that the law of nature—the divine law promulgated to humans through reason (Locke, *Second Treatise*, § 6)—forbids the destruction not only of another's life or possessions but also of one's own. And so Locke is appealing to the idea that our acts, both with respect to ourselves and with respect to others, fall under divine authority because of the status of human beings as divine property. Recent writers have argued for the authority thesis along similar lines. Brody suggests, tentatively and leaving a number of issues for later resolution, that our obligations to obey God can be understood in terms of God's property in all creation (1981; see, for further defense of Brody's view, Taliaferro 1992). Swinburne argues, though in a more limited way, for a divine capacity to create moral obligations by appeal to God's property in created nonrational nature (1977, pp. 206–207).

To be more explicit about the connection between property and divine authority: the general principle to which property arguments for divine authority appeal is that if x is A's rightful property, then B has prima facie reason to refrain from using x except on A's terms. (This is labeled by Honoré as the "right to manage": see his 1961.) If the property right is *absolute*, then if x is A's rightful property, then B has *decisive* reason to refrain from using x except on A's terms. The prima facie version of the principle is plausible enough. If this harmonica is yours, then I have reason to refrain from using it in any way that is incompatible with your wishes with respect to it. If you do not want me to play it at all, then I have reason not to play it at all; if you want me to play it only with accompaniment, then I have reason not to play it unless I have accompaniment. If I use your property at all, it should be on your terms. And if the prima facie version is plausible enough, then it would appear that the absolutized version is plausible as well: if a property right confers some reasons on others to respect the owner's wishes, then an absolute property right will confer absolute reasons on others to respect the owner's wishes.

How, then, does this principle, conjoined with the assumption that God owns—and, we will assume, owns absolutely—created rational beings imply the authority thesis? In most cases, if x is owned by A and not by B, then B has a choice whether to use x or not; only if B chooses to use x will B be governed by A's wishes with respect to x. But if God has property rights over created rational beings, created rational beings will have no such choice available: each created rational being will use itself whenever it acts. Since every created rational being is absolutely owned by God, every created rational being has decisive reasons to act only on God's terms. Those terms include the directives set by divine command. And so created rational beings have decisive reason to obey divine commands.

Perhaps the expression 'the created rational being uses itself whenever it acts' is in need of some explanation. It certainly is a strange locution, but its strangeness does not, I think, cast doubt on the argument's success. The peculiarity will lessen a bit if we provide a clearer understanding of the notion of 'use' that is relevant in the account of the moral principle employed in the property argument. Suppose that we label a 'plan of action' a description of an ordered set of performances by some agent (see also Murphy 2001a, pp. 157–158). Plans of action are objects of deliberation by agents; agents settle upon such plans and then carry them out. For an agent to use an object is for an agent to settle upon and carry out a plan of action that mentions that object. Understood in this way, it is clear that any plan of action that an agent settles upon which concerns how that agent him- or herself will act is one in which the agent uses him- or herself, and that suffices for the argument from property to establish divine authority over all created rational beings.

In a moment I want to consider how to make sense of God's having property in created rational beings. But first we should note that it is far from clear that this argument can reach as its conclusion the Strongest of the authority theses. Even if it were conceded that, through being God's creation, every created rational being comes into existence owned by God, it would *not* follow that necessarily, every created rational being is under divine authority. For property can be *alienated* from one: you can transfer ownership of your harmonica to me, or you can let it revert to the state of nature, a state in which it is owned by no one. It would seem, then, that God could alienate God's property in created rational beings. If so, then even if God originally owns every created rational being, it would not be true that every created rational being is necessarily under divine authority. So any successful argument from property to the Strongest authority thesis would have to be supplemented by some argument that God necessarily could not alienate God's property in rational beings.

Even apart from the difficulty that God's having property at one time in each created rational being does not show that God permanently has authority over all such beings, the argument from property would not be persuasive in the absence of a showing that God's creating rational beings makes those beings God's property. In order to offer such an account we may turn back to Locke, in whose writings there may be found a number of arguments connecting an agent's making something with that agent's having, by nature, a property right in that thing. While I will put to the side the most famous of these strategies, Locke's argument from a being's owning him- or herself and his or her labor to the conclusion that he or she owns the product of the labor—I know of no way to make sense of the idea that God owns God—there is an argument strategy that is independently more plausible and initially more likely to provide a successful account of God's natural property in rational beings.

The core of the idea is an appeal to the Lockean proviso governing just appropriation, that is, that in appropriating what was previously unowned one must leave enough and as good in common for others (Locke, *Second Treatise*, § 27). If we can provide some intuitively plausible conditions under which one would have a prima facie claim to ownership, that prima facie claim will likely be undefeated if it can be shown that the Lockean proviso is satisfied, that no one is made worse off. Now, there are notorious difficulties specifying what would count as a positive reason for holding that one would have a claim over a previously unowned object: Locke says that one who mixes one's labor with the land has a right over it, leaving philosophers to puzzle over the necessary and sufficient conditions for such mixing and over the question of why such mixing results in the gain of the object rather than the loss of one's labor (cf. Nozick 1974, pp. 174–175). But putting to the side questions about the source of one's ownership in the materials that one uses, it is plausible to think that the fact that one conceived and made an object gives one a special claim over it, and that this claim is undefeated if the existence of the owned object renders no other party worse off—perhaps if we also provide, as Mill suggested, that the making of that object was not itself something that one was bound to do (*Political Economy*, II, 2, § 6). As Becker reconstructs the position, if "the labor is beyond what is required, morally, that one do for others; [if] it produces something that would not have existed except for it; and [if] its product is something that others lose nothing from being excluded from," then one who produces an object by his or her labor has an exclusive property right to that object (1977, p. 100). We may call the three clauses of this sufficient condition for property rights over produced objects the *no-moral-requirement*, the *source-in-labor*, and the *no-loss* clauses, respectively. In order to make a plausible case that God's creation of rational beings satisfies these criteria and thus makes rational beings God's property, I will need to provide glosses on, and in one case a revision of, each of these clauses.

With respect to the no-moral-requirement clause: it is undoubtedly broader than it need be. Suppose that I am exquisitely talented in making harmonicas, yet have a tendency to fritter away my time doing philosophy. Distressed by this waste of talent, you extract a promise from me to spend an hour each day harmonica-building. I am under a moral requirement to build harmonicas, but that fact itself does not call into question any right that I have over the harmonicas produced by my labors. A promise to you to build harmonicas is not a promise that you may have my harmonicas, which would indeed threaten my right to them. (Though it is to be noted that to make sense of my capacity to give you a right to those harmonicas we need to assume that I have some sort of prior right over them.) It is plausible to insist only that there be no moral requirement sufficient to strip one of a claim-right over the product of one's labor, should such a right come to hold. A moral requirement to produce the object would not be enough to meet this condition.[1]

With respect to the source-in-labor clause: it is included simply to make clear that for this particular sufficient condition of entitlement over an object to be satisfied, the object must have been brought into existence by one's labor. That labor was a necessary condition for its coming into existence. (It is at least plausible that the source-in-labor clause is satisfied every time one's labor in fact causally contributed to the coming into being of the object: for it is at least plausible that objects have their causal origins of necessity.)

With respect to the no-loss clause: first, the idea that the object must be something exclusion from which causes others to suffer no loss obviously requires some elaboration with respect to the baseline from which we are to assess any possible losses. The 'exclusion' part is more straightforward: to be excluded from an object is just to lack the benefits that one could receive from exercising one's liberties with respect to the object that one would have were that object not owned by its producer. So what, then, is the baseline with which to compare this situation? Surely not that in which one reaps any benefits that one could receive from exercising one's liberties with respect to the object that one would have were that object not owned by its producer: on that view, very few objects other than those of no interest to anybody other than their producers could be items to which their producers are nat-

---

1. Indeed, Mill seems to understand the disqualifying moral consideration not simply as a requirement to produce the object but instead as a prior claim that another person has over it: "It is no hardship to any one, to be excluded from what others have produced: they were not bound to produce it for his use" (*Political Economy*, II, 2, § 6).

urally entitled. No: the relevant baseline is one in which the object is not produced at all. If one is not worse off being constrained by another's having property rights over an object than one would be if the object were not produced at all, then the no-loss clause is satisfied.

Second, the no-loss clause requires a bit of broadening: the existence of an entitlement by the owner in a produced object can be undercut not only by a loss resulting from exclusion but by other imposed losses. If the process of making an object itself imposes losses—if it generates externalities that worsen the condition of other parties—that itself seems to threaten the full entitlement of the producer to the produced object. And if the continued existence of the object imposes losses—if its very existence makes others worse off, apart from their being excluded from use of it—that would be enough to make us question the entitlement of the producer to the object produced. A clear entitlement over a produced object would result from the generation of a produced object that caused no loss to others in any of these ways.

Given these glosses on the three clauses, one can offer the following case for the view that all created rational beings come into existence owned by God. There is no being that has a prior claim-right on rational beings: apart from God's creative activity, there are no other rational beings. So it seems that the no-moral-requirement clause is satisfied. Created rational beings would not exist were it not for God's creative act. There is no other possible source for such beings other than God. So the source-in-labor clause is satisfied. And while created rational beings might rather have the freedom to decide how to live their lives than to be subject to God's dominion, it can hardly be said that it constitutes a loss to created rational beings in the relevant sense. The only way that one could claim that it constituted a loss would be, I suppose, to hold that the lives of created rational beings as God's property are not worth living, so that one could rationally regret ever having come into existence. (In 5.4 below I argue that it is true of *no* created rational being that his or her life is not worth living. Here I will merely note that the no-loss clause is plausibly held to be satisfied, and could only be shown not to be satisfied here by appeal to a response something like the not-worth-living line.)

There is a decent case to be made, then, that these conditions for a natural entitlement in a produced object are satisfied in the case of God's creation of rational beings. If the three clauses do in fact jointly make for an entitlement, then it would seem to follow at least that rational beings come into existence under divine authority. This is the best formulation of the argument that created rational beings come into existence as God's property that I can offer, and so I will treat the property account of divine authority as resting on it.

I want to raise one objection concerning the no-moral-requirement clause and one objection concerning the no-loss clause. (I assume that the source-in-labor clause is satisfied, and unobjectionably so!) First, the fact that there are no rational beings prior to God's creative act that could have any sort of claim over the products of that act does not show that the no-moral-requirement clause is satisfied. For it could be that since what is brought into existence by these divine creative acts are rational beings, the sorts of beings that are capable of enjoying rights and exercising liberties, one of these rational beings could come into existence with a set of claim-rights that would cause the no-moral-requirement to remain unsatisfied. If, for example, rational beings are the sorts of things that naturally have a set of claim-rights over their own lives and activities, then they would come into being with claims over God's products of labor that would deny God title to them.

Whether rational beings necessarily have such claim-rights over themselves is a difficult question. Certainly human beings have something like such rights against other human beings by nature, even if the Lockean rights-language is not the most perspicuous way of understanding these moral claims. Indeed, to ascribe such rights to human beings strikes me as the crucial move for Locke to make to avoid the implication that parents who set out to have children thereby own those children. One might say: there is no problem about parental ownership of children, for the sense in which God creates rational beings is of a wholly different order than that whereby human beings generate other human beings. But there *is* a problem here. Everything has its existence due to God's creative activity, so God owns it all. But there must be a sense in which humans can nonetheless gain entitlements over those created things—perhaps the entitlements they gain are complete save for the rider 'unless God directs otherwise.' If so, then we would still have the problem about parents' owning children—the conditions for entitlement would be met with respect to parents' ownership of children, even if that ownership would be limited by God's directions to the contrary. One way to avoid this implication is to hold that rational beings necessarily come into being with a set of claim-rights against other created rational beings. But the question would then become why one has those claim-rights against other created rational beings but not against God.

So there are some cases in which we want to ascribe such rights to rational beings. Why, then, would we fail to allow that there is such a prior right with respect to God? Obviously the situation of one created rational being vis-à-vis other created rational beings differs in a number of crucial respects from the situation of one created rational being vis-à-vis God. But in attempting to identify the difference that is relevant we are back on the path to trying to provide an account of divine authority, or something that would underwrite divine authority. The reason that created rational beings are not owned by their parents, but are owned by God, is that there is some superiority in God that makes God's claim to govern the use of a particular rational being stronger than the claims of that being's fellows. That looks like the makings of an argument that there are independent grounds for ascribing authority over created rational beings to God.

The second criticism concerns the appropriateness of the no-loss clause in this undoubtedly special case. Characteristically, the no-loss clause is employed by comparing the condition of a rational being precluded from exercising liberty with respect to an object with the condition of that rational being if that object were never produced. But in the case of God's creation of rational beings, the no-loss clause is satisfied, as it were, on a technicality—there is no such thing as the condition of that rational being if the relevant object were never produced. This should make us suspicious of the argument, but on its own the fact that the no-loss clause is satisfied in a peculiar way is not telling against it. Surely the case of the creation of rational beings is a special case, so it should not be surprising if the no-loss clause is satisfied in a special way. (Indeed, I endorse a similar response to a criticism of the argument from gratitude in 5.4.) To transform this point into an objection against the argument that created rational beings are God's property, we need to look at the rationale for the no-loss clause, and see why the unusual way that the no-loss clause is satisfied here is out of line with the rationale for the no-loss clause. The plausibility lent to natural entitlements by the no-loss clause is not present in the case of God's alleged property in created rational beings.

Here is why. What makes the no-loss clause a plausible condition to build into the conditions of a natural property right is the way that it respects the separateness and autonomy of the rational beings affected—both the potential laborer and others. Grant that the no-moral-requirement obtains—the potential laborer is not bound by any moral requirement to others to produce the object for their use. If this is true, then it would be an unjustifiable *further* infringement on the potential laborer's autonomy not to be able to devote his or her energy to making whatever he or she might wish to make for his or her (or others') use and benefit—unless in making that object the laborer would thereby make ingresses upon others' autonomy. What is key is the autonomy of the potential laborer to create an object and employ it in his or her plans of action and the autonomy of others not to have their capacity to make and carry out plans of action undercut by others' productive acts.

But if this is the correct understanding of the rationale for the no-loss clause, then the special way that it is satisfied in the case of God's creating rational beings *does* call the relevance of the satisfaction of that clause into question. For in this case God's possessing a right over a created object is *essentially* an ingress onto another's autonomy—the autonomy of the very thing that is created. It cannot be plausibly claimed that no being's autonomy is affected by the acknowledgment of the producer's entitlement to the produced object if the produced object is itself a rational being. All of this, I agree, may be just a fancy way of putting a common objection to Locke's idea that we are all God's property—that rational beings are just not the kind of thing that can be property. But I hope that the way that the good of autonomy is connected to the no-loss clause moves this common objection beyond the status of a bare counterassertion to the Lockean idea that humans are God's property and thus under God's authority.

Now, one might respond: even if the no-loss principle is not satisfied in this case in a way that vindicates God's property in created rational beings, there are alternative ways to formulate the no-loss clause. Earlier I noted that it would be too stringent to claim that the baseline for the application of the no-loss clause is the position of the other parties if the object is produced yet the producer has no rights over that object. But while this clause is too stringent generally, one might say that surely it can serve as part of a sufficient condition for entitlement. If one made the object, no one has any moral claim over the object that conflicts with the producer's gaining an entitlement to it, and others are no worse off lacking use of the existing object than they would be if they could use the existing object, then surely the producer is entitled to it. But one might claim that created rational beings are, in fact, better off being God's property than not being God's property. In part, one might claim, this is because it is better for one, overall, to be under divine authority than to not be under divine authority.[2] (We will consider these reasons in some detail in 7.6.) Does this line of response succeed in showing that there is no serious obstacle to thinking of created rational beings as God's property?

It does not succeed. One thing that we *necessarily* lack if we are God's property is the opportunity to place ourselves under divine authority, to submit entirely to God, to make ourselves God's own. This strikes me as a very important good, assuming for the moment that it is an available good. (It would not be available if the Strongest authority thesis is true.) And this is a good that created rational beings would lack by God's having an initial entitlement over all. So there is one very important way that such beings could be worse off by not being initially unowned by God. This gives us some reason to think that this revised no-loss clause is not satisfied: for if one is not initially owned by God, one can gain the relevant benefits of being owned by God by submitting to God, while *also* enjoying the goods involved in this submission itself. One might say: this assumes that one will recognize the importance of submission and have the will to act on it. But one who cannot recognize or cannot act upon the good of being under divine authority by submitting would be similarly unlikely to be able to recognize one's given status as under divine authority or to be able to act on the fact that one has that status. We do not have reason to believe that there is no loss involved in being naturally owned by God.

There is more to be said in favor of property arguments for divine authority than many are wont to allow, but there is not enough to be said in favor of those arguments to establish the authority thesis. There are, however, other relevant moral considerations resulting from God's creation of rational beings besides those of justice: one might hold that obedience is to be

2. If this claim could be shown to be true, it would also provide some answer to the question why the status of created rational beings as God's property is not merely contingent: God would not alienate us from his ownership if so doing would make us worse-off.

rendered to God not out of justice but out of gratitude. To this argument for divine authority we now turn.

5.4 GRATITUDE

Suppose that we grant that gratitude is a requirement that would bind any created rational being. Now, gratitude requires one who has received gratuitous benefits from another to be willing to perform beneficial acts for that other. The extent of the beneficial act that is owed on account of gratitude depends on the character of the gratuitous act performed by the benefactor: ceteris paribus, the more gratuitous a benefiting act is, the greater the grateful response that is due; ceteris paribus, the more beneficial the benefiting act is, the greater the grateful response that is due. But it is a necessary truth that all created rational beings receive gratuitous benefits from God: God's creating and conserving in existence rational beings is an act that is both gratuitous (God is not required to perform any creative act) and beneficial (rational beings are benefited by this creation and conservation). And given the character of this creating/conserving act as overwhelmingly gratuitous and beneficial with respect to created rational beings, the extent of the grateful acts owed by created rational beings to God can extend no less than to obedience to all of God's commands. Nothing less would constitute an adequately grateful response. (See, for example, Swinburne 1977, pp. 205–206, and 1996, pp. 14–15; see also Adams 1999, pp. 252–253.)

The gratitude argument has recently attracted quite a bit of negative commentary, much of it undeserved. Some objections to it hold that the conditions that must be met by a gratitude-engendering act, even those conditions as set out in the sketchy version of the argument discussed in the previous paragraph, fail to be met. Some objections to it hold that there are further conditions on gratitude-engendering acts that are not met by God's creation and conservation of rational beings. And some hold that even if all such conditions are met, they fail to show that obedience is picked out as the sole appropriate response to this debt of gratitude, or even that obedience out of reasons of gratitude makes any sense.

The ought-implies-can objection. We may begin our consideration of objections to the gratitude account by dealing with an argument against the very idea that gratitude can engender moral obligations. It appeals to three premises: first, an *ought-implies-can* premise; second, a premise affirming the involuntary character of one's attitudes and emotions; and third, a premise concerning the nature of the gratitude-requiting act. The argument is as follows. One cannot be morally required to perform an act that it is not possible for one to perform. Now, if there were moral obligations of gratitude, they would be obligations to perform grateful acts. But a grateful act is necessarily one that flows from, and is an expression of, certain attitudes; one cannot perform a grateful act without having grateful attitudes, just as one cannot jump for joy without being joyful. But attitudes are not the sorts of things that can be voluntarily summoned up. One cannot, then, be morally obligated to perform grateful acts. (See, for example, Simmons 1979, pp. 166–167, and Lombardi 1991, p. 108.)

This objection fails. First, with respect to *ought implies can*: while I will not belabor the point here, it appears that *ought implies can* does not hold in cases where one's inability to perform a certain act is due to one's unreasonableness. If I am so unreasonable that I cannot restrain myself from committing murder, we should not conclude that it is not true that I ought not murder. (We should say, rather, that I am inculpable for the performance of that wrongful act—assuming, that is, that my unreasonableness was not itself culpably induced.) But one's attitudes can be reasonable or unreasonable. If one is a recipient of gratuitous, benevolent acts yet fails to have the grateful attitude fitting for a recipient of gratuitous benevolent acts, this is a failure of reasonableness. One who is unable to act gratefully because his or her attitudes are out of line with what is practically reasonable is not thereby immune from obligation.

Second, gratitude is not necessarily an expression of certain attitudes—unless we hold that any act that displays a certain intentionality ipso facto counts as expressing the requisite attitude. We can think about it this way. Gratitude-engendering and gratitude-discharging acts are benevolent acts. But benevolent acts are themselves not necessarily the expression of preexisting attitudes toward the recipients of such acts. Consider, for our purposes and not for his, the characters described by Kant who are lacking in ordinary moral sentiments yet nevertheless are capable of acting with the aim of benefiting others (*Grounding*, p. 398). Suppose that these characters are the intended beneficiaries of gratuitous benevolent acts, and are in fact benefited by those acts. While lacking the characteristic warm and friendly emotions of gratefulness, they nonetheless view these acts correctly, as calling for a benevolent response, and act on that view. There is nothing essential to gratitude-requiting acts that is lacking in this case.

Third, even if it were conceded that it is a substantive condition and a real constraint on gratitude-requiting acts that the one performing such acts possess the requisite attitudes, there must be something wrong with the argument. For if such an argument can be run in the case of putatively morally required actions that are necessarily expressions of certain attitudes, then the same argument can be run in the case of putatively morally required actions that are necessarily expressions of certain beliefs. For beliefs are no more voluntary than attitudes are. But it would be disastrous to affirm this argument in the case of actions that express certain beliefs, because *every* action expresses beliefs. If the fact that an action is essentially an expression of an involuntarily possessed attitude shows that this action cannot be morally required, then the fact that an action is essentially an expression of an involuntarily possessed belief would show that that action could not be morally required; but every action is essentially an expression of an involuntarily possessed belief; and so no action can be morally required. (RAA.) The *ought-implies-can* objection to the existence of obligations of gratitude fails.

The benefits objection. More promising are objections that deny not the very possibility of obligations of gratitude but rather the necessary presence of the conditions by which rational creatures would be under a debt of gratitude to God. One such objection concerns whether creation can count as a benefit and so trigger the application of the gratitude principle. Here is one version of the worry. To benefit someone is, characteristically, to improve that person's position. But if this feature is not merely characteristic of benefiting but definitive of it, then creation cannot be a benefit. For there is no person whose position is improved by being created; rather, the person comes into being with creation, and so it is false to say that his or her position was improved and false to say that he or she was benefited.

The first point to make in response to this objection is that creation is not the only divine act with respect to rational beings to which a defender of the gratitude account might appeal. Any benefit to which the defender of this argument may appeal must be one such that, necessarily, if one is a created rational being, then one enjoys that benefit. *Being created* is the obvious candidate. But rational beings are not only created by God but also conserved in existence. Conservation is, however, an act that takes as an object an existing thing. So, if one does not want to deny that other existence-preserving acts—being given enough water, food, etc.—can count as benefits, one had better allow that being conserved in existence can count as a benefit. Even if we grant the objection and allow that creation cannot be a benefiting act for the being that is created, then, the only rational beings that would not be benefited would be those that are created but not conserved, that is, those beings that are brought into existence but then immediately let to slide into nonexistence.

This does not suffice to answer the objection entirely, for it might be possible that a created rational being come into existence and then immediately slip out of existence, being not conserved in existence by God, and if we rely entirely on conservation as the benefit grounding the obligation of gratitude, then we would lack an argument that such beings would be under divine authority on account of the requirement of gratitude. (Consider, for example, Swinburne's formulation of the argument from gratitude, on which we are bound by a debt of gratitude to God because "we owe our existence from moment to moment to the conserving action of God" [1996, p. 14].) One might find silly the idea that God would create a rational being while immediately letting it slip out of existence. Consider, though, the following. On Aquinas's account of the fall of the angels, there was no interval between the creation of the angels and the fall of some of them (*Summa Theologiae* Ia 63, 6).[3] God conserved the being of these bad angels and sent them to Hell. But now suppose that God had chosen to deal with these angels not by damning them but by annihilating them. If so, then we could not say that these angels were under divine authority on account of a requirement of gratitude. One might accept this consequence and hold that if this is a genuine possibility, then gratitude cannot establish the Strongest authority thesis. But it seems to me that the defender of the gratitude argument should want to hold firm, saying that the angels that fell did owe a debt of

3. It should be noted that Aquinas denies, however, that the devil's fall occurred in the same instant as its creation (*Summa Theologiae* Ia 63, 5). For, according to Aquinas, while there is nothing impossible about a thing's acting in the same moment as it comes to exist, that act can only be defective if the thing is defective in its created nature. But the devil's created nature is good. Therefore, etc. If conservation is necessary to keep the devil around long enough to sin—even if there is, as Aquinas thinks, no interval between the devil's being created and his fall—then we would need to reject Aquinas's argument against the devil's instantaneous fall or find another way to make plausible the possibility of God's creating a rational being and immediately failing to conserve that being.

gratitude to God in that first moment of creation, a debt of gratitude (among other requirements, one imagines) that they failed to honor in the act that occasioned their fall.

It would help the argument from gratitude, then, if creation itself constituted an act of benefiting; but if we adopt the notion that to benefit another is to improve that other's condition, it seems that we cannot so understand creation. It is wrong, though, to think that we are forced to this conception of benefiting. As Parfit remarks, surely it can be *good* for someone that he or she was brought into existence, even if it was not *better* for him or her; and even if characteristically benefiting involves improving one's condition, bringing into existence is obvious a special case with respect to which some characteristic features of benefiting might well be absent (Parfit 1984, pp. 489–490). Perhaps the following can serve as a rough test for (not an analysis of) benefiting, one that captures both the usual and the special case: A is benefited by an act of ϕ-ing if and only if, from a personal point of view, it would be reasonable for A to be glad that the act of ϕ-ing took place. (I say 'personal' rather than 'self-interested' because I want to leave open the possibility that one can be benefited by improvement in others' good, if those others are related to one in a special way.) I am very glad that I got a good job and have a loving family, and I am reasonable to be glad about these things; I am also very glad that I came into existence, and I am reasonable to be glad about that. If one wishes to stipulate that my coming into existence was not a benefit to me, I will be happy to oblige, so long as we allow that requirements of gratitude might be engendered not only by acts of benefiting in this stipulated sense but also by any act that can make its recipient glad in this way.

A distinct line of objection calling into question the satisfaction of the benefit condition argues not that the creation of a rational being is necessarily not an act beneficial to that being but that it is *possibly* not beneficial to that being. Since some lives, it is sometimes said, are not worth living, being brought into existence is not good for beings with those lives, and those people would not be reasonable to be glad about being brought into existence. This objection is much more troubling and I am confident that I will not be able to offer anything fully persuasive to those who accept it. Here is why I reject this line of reasoning.

I deny the possibility of a life that has no value for the being that lives it. For, first, I think that life is, at whatever level of vitality, an intrinsic good for the being that has it. The good of life is, as I understand it, the proper functioning of one qua animate being. Now, it is not implausible that the proper functioning of one qua animate being as such is intrinsically good for one; if the notion that life is an intrinsic good is implausible, it is because there is not much to be said in its favor when very meagerly instantiated. But to say that there is not much to be said in its favor when very meagerly instantiated is not to say that there is *nothing* to be said in its favor: if life is an intrinsic good, then one would think that the meagerness of an instance of life would make it merely much less good than a much fuller participation, and not entirely valueless. (I argue this point at greater length in Murphy 2001a, pp. 103–104.) If this is true, then in virtue of life, which is sine qua non for any existing created rational being, each created rational being has a life with some value for that being.

Some may find unpersuasive the notion that life is an intrinsic value.[4] Here is an alternative intrinsic good that can plausibly be held to be instantiated in every created rational being, even those whose lives are absolutely miserable. A defender of the gratitude argument might appeal to the good of being the kind of thing whose misery (or, more positively, whose joy) *really matters*—the good of being a thing with *dignity*. Even if one is miserable, it is a precious thing to be a being that is so important that its misery is something worth crying to the heavens about. I am not here simply affirming the tautology that if one is the sort of being whose misery is bad from the point of view of the universe, then if it is miserable, that is bad from the point of view of the universe. That triviality is distinct from the substantive claim that I am making, that is, that having dignity is good *for* the being with dignity. It is good for one to be a being of the sort whose misery matters from the point of view of the universe.

My reason for thinking that having dignity is valuable for the being that has it is as follows. Even for those of us whose lives are remarkably fortunate, there are bad stretches; yet during those bad stretches one thing that makes one's life not so bad as all that is the fact that one's suffering *matters* to at least some others. (It is not merely the fact that one *believes* that one's suffering matters to others, and the fact that such belief can give solace: if one has such

---

4. Though it would seem strange for Christians to hold this, given the way that "life" is used by Christ by way of synecdoche for all good: "I came that they may have life, and have it abundantly" (John 10:10).

a belief, and it is false, one is even more pathetic and badly off.) If one's suffering matters, then, not just to oneself but *from the point of view of the universe*—and, presumably, to God—this fact about oneself makes one's life not *as* bad. If, then, it is necessarily true that rational beings are beings with dignity, and this dignity is the sort of thing that is good for a created rational being, then there is further reason to suppose that being created is not merely contingently but necessarily good for created rational beings.

If either life or possession of dignity is intrinsically good for created rational beings, then there is necessarily realized in the life of every created rational being some intrinsic good. The only way for such beings to have a life not worth living is, then, to have the intrinsic goods essential to created rational life *negated*—that there be other aspects of those beings' lives that are *evil* and that *cancel out* the good of life, or dignity. But I reject this possibility, because it seems to me that the classic doctrine—that all evils are simply privations of goods (Aquinas, *Summa Contra Gentiles* III, 6)—is correct. The concept of *negative value* is thus without application.

The only really persuasive instance of a positive evil that I know of is that of pain, which seems not at all like a deprivation but like a genuine, on-its-own-account evil. But I say that even pain, when its basic badness is made manifest, is privation of good. For what is bad about pain is its being unwanted; as Parfit writes, we would regard drugs that made us no longer mind the sensation of pain as effective analgesics (1984, p. 501). It is wrong to say that a sensation of pain is an evil, bad for one, if one has that sensation yet does not dislike it. The evil of pain, as I see it, is its being a privation of a genuine good: that of inner peace, the state of having only fulfilled desires. Pain, a sensation characteristically accompanied by a desire not to have it, is a disruption from and a lack in the good of inner peace. And so pain does not constitute an ultimately plausible counterexample to the notion that all evil is privation of good. (I argue this point at greater length in Murphy 2001a, pp. 97–100, 118–126.)

If life or dignity is intrinsically good, and the notion of negative value is empty, then, necessarily, every created rational being is benefited by coming into existence. One might respond, of course, that the benefit is relatively meager in some cases, while relatively rich in others, and might claim that this causes problems for the idea that everyone is equally bound to full obedience to God out of gratitude. But this is not persuasive. First, there is the obvious point that for the poorly off and the well-off, each owes *all* the good that he or she is and has to God. Second, though the poorly off and the well-off are differently situated with respect to received benefits, they are also correspondingly differently situated with respect to sacrifices that God can, through the exercise of God's commands, call upon them to make. The idea of the gratitude argument is that because we received all good that we enjoy from God, we owe, out of gratitude, everything we have to God: so those that have much, owe much; those that have little, owe little. The fact of differences in benefit does not call this line of reasoning into question.

The particularity objection. Even if one grants that creation necessarily counts as a benefit to the created rational being, there is another line of objection that appeals to the prior nonexistence of the beneficiary that can be pressed. This line of objection is based on the idea that obligations of gratitude are generated only when the acts that in fact benefit a person are *aimed at* benefiting a person. More strongly, one might say not only that benefiting acts must be intentionally beneficial; they must be intended to benefit the particular person putatively bound by a debt of gratitude. For A's act of benefiting B to be gratitude-engendering, it would have to be the case that A intended to benefit B. It would not be enough if A intended to benefit only C $(B \neq C)$, yet B was accidentally benefited by that act; nor would it be enough if A intended to benefit the members of some class of persons P (read *de dicto*, not *de re*), and B happened to be a member of P. (This is true even if A *knows* that B is a member of P.)

But to place this constraint on acts of benefiting that can engender obligations of gratitude would raise a difficulty for the idea that creation constitutes a gratitude-engendering benefit. For one cannot have *ex ante* an attitude toward the particular being that one creates, for there does not yet exist the object about which one can have the requisite attitude. Consider, as an analogous case, an act by which parents conceive a child. If I were to put to my daughters the notion that they owe their mother and me gratitude for having conceived them, they could respond that we did not set out to conceive *them*; we set out to conceive some children or other, and they were the ones that we succeeded in conceiving. "Of course you two were trying to have children, and we are the children that you had," they might say. "But it does not follow from those facts that you were trying to have *us*. Since you could not have tried to have *us*, there is no offense taken. But since you did not try to have us, even though we are very glad that you had us, those benefiting acts do not call for gratitude on our part. If we owe the two of you any gratitude, it is for the care that you two gave us while we were in utero, and for the care that the two of you have given us since." If this line of argument is persuasive with respect to the relationship between parents and the children they conceive, and if the relationship between God and the rational beings that God creates is similar to the parent-child relationship in relevant respects, no rational being could owe God a debt of gratitude for the beneficial act of creation.

I will argue later in this section that the requirement that a benefiting action must be aimed at an agent in his or her particularity for a debt of gratitude to be generated is an overly strong interpretation of what counts as intending to benefit some person. But I want first to explore whether this interpretation, strong as it is, would really rule out gratitude based on creation. I say that it would not, for there is a relevant difference between the parents' conceiving a child and God's creating a rational being. Consider the notion of a *haecceity* (see, for example, Plantinga 1970, pp. 489–490). A haecceity is an individual essence: H is a haecceity of O's if and only if necessarily, if O exists, then O exemplifies H, and necessarily, for any object O^*, if O^* exemplifies H then $O = O^*$. Let α designate the actual world. *Being the only rational being in 235 New North on September 17, 2001, at 1:15 P.M. in α* is one of my haecceities. So is the more homely *being identical to Mark Murphy*. Defined only in these terms, it does not strike me as very controversial to think that there are haecceities. What is controversial are additional claims that one could make about them: that they are (or are not) reducible to qualitative properties; that they can (or cannot) be used to provide informative criteria of identity over time, or across worlds; that they are (or are not) necessary existents. If haecceities preexist the objects that instantiate them—if they are, for example, necessary existents—then we can answer the particularity objection. (For an argument that haecceities are indeed necessary existents, see Plantinga 1983.) For if haecceities preexist the objects that exemplify them, then the knowledge of haecceities would enable God to aim at creating particular individuals.

This, then, is one of the many dissimilarities between the human and divine situation with respect to human conceiving and divine creating of rational beings. For a human's knowledge of haecceities is entirely dependent upon his or her acquaintance with the objects exemplifying those haecceities—or, perhaps, dependent on someone else's acquaintance with the objects exemplifying those haecceities, which knowledge is then transmitted through testimony. Because of this constraint on human knowledge of haecceities, I lack any acquaintance with unexemplified haecceities (though I can pick out *classes* of such haecceities). But this is a relevant dissimilarity between the parent–child and God–created rational being relationships. God knew my essence, even before I was created. Through that knowledge God could have aimed at creating *me*, not just one of some class of rational beings fitting a certain Murphy-like description. But my wife and I, in our state of knowledge, could not have aimed at conceiving Ryan Elizabeth Murphy or Flannery Jane Murphy. We could aim at conceiving children, and even at conceiving children with certain qualities; but we could not aim at conceiving *these* children. So the particularity desideratum for gratitude-engendering acts can be met in the case of divine creation but is not met in the usual parent–child case.[5]

If the haecceities exemplified by created rational beings preexist those rational beings, then God can know these haecceities, and intend the creation of particular rational beings. Any objection that rests on the impossibility of God's acting to create a particular created rational being would therefore fail. But there is a successor particularity objection that may yet have force. This successor objection holds that even if it is possible for God to create particular rational beings, we would nonetheless fail to owe God debts of gratitude because of the way that God selected which particular rational beings would be created.

The argument would go something like this. God's creative decree with respect to the creation of rational beings may be, as Peter van Inwagen suggests with respect to God's actualization of one among many feasible possible worlds, a decree *that some rational beings be*: from this decree would result the creation of certain particular rational beings. Or God's creative decree might involve the random selection of certain particular rational beings to create, followed by God's creative decree that these particular beings be: from this decree would result the creation of certain particular rational beings (cf. van Inwagen 1995c, pp. 48, 56–60). In either case, we might argue, no debt of gratitude for creation could emerge. In the former case, there is no particularity to God's creative intention, thus blocking the gen-

---

5. I suppose it is possible in the human case, if the intentionality of the parents' conceiving the child were adequately *divinely* informed.

eration of a debt of gratitude in response to this act of benefiting. In the latter case, there is the requisite particularity to God's creative intention, but the randomness by which God settles on a particular event of haecceity-exemplification disqualifies the creative act from constituting a gratitude-engendering act. In neither case does creation generate a debt of gratitude binding on the rational beings thus created.

But this argument is, upon reflection, not very plausible. Here is an analogy. Suppose that I have two relatives, both of whom are in need of a kidney transplant. Fortuitously, I am an eligible kidney donor with respect to each. I love each of them, but can give up only one of my kidneys. To choose the recipient, I settle on a policy: I will decide who gets the kidney by means of a coin flip. If the winner of the coin flip judges that she owes no debt of gratitude because I did not direct the benefit toward her *as such*, we would rightly judge her an ingrate. The relevant feature of the case is my prior love for both, which is for each of them in their particularity; the randomness by which a scarce good is channeled to a recipient does not prevent the particularity desideratum from being met. Now, it may well be that for every unexemplified haecceity of a created rational being, God thinks lovingly about that haecceity's being exemplified as a real, live person. But some haecceities are such that they cannot be co-exemplified. And, since for every number of haecceities exemplified in some world there could yet be another, God will simply have to pick some number of rational beings to create. If God's reason for creating rational beings is love for rational beings, and the randomness of the selection of which rational beings are created is due to necessary limits on creation, then we should not deny that creation in these cases counts as a gratitude-engendering benefit.

This completes the part of my response to the particularity objection based on the assumption that particularity of intention is a necessary feature of gratitude-engendering benefactions. Suppose, though, that one finds the appeal to preexisting haecceities dubious metaphysics. Is there any way to defeat the particularity objection without casting about for a way to characterize God's intentionality in creating as aimed at creating rational beings in their particularity? Yes: we can deny that the particularity requirement is a plausible constraint on gratitude-engendering acts.

The particularity requirement is very implausible. Consider a modified version of the transplant situation. Suppose that I, moved by the plight of patients badly in need of kidney donations, register as a donor. I am willing to give my kidney to the first person in need who is sufficiently biologically compatible that chances of rejection will be within an acceptable range of risk. I am informed that a match has been found; I undergo surgery, and yield my kidney; it is successfully transplanted. Later, my meeting with the recipient goes less than smoothly. "I would thank you for your sacrifice," he says, "but you didn't do it *for me;* you didn't even *know* me. You did it simply for anybody who needed a kidney, and I happened to fall under that description. You didn't intend to give it *to me;* you intended to give it to anyone who happened to be in need." Such a person is a terrible ingrate.

The strong interpretation of benevolent acts, the interpretation requiring particularity, cannot be faulted for holding that *A*'s intending to benefit someone in class *C*, even together with *A*'s believing that *B* is a member of class *C*, does not constitute a case of *A*'s intending to benefit *B*. The mistake must be just that of thinking that gratitude-engendering acts require that sort of particular intention. I agree that if one's benefiting were not for the sake of benefiting—if, for example, rational beings were simply the precipitate of God's creating an orderly universe—then gratitude would be out of place, as not aimed at any rational creature's good. But we need not understand God's benefiting as aimed at the creation of particular rational beings in order to understand God's creating as an instance of intentional benefaction. If God's purpose in creating rational beings was for the sake of those beings and the good to be realized in their lives, then we lack grounds to think that no gratitude could be owed, even if God did not have, or could not have had, intentions that bore on the particular identities of the rational beings thus created.[6]

The self-defeatingness objection. The objections from *ought implies can,* benefiting, and particularity are unsuccessful. We have, I think, some reason to think that all created rational beings are bound by a debt of gratitude to God for their creation. One might, however, grant the existence of such an obligation while rejecting the notion that a requirement of obedience could be generated out of that obligation.

This objection takes its lead from the idea that since gratitude-engen-

---

6. This seems to me right in the case of parents and children as well. There may be other grounds for thinking that children do not owe their parents gratitude for conceiving them. But it does not seem to me that the fact that their attempt to conceive was not aimed at the child in its particularity is not such a ground, so long as the attempt to conceive a child is performed out of an anticipatory love directed at whatever particular child may come into existence.

dering acts are gratuitous acts of benevolence, obligations of gratitude are not engendered when the benefiting act was performed precisely to obligate the beneficiary. As Berger writes, when a beneficial act is "done in order to gain favor, . . . the duty to show gratitude is diminished" (1975, p. 300). Berger suggests that because this is true, "we do not feel at ease in saying that something is owed the grantor in the sense that he has the right to demand it" (1975, p. 300). And Lombardi, applying this view specifically to the relationship between gratitude and divine authority, agrees, holding that the gratuitous character of gratitude-engendering acts implies that the benefactor cannot demand a grateful response from the beneficiary (1991, pp. 109–110).

The conclusion may be true, but the argument is confused. The fact that an obligation of gratitude is not generated when one benefits another solely in order to create that obligation does not at all show that a benefactor can never demand a grateful response from the beneficiary. To make the argument work, it would have to be assumed that whenever one demands a grateful response from another that he or she has benefited, the initial act of benefaction was performed in order to bring about the obligation. But there is no reason to suppose this is true. Suppose that out of love for my children I raise and nurture them. When they become adults, I demand that they pursue philosophy as their life's work. When they demur, I insist that they do so, citing the gratitude that they owe to me as the reason that backs up my demand. Now, I do not deny that my demand is entirely unreasonable. But it would be just false to insist that my initial acts of benefiting must have been solely, or at all, for the sake of producing obligations that I could exploit later. And this could be true in the divine case as well. God's reasons for creating rational beings may be simply love for those beings. If there is something amiss in the idea of God's backing up commands with reasons of gratitude, it is not because it implies that those acts of benefiting were ipso facto not of the sort to engender obligations of gratitude.

It is true, though, that there is *something* amiss in the idea of demanding that another act out of reasons of gratitude. As Berger writes, using Austin's label, such demands are "misfires." But it does not follow from the fact that such demands are misfires that those under requirements of gratitude are not bound to adhere to such demands, bound to adhere to them out of gratitude itself. I owe my parents a large debt of gratitude. If my father were to demand that I, say, hang his portrait in my living room, and if he were to offer reasons of gratitude as his basis for so demanding, this would be a major misfire. But it is not obvious that I would thereby lack a reason of gratitude for doing what my father wills with respect to the hanging of his portrait. The misfiring of the demand indicates that it is not one that a reasonable person would make. But it does not follow from the inevitable misfiring of such demands that grateful persons lack any reason to adhere to those demands. So we cannot reason from the fact that demanding that another ϕ out of gratitude is inevitably a misfire to the conclusion that gratitude cannot provide reasons to act in accordance with that other's demands, indeed, even with demands to ϕ out of gratitude.

But *God's* commands surely never misfire. So, in giving any command, God must be relying on reasons for those commanded to comply other than reasons of gratitude. Since God gives commands only when there are decisive reasons for compliance on the part of those commanded (Chapter 2), it follows that God's commands are always backed by reasons that would be decisive even apart from reasons of gratitude. So even if it were true that every created rational being has decisive reasons of gratitude to adhere to God's commands, we would never need to appeal to those reasons of gratitude in explaining how it is possible for God to give any particular command, nor could we ever licitly appeal to such reasons in providing such explanations.

It is important to understand in what ways the self-defeatingness objection calls the gratitude account into question, and in what ways it does not. In posing the problem of divine authority, most of us would assume that if God has authority then God can *extend* the range of actions that we have decisive reasons to perform. It would turn out to be quite a surprise if God's authority were restricted to overdetermining reasons for action, to adding further reasons to do what there is already decisive reason to do. But that is just what the self-defeatingness objection shows: necessarily there is no action that God might command rational beings to perform that, but for reasons of gratitude, God could not have commanded rational beings to perform. Divine authority explained solely by reasons of gratitude would not enable us to enlarge the range of actions that we rational beings might be required in reason to perform.

While the self-defeatingness objection shows that if divine authority comes from considerations of gratitude, then its exercise is extremely limited, it does *not* show that God does not possess authority as a result of the requirements of gratitude. The self-defeatingness objection does not undercut the gratitude account's conclusion that if God gives a command to perform some action, that command partially constitutes a decisive reason to perform that action. It shows only that God would not give that command unless there were already decisive reasons to perform that action.[7]

The specificity objection. A similar line of argument comes to the same result. It has been suggested that divine authority cannot be grounded on a requirement of gratitude because it is contrary to the nature of that requirement for the benefactor to specify precisely how the beneficiary must requite that obligation: any statement by the benefactor that the beneficiary is to fulfill the obligation of gratitude in a particular way is a misfire (Berger 1975, p. 306; Lombardi 1991, p. 110). In laying down commands, though, God would be specifying precisely how created rational beings must act in satisfying the requirement of gratitude. Therefore, gratitude cannot provide an account of divine authority.

The argument fails, since it does not follow from the facts that in cases where gratitude is owed it is a misfire for the benefactor to specify how the gratitude debt is to be met and that God's directives never misfire that we do not have reasons of gratitude to obey God's commands. All that follows is that God does not issue these specific directives qua backed by requirements of gratitude. And since God's commands are always backed by decisive reasons, no appeal to reasons of gratitude is needed to account for the decisive reasons to obey those commands that created rational beings have.

The insufficiency objection. The final objection provides, in my view, the greatest difficulty for the gratitude account. The self-defeatingness and specificity objections, while stripping the gratitude account of any pride of place in the explication of reasons to do what God tells us to do, do not succeed in striking at the central contention of the gratitude account, which is that a requirement of gratitude binds all created rational beings to act on God's commands. The insufficiency objection calls this conclusion more successfully into question, suggesting that the existence of a maximally pow-

---

7. Even if divine commands could only overdetermine reasons for action, the gratitude account (if otherwise successful) would be useful in the task of explaining how agents can intelligibly act out of the motive of obedience to God's commands. Indeed it may be that acts of obedience out of the motive of obedience, and perhaps out of the motive of obedience in light of gratitude, are more pleasing to God than those performed for the other reasons that back a divine command.

erful debt of gratitude to God is nevertheless insufficient to generate divine authority.

Begin with the question: How are we to support the notion that the benefit of creation and conservation dictates that *every* appropriately grateful response will include *entire* obedience? The answer, so it seems to me, is that the benefit is so great that the created rational being owes God *everything* out of gratitude. And this includes one's capacity to choose freely with respect to what is to be done, within the limits set by the requirements of practical reasonableness. To hold back obedience to God is thus to be ungrateful.

It is the idea of 'holding back' obedience to God that is in need of spelling out. Suppose that gratitude is the sole source of divine authority. If so, then apart from the requirement of gratitude, created rational beings are free to make their own choices with respect to what is to be done. But since all such created rational beings necessarily owe God a debt of gratitude, this freedom should be yielded up to God. *Even if it is true, though, that the practical freedom of created rational beings is owed to God out of gratitude, it does not follow that created rational beings are necessarily under an obligation to obey God.* Let me explain.

Suppose that my life is saved, at great risk, by someone who is but a slight acquaintance of mine. She herself is badly injured in the rescue. A lover of philosophy, she would like nothing more than to read a particular philosophy book during her convalescence. But copies of the book are hard to acquire within a reasonable time; and by the time she could acquire a copy on her own, she would no longer be bedridden and in particular need of diversion. Luckily, I own a copy. Surely I ought to give her the book. But from the debt of gratitude the book is not hers yet. This is not the point that she cannot, without 'misfiring,' demand the book, which is of itself consistent with the view that it is hers by right. It isn't anything of the sort; it's *mine*. But I ought to yield it to her. And only when I do what is right by yielding the book to her does it become hers.

Now, if gratitude is our sole account of divine authority, then we should understand the position of rational beings and obedience along the lines of this analogy. If the freedom for self-direction within the range of otherwise eligible choices is part of the 'original equipment' of created rational beings, then we should yield this freedom to God, out of gratitude for creating and sustaining us. But that debt does not immediately translate into a requirement of obedience, just as the debt of gratitude in my example does not immediately translate into a transfer of book-ownership. If, in the book case, I am not an ingrate, I will yield the book to her, and it will become hers by right; but if I am ungrateful, I will not yield the book, and it will remain mine by right. If created rational beings properly acknowledge their debt of gratitude to God, they will submit to the divine rule, and become subjects of God; but if they are ungrateful, they will not submit, and will remain outside of divine authority. Remember: I am reasoning here under the assumption that gratitude is our sole account of divine authority. If our sole appeal is to gratitude, we cannot show that created rational beings are necessarily under divine authority; all it can show is that such beings are bound to submit to God and place themselves under divine authority. This leaves open the possibility that some other account of divine authority— whether an argument from divine perfection, or some other moral argu- ment—will be able to accomplish what the gratitude account, for all its strengths, cannot.

5.5 COORDINATION

Recently there has been an interest in coordination accounts of political au- thority, accounts that purport to explain the practical authority of the state in terms of the need for coordination of citizen action with respect to the realization of some common good. (See Green 1990, pp. 89–121, for a dis- cussion of these views.) It is, defenders of these accounts claim, the salience of the state with respect to the solution of the coordination problem faced by citizens in realizing the common good that makes the state's dictates con- cerning the realization of that good reasons for citizen action. It might be thought that once the analogies between the state's role in coordinating ac- tion for the common good and God's role in coordinating the action of all created rational beings toward the good of the universe as a whole are made out, and the limitations on the state's authority shown not to hold in the case of God, it would turn out that a defensible coordination argument for the authority thesis can be made.

Here is the most basic form of coordination arguments. Suppose that there is some end E that agents A_1 through A_n have reason to promote. This end is best promoted through coordinated, cooperative action. Since there are, however, a number of incompatible ways for A_1 through A_n to coordinate their activities in pursuit of E, some common decision must be made. If, then, there is some salient person or set of rules L that offers a common decision concerning A_1 through A_n's acting to promote E, then

A_1 through A_n would be acting unreasonably if they were to pursue E without adhering to L's plan of action. Generically considered, this account of authority offers as its conclusion only that if agents pursue E, in these conditions it is reasonable only to act in accordance with L's prescriptions concerning its pursuit. But there is, of course, a way to strengthen the account: if the end E were a mandatory end, an end that A_1 through A_n were bound to promote, then the antecedent of the conditional could be dropped: those agents would simply be bound to act in accordance with L's dictates.[8]

It is important, though, that the circumstances in which the existence of a salient coordinator is sufficient to generate practical authority are likely to be few and far between. On the salient coordinator view, a salient coordinator exists only if for some end E, agents in pursuit of E would be acting in a practically unreasonable way if they did not adhere to the dictates laid down by that coordinator. But the end E must be of a very particular sort in order for us to be confident that these conditions are met: it must be either determinate or in need of only arbitrary specification. (To be 'in need of only arbitrary specification' is for the end to be to some extent indeterminate, and for there to be no way to make the end determinate that we have any good reason to prefer over any other way to make the end determinate.) Suppose that an end meets this condition. If so, then the need for authority in coordinating action for the sake of this end results from there being at least two plans of action, P_1 and P_2, of which the following is true: (a) P_1 and P_2 are no worse than any other plan of action that might be put into place to realize E and (b) P_1 and P_2 are 'arbitrary with respect to E,' that is, there is no reason available in terms of E for choosing P_1 over P_2, and vice versa. In these circumstances the salient coordinator account has sufficient basis for the claim that some salient authority has genuine practical authority to decide whether P_1 or P_2 is the plan to be followed to achieve E. Suppose, for example, that the end in question is that of everyone's driving on one side of the road. While this end is not totally determinate—there is more than one side to choose from—how this end is realized is an indifferent matter; it is in need only of arbitrary specification. Given this end, if there were a salient standard that proclaimed 'all are to

---

8. The agent would be bound given the assumption that L's dictates were not themselves otherwise precluded by some principle of practical reasonableness.

drive on the right side of the road,' then it would follow from the adherence to this end, the need for a standard, and the likelihood of general compliance with that standard that for each agent that standard is authoritative. In acting for this kind of end, and in conditions where there exists such a standard for action, the best way to realize that end would be to adhere to the standard, and agents would be able to offer no reason in terms of that end for failing to adhere to that standard. Thus, in terms of the end E, agents would be practically unreasonable not to adhere to the standard laid down by the salient coordinator.

Note, though, how different this is from any case in which the end is indeterminate yet not arbitrary: indeterminate either because that end is general or because that end is complex yet unordered; nonarbitrary because there are reasons to prefer one specification of that end rather than another, and vice versa. Assume that E is indeterminate either through vagueness (for example, 'the common good') or through complexity (for example, 'lowering crime and promoting beautification'). With respect to such ends, it is typically the case that there are at least two plans of action P_1 and P_2 such that (a) P_1 and P_2 are no worse than any other plan of action that might be put into place to realize E yet (b) P_1 and P_2 are *not* arbitrary with respect to E: one can give a reason in terms of E for preferring P_1, and a distinct reason in terms of E for preferring P_2. For example: given the complex end of lowering crime and promoting beautification, P_1 might be slightly better at lowering crime while P_2 is slightly better at promoting beautification. But the nonarbitrariness with respect to E of P_1 and P_2 raises difficulties for the salient coordinator account. Where the plans of action among which the salient coordinator chooses are arbitrary with respect to the end, those concerned to promote the end can offer no reason in terms of that end for failing to adhere to the authority's dictates. But where the plans of action involved are not arbitrary, those concerned to promote the end can offer reasons in terms of the end sought for failing to adhere to the authority's dictates. In such cases, the defender of the salient coordinator account cannot claim that the best way for the end to be realized must be for the agent to act in accordance with the salient standard. It will often be the case that even if others generally comply with the putatively authoritative standard, one can through defection from such compliance bring about a state of affairs that better approximates a different, eligible specification of the end.

These remarks suggest that while the salient coordinator account of practical authority can, in principle, generate authority, its application will be extremely limited, for most of the ends that are pursued in common are in need of nonarbitrary specification.[9] If this is true of any end pursued in common, it is true of the ends pursued in political community. But some writers have held that even if the common good of the political community is in need of nonarbitrary specification, the salience of political authority as the organizer of efforts to promote the common good confers authority on de facto authorities. John Finnis writes that the law is a salient coordinator because

> The law presents itself as a seamless web. Its subjects are not permitted to pick and choose among the law's prescriptions and stipulations. It links together, in a privileged way, all the persons, and all the transactions, bearing on [one's] present and immediate future situation. It also links all the people and transactions which have borne on [one's] well-being or interests in the past. And finally, it links too all the people and transactions that may bear on [one's] future interests and well-being as [one] moves into other occupations, into retirement, old-age, illness, and death. (Finnis 1984, p. 120)

And so the law is uniquely *normatively* salient: of all candidates to fill the role of authoritative specifier of the common good, it is the law that is normatively privileged. We can have far greater confidence in the law as the decider of these questions about the promotion of the common good: it is more likely to be just, evenhanded, persisting, and common than any other candidate authority. Given the need for some authority to fill the role of co-

9. I have not pressed here another severe difficulty for salient coordinator accounts: they do not show that under certain circumstances a salient coordinator's dictates *constitutively* actualize reasons for action; they show, rather, that under certain favorable circumstances a salient coordinator's dictates *merely causally* actualize reasons for action (for the distinction see 1.1). Suppose, for example, that the end in question is that of everyone driving on the same side of a given road. If the salient coordinator is a large sign at the entrance to that road that says 'Everyone is to drive on the right side of the road,' then it does seem that, under normal circumstances, one would be unreasonable to drive on the left on that road. But one's reason for driving on the right here is just that, because others are likely to drive on the right, one's driving on the left would likely be dangerous in a way that one's driving on the right would not be. The sign surely had a central role in bringing this reason about: if the sign were not posted, the driving pattern that holds sway on that road might well not have. But the sign's role here is causal, not constitutive. For further argument against the salient coordinator account along these lines, see Raz 1979, pp. 247–248; 1984, pp. 151–152.

ordinator of action to the political common good, and the salience of the law in filling this role, we have decisive reason to obey the law with respect to the promotion of the common good.

Granting for the moment that this extended coordinator argument might be successful in explaining why we have reason to adhere to the law's dictates, how can this argument be reasonably extended to the case of divine authority? As follows. God has adequate (!) comprehension not only of all the reasonable ends of action within a given political community, but of any reasonable ends besides these. If the realization of a common good within a particular, highly circumscribed human community requires coordination by some salient authority, then a fortiori any good that includes the goods of such communities will require coordination as well. The only party that could in fact coordinate the activity of rational agents toward such a comprehensive good would be God. And, furthermore, God is not subject to any of the limitations that require qualifications of the requirement to adhere to the dictates issued by human authorities. God is omniscient, so no failures of knowledge of the sort that can vitiate the authority of particular dictates of human law can occur. God is perfectly morally good, so God's concern with the good will be fully appropriate. And since God can comprehend all reasons for agents to act, and not merely some subset of them, the reasons for action provided by God's dictates cannot be overridden by other concerns, as one might take to be the case with respect to reasons for adherence resulting from the need to promote the common good. An argument structurally identical to the coordination argument for political authority seems to support divine authority with even greater plausibility.

But the coordination argument is not ultimately successful with respect to political authority, and the coordination argument for divine authority inherits its failings. The problem with the salient coordinator argument, as I have portrayed it, is that it does not show why we ought to obey in cases where there are materially different, nonarbitrary specifications of the common good available—one could have, under such circumstances, adequate reason to depart from the specification offered by the salient coordinator. An argument like Finnis's establishes the conclusion that the best candidate to fill the role of salient coordinator is the law. But even if it is true—and I think that it is true—that practically reasonable agents will recognize the need for authority in coordinating practically reasonable agents to the common good, the existence of a need for political authority does not translate into the existence of political authority. The need for *x* never implies the existence of *x*. While the requirement that citizens seek to promote the common good gives each agent reason to do his or her part in putting into place a political authority, the acknowledgment of the need for a genuinely authoritative institution to guide action to the common good is not sufficient to show that where the law exists citizens are under a moral requirement to adhere to it. (See also Murphy 2001c, pp. 79–83.)

Now, it is possible that while the coordination argument for *political* authority fails, there is some special feature of the coordination argument for *divine* authority that prevents its failing in this way. But I don't see that this is true. As far as we can see, there are a number of incommensurably good ways for the universe's history to go on, and so the good of the universe can be nonarbitrarily specified in incompatible ways. Now, it may be best for there to be a coordinator of agents toward the common good of the universe, and so all agents would have reason to do their part to make such a coordinator authoritative; and it is obvious that God is the only serious candidate for this role. But all that this shows is that created rational beings have decisive reason to do their part in making God authoritative over them—that is, to submit to the divine rule. This argument does not militate in favor of the conclusion that God is in fact authoritative over all created rational beings. It militates in favor of the conclusion that all created rational beings ought to make God authoritative over them. The true upshot of the coordination argument is not that all created rational beings *are* under divine authority but that all created rational beings *ought to be* under divine authority.

How is this possible? Why would it not follow from the fact that created rational beings ought to be under divine authority that they actually are under divine authority? The point is just that created rational beings can see that it would be good to have certain reasons for action without thereby having those reasons. Here are two examples, one concerning moral reasons and the other concerning prudential reasons. Suppose that you are responsible for the care of a sick friend, and a pharmacist will give you a drug that will significantly ease the illness only if you are under an obligation to pay her twenty dollars within the week. In this case, it would be good for you to have this reason—your friend's health depends on it—but its being good to have this reason does not give you the reason to pay the twenty dollars within the week; you will need to do something—make a promise, perhaps—in order to generate the requisite reason (see Murphy 1994, pp. 276–277). Or: suppose that you are the character described in Warren Quinn's "The Puzzle of the Self-Torturer" (W. Quinn 1993b). The Self-Torturer has a standing offer to receive ten thousand dollars in return for willingly undergoing an imperceptible increase in electric shocks. Since each increase in the level of the electric shocks causes you no further suffering, yet the accumulation of such steps is (unfortunately) easily perceptible, you are willing to take each step but know full well that eventually you will find yourself in a position in which you are much worse off than when you started. It would be good if you had some reason never to begin this game, or some reason to stop playing at a level at which the total increase in the shocks is worth the total reward reaped. But that it would be good to have a reason to stop does not yet give you a reason to stop; that is what makes the Self-Torturer case *puzzling*. The best way to resolve the paradox is to identify some way of generating a reason never to start playing the game, or to stop playing the game at some point, perhaps through a commitment of some sort. That the goodness of having a reason to ϕ does not imply having a reason to ϕ is what makes the problem of the Self-Torturer a hard case rather than an easy one.

To be under another's authority is for that other's dictates to constitute decisive reasons for action for one (1.1). It can be desirable to be under another's authority; it can be desirable for another's dictates to constitute decisive reasons for action for one. But we can move from the desirability of this state of affairs to the conclusion that this state of affairs is actual only by affirming the further premise that if it is good for one to have a reason to ϕ, then one has a reason to ϕ. Since this premise is false, we are left with a gap: that created rational beings ought to be under divine authority does not imply that they actually are under such authority.

5.6 OBEDIENCE TO GOD AS AN INDEPENDENT MORAL PRINCIPLE
In the Introduction I distinguished between the task of showing that a normative version of divine command theory of ethics is true and that of showing that the Strongest authority thesis is true. To recapitulate briefly: normative versions of divine command theory entail, but are not entailed by, the authority thesis, because normative versions of divine command theory claim not only that the Strongest authority thesis is true but that its truth is

prior to all other moral norms. We could not prove a normative version of divine command theory without also proving the Strongest authority thesis, and more besides. Nonetheless, any arguments in favor of normative divine command theories are worth considering. What makes such views worthy of consideration is that because they treat the requirement to obey God's commands as being *supreme*, the principle from which all other moral norms derive, they must also think of the Strongest authority thesis as *independent*, not merely an implication of some other moral principle. And so any arguments such views offer for the authority thesis as an independent moral principle may be available for adoption, even by those who reject divine command theories.

Unfortunately, classic defenses of divine command moral theories do not distinguish between divine command theory in its metaethical and its normative versions, and arguments offered for divine command theory tend to be arguments for metaethical versions of divine command theory. Here are two famous arguments for divine command theory along metaethical lines. First: if God is omnipotent, with the power to do anything within the realm of the broadly logically possible, and God is impeccable, unable to act contrary to what is morally good, then God must be able to control the content of the morally good, for otherwise God would not have the power to do everything that is within the realm of the broadly logically possible. Or: if God has absolute liberty, with the freedom to do anything within the realm of the broadly logically possible, and God is impeccable, unable to act contrary to what is morally good, then God must be able to control the content of the morally good, for otherwise God would not be free to do anything that is within the realm of the broadly logically possible. (For a discussion of the historical sources of these arguments, see Idziak 1979b, pp. 8–9, and Idziak 1989, pp. 51–53.) In this tradition of argument for divine command theory is Philip Quinn's argument from divine sovereignty, on which all states of affairs wholly distinct from God depend on God for their obtaining; on his view, this includes (most) deontological states of affairs, so that such states of affairs depend on God for their obtaining (1990). What all of these views would establish is, at most, a metaethical version of divine command theory, on which the content of morality is causally controlled by God's will. But such causal conceptions are not to be identified with, and do not entail, divine authority, as I argued above (4.3). For it is consistent with these accounts to hold that created rational beings do not have reason to obey God; they do not entail that God's commands partially constitute reasons for action for any rational being.

To compound the misfortune, recent defenders of explicitly normative versions of divine command theory have not offered arguments in favor of the principle except to note that it is not obviously incoherent and that the most central objections to it are not decisive (see, for example, Wierenga 1989, pp. 213–234). One can imagine why this might be. It might be thought that if this principle really is independent, indeed supreme, there could not be a proof of it: for any proof would appeal to some independent, indeed superior, moral principle of which the requirement of obedience to God would be but one application. But this would be an unwarranted step. Even aside from the possibility that the divine perfection establishes God's authority—a possibility that I attempted to foreclose in Chapter 3—there are modes of argumentation for moral principles that do not presuppose the existence of superior moral principles, or indeed the existence of any other moral principles.

We might appeal to the moral version of inference to the best explanation: there is a set of cases about whose moral status we are confident; that these cases have this moral status is best explained by the affirmation of a certain general moral principle; therefore, we have reason to affirm that general moral principle. If we have a set of cases of slavery, otherwise very different, yet about which we are confident in our moral condemnation, then we can be justified in holding that there is a moral prohibition on slavery. We could make the same sort of case with respect to an independent principle of obedience to God's commands. If it turns out that there is a set of cases about which we have confident moral judgments and which are best explained through the affirmation of a principle of obedience to divine commands, then we would have a basis for affirming the authority thesis as an independent moral principle.

The compliance thesis, as we have seen, already guarantees that there could never be an occasion on which God gives a command with which those commanded do not have decisive reason to comply (2.1). So we do not need to posit the authority thesis in order to explain why on every occasion on which God gives a command, there is decisive reason to comply with God's command: such cases are all accounted for by the already established compliance thesis. So the strength of the argument for the authority thesis from cases is going to depend on the *range* of cases in which one thinks that it is genuinely possible for God to give commands. It will not suffice to say, "Well, obviously, on any occasion on which God gives a command, it is clear that the thing to do is to follow that command." This is already given by the compliance thesis. The real issue will be: On what occasions can God in fact give commands? Can God give commands when there are not other reasons for compliance—either independent moral reasons, or independent prudential reasons, or moral or prudential reasons attached by God to the command (for example, punishments and rewards)?

Given this point about the limiting role of the compliance thesis in this argument, I have two worries about the inference to the moral principle requiring obedience to God. The first is just that I lack clear intuitions about the range of cases in which God can give commands, and so I lack confidence that an appeal to a principle as strong as the Strongest authority thesis is warranted in order to account for those intuitions. The second is that even of those intuitions about cases that I do have, I am not confident in those intuitions, for the following reason. If I imagine a case in which God gives a command, and in which (of course) the person commanded has decisive reason to adhere to the command, it may seem possible to me thus conceived. But if I were pressed on whether I thought it was *really* possible, I would feel compelled to add the following proviso: "if there is nothing else about that state of affairs such that God's giving that command is out of line with God's goodness." We need to stipulate the hidden moral variables out of the state of affairs. But as we saw in 3.4, one of the hidden moral variables is just the presence or absence of divine authority. My judgment about whether one of these states of affairs is really possible may well depend on a prior judgment about whether God is authoritative in that state of affairs, and so my judgment about whether one of these states of affairs is really possible cannot be used in support of the judgment that God is authoritative in that state of affairs.

Others may have more confidence in, and even greater sheer numbers of, intuitions about the range of situations of divine commands that are genuinely possible. But I must say that I harbor suspicions about whether such persons are genuinely arguing from more immediately known particulars to a general principle of obedience to God. I suspect that those who have such 'intuitions' are really just making deductions. Is this a case in which God might give a binding command? Of course—because God has intense and wide-ranging practical authority, there are no situations in which God could not give binding commands. But to think this way is not to engage in an inference to the best moral principle; it is to reassert one's brute intuition that all created rational beings are under divine authority.

And what of it? Why not say, as was suggested with respect to authority as a divine perfection (3.5), that it is just a brute truth that obedience to God is absolutely morally required? I have but two arguments against this stance. The first is just that to embrace this principle as a mere intuition is to make it entirely free-floating, objectionably disconnected from other moral principles and moral judgments about particular cases. The second is to bring back to mind how easy it is to confuse the terrific variety of true and relatively well-grounded claims we can make about the relationship between God's dictates and reasons for action, claims that nevertheless fall short of the thesis that obedience to God is morally required, with the authority thesis. We have all of the considerations drawn from Chapters 2 and 3: that there is always decisive reason to do what God commands (Chapter 2); that God's commands are perfectly wise (3.2); that God's commands reflect perfect moral knowledge (3.2, 3.3); that God's commands are perfectly responsive to rational beings (3.3); that God causally determines what reasons rational beings have to act (3.4); and so forth. And, further, considerations raised during our considerations of arguments from property (5.3), gratitude (5.4), and coordination (5.5) suggest another principle in the vicinity: that created rational beings have decisive reason to submit to divine authority. (I consider this point in greater detail in Chapter 7.) One's confidence in the truth of a thesis that one holds in the manner of an ungrounded intuition should be tempered in the face of a slew of claims, all of which are better grounded, in the vicinity of the ungrounded thesis, and able to explain why one is tempted to assert the ungrounded thesis. We have seen a number of good reasons to accept a number of claims that fall just short of the authority thesis, but we have not seen good reasons to accept the authority thesis itself.

CHAPTER 6

The Authority Thesis and Orthodox Christianity

6.1 THE STRONGER AND STRONG AUTHORITY THESES

In Chapters 3, 4, and 5, our attention was entirely on the Strongest of the three authority theses. Recall the justification for disproportionately close attention to this version of the authority thesis: those who think that God is authoritative over all created rational beings in the actual world tend to affirm that claim on the basis of the view that God must be authoritative over *any* rational beings that God might choose to create (1.2). But even if one accepts the arguments offered in the previous three chapters against the Strongest authority thesis, one might nevertheless take the lesson of those arguments to be that we should retreat only to the Stronger or the Strong authority thesis, not that we should give up on all three of the authority theses. Even if it is metaphysically possible for God to create rational beings not under divine authority, one might say, *we* are not those beings.

But, on the assumption that the last three chapters have been successful, the defender of the Strong or Stronger authority thesis finds him- or herself in a difficult argumentative position. To show that the Stronger authority thesis is true, one would have to make an argument for divine authority that relies on relevant facts about us actual rational beings and which entails that we actual rational beings, but not rational beings of every possible sort, are necessarily under divine authority. To show that the Strong authority thesis is true, one would have to make an argument for divine authority that relies on relevant facts about us actual rational beings, and perhaps also other features of the world that we actual rational beings inhabit, and which entails that we actual rational beings, but not rational beings of every possible sort, are under divine authority.

I cannot see my way clear to how any such argument would go: any argument that I can think of for divine authority appeals directly to God's nature or to moral principles that bind all created rational beings. I cannot see what there is specifically about actual created rational beings—humans and angels, at least—that would provide for us an argument that we are all actually under divine authority.

Note that the most prominent moral theories constructed by and for us actual rational beings—Kantianism, utilitarianism, virtue ethics—offer no hint that we rational beings are under divine authority. The Kantian principle, requiring us to treat rational beings as ends in themselves and not as means only, requires us to respect God as a rational being, but it does not give us a basis to suppose that God's commands constitute decisive reasons for us to act.[1] If we knew that obedience to God would inevitably bring about greater amounts of good overall than any course of action involving disobedience to God, then there would be, according to the utilitarian principle, reason to do what God tells us to do. But even supposing the assumption connecting obedience and the promotion of the good to be correct and the utilitarian principle to be true, all this provides is another proof of the compliance thesis (2.1): it does not give a basis for supposing that God's commands themselves partially constitute reasons for action. Virtue ethics, which holds that the most complete standard for reasonable action is what the virtuous person would do, provides us with no basis—without the addition of further, controversial premises—to think that virtuous persons

---

1. This is true not only if we appeal to the substantive Kantian ethic but even if we appeal to Kant's discussion of the postulate of pure practical reason that there may be a God that rewards the virtuous. The rewards themselves constitute reasons for action, but God's dictates do not.

would take divine commands to be decisive reasons for action.[2] And if one were to respond to the inability of the moral theories that we actual rational beings have constructed and defended to support the Strong or the Stronger authority thesis by asserting that one of these theses is to be accepted in the manner of a moral intuition, I would merely repeat, mutatis mutandis, my criticisms of the attempt to put forward the Strongest of the authority theses as an intuition (5.6), along with a challenge: once we allow that there could be rational beings not under divine authority, why would we not take seriously the possibility that we are those beings?

This is, no doubt, a rather quick response to the suggestion that even if we lack an argument for the Strongest of the authority theses, we might nonetheless safely affirm the Stronger or the Strong thesis. One might well fail to be impressed by the inability of the theories now dominant in academic moral philosophy to provide support for any authority thesis. Kantian deontology, Benthamite or Millian utilitarianism, Platonic or Aristotelian virtue ethics—none of these is a view articulated in a framework built around a personal, omniscient, omnipotent, perfectly good, and loving Creator. One might suggest, following van Til, that these moral theories take humanity rather than God as their ultimate frames of reference, and so blind themselves to the truth about God's status with respect to us (1955, p. 94), including the truth about God's status as an authority over us. It is therefore unsurprising that such moral views do not capture God's authority over us created rational beings.

So perhaps we need to consider the possibility that the affirmation of one of the authority theses is essential to a religious worldview. Since it is the Christian standpoint whose content has shaped and limited the philosophical theses I have defended in this work (see the Preface), it is in terms of this standpoint that I will frame the questions of this chapter. Is it, we may ask, a presupposition or an implication of orthodox Christianity that one of the

2. There is a complication here. Created rational beings, on my view, ought to place themselves under divine authority (5.5, 7.6), and so virtuous beings would place themselves under divine authority and would thus end up having decisive reasons to obey God. But this is, on every plausible virtue ethics, going to count as an exception to the standard that agents should do what the virtuous person would do. For some of the actions that the virtuous person performs are actions that not all persons have reason to perform, because those reasons depend on prior virtuous action. This is the case with virtuous persons' obedience to God: their reasons to obey depend on their having made God authoritative over them, and so only those persons that have submitted to the divine rule would have those reasons.

authority theses is true? One might think that the answer is obviously 'Yes,' for surely a lot of Christians would affirm that thesis. But there are a lot of theological claims that a lot of Christians would affirm—such as the claim that transubstantiation does not occur during Catholic Mass—that are not plausibly considered presuppositions or implications of orthodox Christianity. (Indeed, they could even be false.) What we need is not a survey showing that a lot of Christians happen to think that one of the divine authority theses is true, but an argument that some set of propositions that are made known through canonical Christian sources implies the truth of the authority thesis.

Again we will confront the difficulty of disagreement among Christians about the canonical character of various sources. But I will here strive for a fairly ecumenical treatment, appealing centrally to standard understandings of the Bible and its claims about our proper practical relationship to God, the history of the Jewish people, and the divine nature. The first argument that I will consider is that the practical stances toward God required by orthodox Christianity—obedience and worship—presuppose the truth of an authority thesis (6.2). The second is that the biblical narrative of God's rule over Israel implies the truth of an authority thesis (6.3). The third is that the frequent claims in Scripture that God is king, and furthermore, king over all the universe and for all time, imply the truth of an authority thesis (6.4). I shall argue that none of these alleged implications holds. I will conclude the case against all three versions of the authority thesis by considering what epistemic stance we ought to take on the authority theses as a result of that case: I will argue (6.5) that we ought not merely to withhold belief in any of the authority theses; we ought, rather, to disbelieve them.

6.2 THE PRACTICAL STANCE TOWARD GOD ENDORSED BY CHRISTIANITY

Christianity takes for granted that one should take a certain practical stance toward God and God's commands. We are, as Peter says, to obey God rather than any human authority (Acts 5:29). This is not to say only that if we are choosing between submission to God and submission to other humans, we should plump for submission to God, of course; it is to say that we are to submit to God's governance and that it is never right to act against God's commands, even if human beings with power over us give commands to the contrary.

But we have already explained why we ought always to comply with God's commands, even should we receive commands to the contrary from some other source. All that we need to establish that we ought always to comply with God's commands is the compliance thesis, according to which we can always be certain that there is always decisive reason to perform the acts that God tells us to perform (2.1). One may have all sorts of questions about how one can know whether a putative directive is a divine command, and indeed one may very well have to draw on one's own independent practical knowledge to help to decide whether a given dictate really comes from God. But orthodox theism holds that if one does come to the view that a command really is from God, then the thing to do is to adhere to it, to have absolute trust that following that command is the thing to do.[3]

Now, what is noteworthy about this practical stance for our purposes is that this description of it does not at all commit one to a particular view on whether God's commands are themselves reasons for action. All that it commits one to is the idea that on any occasion in which God actually gives a command, there will be some reasons—reasons of prudence, or independent moral reasons, or reasons of divine authority, or some combination of such reasons (etc.)—that render the action that God commands *the* reasonable thing to do on that occasion. Compliance with God's commands, a compliance deemed absolutely necessary by orthodox Christianity, is adequately underwritten without appeal to an authority thesis.

One might rightly respond: compliance, even out of the sort of supreme trust in God mandated by the compliance thesis, is surely not obedience in the strictest sense. For one to be obedient to God is not simply never to perform actions that God has commanded one not to perform; it is, positively, to take those commands as one's guide to action. One could affirm the compliance thesis, trust that God will never tell one to do something that one does not have decisive reason to do, yet never take God's commands as themselves reasons for conducting oneself one way rather than another. But this is not obedience. To be obedient is to act in a certain way *in order to* act so as to fulfill another's commands. But one can make sense out of obedience as a reasonable stance to take toward another's commands only if one has reasons to adhere to those commands, if those commands themselves at least partially constitute reasons for action. And so the stance of obedience that is

---

3. This absolute trust is emphasized in MacIntyre 1986.

mandated by Christian theism can be accounted for only if the authority thesis is true.

This argument fails. It is true that obedience in the strict sense entails that one act so as to fulfill another's commands. But it is not true that the only way that one can make sense out of obedience as a reasonable stance to take toward another's commands is that one has reasons to adhere to those commands. There are two reasons why one might submit oneself to another's guidance in the manner of obedience. One reason is, surely, that one recognizes the other as an authority, and so in occupying the stance of obedience one is committing oneself to perform those actions that reason already requires. But there is another possible reason: it could be that one is rationally required to occupy a stance of submission to another party *in order to* make that party an authority over one. It is not that the other is, prior to that act of submission, an authority over one; it is that the other becomes an authority over one through one's taking a certain practical stance. (I argue for this claim further in Murphy 1994, pp. 273–276.)

I concede that the practical stance of obedience to God is required by orthodox Christianity. What I do not concede is that this implies that God is authoritative. What it implies is that one who fails to enter that practical stance is unreasonable. But the unreasonableness of the failure to enter that practical stance can be accounted for without appeal to the claim that God is authoritative. Since I have given arguments for the conclusion that attempts to prove God's authority fail (Chapters 3, 4, and 5) and I have given (and will offer further) arguments that we are rationally required to take an obedient stance toward God (5.4–5.5, 7.6)—a stance that *makes* God authoritative over us, once it is occupied—the fact that orthodox Christianity affirms that this stance of obedience is mandatory gives us no grounds to believe that any of the three authority theses is true.

But what, one might ask, of the stance of worship? Surely worship presupposes divine authority? Again, I think not. Worshipfulness requires that one think of God as unsurpassably great and that one have dispositions, attitudes, and desires with respect to God that are fitting dispositions, attitudes, and desires to have with respect to one that is unsurpassably great. But we cannot say that God's being unsurpassably great entails that God has authority, at least if the arguments of Chapter 3 were successful: there I argued that there is no good argument from perfect-being theology to the authority thesis. Neither does the fact that worshipfulness requires one to have certain dispositions, attitudes, and desires show that the authority thesis is correct. I will grant for the sake of argument that if one has those dispositions, attitudes, and desires, one will submit oneself entirely to God's governance, and will thus be under divine authority. But the fact that *if* one responds properly to God's greatness, *then* one will be under divine authority obviously does not entail that one is under divine authority. It is consistent with the view that if one responds properly to God's greatness, then one will be under divine authority that those who do *not* respond properly to God's greatness are *not* under divine authority. Such persons can be criticized for failing to respond properly to God by subjecting themselves to the divine rule, but we cannot conclude straightaway that they are as yet under divine authority.

6.3 GOD'S KINGSHIP OVER ISRAEL

The second argument from orthodox Christianity to an authority thesis appeals to the narrative of God's kingship. We have in the Hebrew scriptures a detailed account of God's exercising rule over a particular people, and we might think that this narrative offers evidence that God is authoritative, at least over all of us rational beings in the actual world. (See, for an extended argument about the narrative of the divine rule over the Jews, O'Donovan 1996.)

But the narrative of God's rule over the Jews—as apart from certain claims about God asserted in the Hebrew scriptures, claims that we will consider in 6.4—offers scant evidence for any claim as sweeping as even the Strong authority thesis, much less for the Stronger or Strongest theses. Given the way that we Jews and Christians characteristically do in fact take God to be authoritative over all created rational beings, it is natural for us to read the story of God's rule over the Jews as a story in which God simply decides to exercise God's rule over a particular subset of us created rational beings. But the narrative itself does little to support the claim that God is authoritative over all actual created rational beings, as opposed to those created rational beings over whom God chose to exercise governance.

To bring out this point, consider a narrative that is not true and that is not about Yahweh. The sketchy narrative that I offer is that of (with apologies to Basil Mitchell [1955]) the Stranger. Here is the (compressed) story of the Stranger, and the Stranger's dealings with one tribe of people, the Wanderers, and with those people who were outside of the Wanderer tribe.

The history of the Wanderers is a history of the encounters between the Wanderers and the Stranger. The Stranger—a being that
showed herself to be extraordinarily intelligent, extraordinarily powerful, and extraordinarily just—appeared to one of the Wanderers and
told her that the Stranger had selected her and her people to have a
special relationship with the Stranger. After initiating this special relationship with the Wanderers, the Stranger governed their lives: the
Stranger issued directives with respect to the conduct of their affairs
with each other, with those outside of the Wanderer tribe, and with
the Stranger herself. The Stranger also initiated and directed their
military campaigns, preserving them in battle and helping them to
conquer their foes; and the Stranger directed the Wanderers to a wonderful place for them to settle.[4] The Stranger often reaffirmed the
special relationship between the Stranger and the Wanderers. But the
Stranger was found to be unsatisfactory by the Wanderer masses, who
wished to have a leader who was a bit less strange, a bit more like the
leaders of the other tribes. The Stranger, acquiescing with their
wishes (though warning them of the dangers of what they were asking for), delivered to them a ruler like the rulers of other tribes. Even
after the accession of the new ruler, the Stranger continued to care
for the Wanderers, while not intervening as often and visibly in their
affairs.

Suppose that we accept the narrative of the Stranger and the Wanderers
at face value and ask what it implies, or even suggests, about the authority
over created rational beings possessed by the Stranger in a world in which
the story of the Wanderers is true. Surely it is *consistent* with this narrative
that the Stranger in fact has authority over all created rational beings in that
world, and that the Stranger has chosen to exercise that authority, through
the giving of general and specific directives, over the Wanderers alone. But
if we move beyond the question of mere consistency and we ask whether
the story of the Stranger militates in favor of the view that the Stranger has

---

4. Cf. O'Donovan 1996, p. 45: "We have identified, then, three affirmations which shape
Israel's sense of political identity and defined what is meant by saying that Yhwh rules as king:
he gives Israel victory; he gives judgment; he gives Israel its possession."

authority over all created rational beings rather than, say, the view that the Stranger has authority over the Wanderers alone, it is clear that the story does not entail, or even suggest, that the Stranger's authority extends beyond the community of Wanderers. It is a natural interpretation of the story of the Stranger and the Wanderers to think that it is something about the special relationship between the Stranger and the Wanderers that renders the former authoritative over the latter; and since this is a special relationship that the Stranger does not have (so far as the narrative goes) with other tribes, we have no reason to suppose the Stranger's authority to reach beyond the Wanderer tribe.

Now, I take the story of the Stranger's dealings with the Wanderers to be sufficiently close to the story of Yahweh's dealings with the Jews for the lessons drawn from the former story to be easily adapted into lessons that we should draw from the latter story. What is portrayed in the Hebrew scriptures is Yahweh's special relationship with and rule over the Jews. It is consistent with Yahweh's rule over the Jews to claim that God, while in possession of extensive practical authority over all created rational beings, chose to exercise that authority over the Jews alone. But the narrative of God's rule over the Jews does not provide any positive grounds for thinking that God is authoritative over all created rational beings, rather than that God is authoritative over the Israelites.

Of course, there are some important claims about God in the Hebrew scriptures that were given no correlate in the condensed story of the Wanderers. We hear nothing of the Stranger before her first encounter with the Wanderers. But the story of Yahweh in the Hebrew scriptures begins not with Yahweh's dealings with Abram, but with Yahweh, the all-powerful, creating Heaven, and Earth, and all nonrational and rational beings in it. So there are some very important facts about God that have no analog in the story of the Stranger. But they are facts about God that I have taken account of elsewhere: in Chapter 3 I considered what we can learn of God's authoritative status from God's being all-perfect, and in Chapter 5 I considered what we can learn of God's authoritative status from the moral requirements that apply to us due to God's creative and providential acts (5.3–5.5). So to the extent that there are elements of the story of Yahweh that I have not included in the story of the Stranger, they are elements that do not give us reason to suppose that God is authoritative over created rational beings.

6.4 IS AN AUTHORITY THESIS AN AFFIRMATION OF SCRIPTURE (OR TRADITION)?

Neither the practical stance toward God endorsed by orthodox Christian theism (6.2) nor the narrative of God's rule (6.3) provides much in the way of support for the claim that one of the authority theses is true. Perhaps we should appeal simply to the direct testimony in Scripture, especially that offered in the psalms, for God's kingship.

> The LORD sits enthroned forever,
> he has established his throne for judgment.
> He judges the world with righteousness;
> he judges the peoples with equity. (9:7)

> For dominion belongs to the LORD,
> and he rules over the nations. (22:28)

> The LORD sits enthroned over the flood;
> the LORD sits enthroned as king forever. (29:10)

> For God is the king of all the earth;
> sing praises with a psalm.
> Sing praises to God, sing praises;
> sing praises to our King, sing praises.
> God is king over the nations;
> God sits on his holy throne. (47:6–8)

> The LORD is king, he is robed in majesty;
> the LORD is robed, he is girded with strength.
> He has established the world; it shall never be moved;
> your throne is established from of old;
> you are from everlasting. (93:1–2)

> The LORD is king! Let the earth rejoice;
> let the many coastlines be glad!
> Clouds and thick darkness are all around him;
> righteousness and justice are the foundation of his throne.
> Fire goes before him,
> and consumes his adversaries on every side.
> His lightnings light up the world;
> the earth sees and trembles.

The mountains melt like wax before the LORD,
  before the Lord of all the earth. (97:1–5)

The LORD is king; let the peoples tremble!
  He sits enthroned upon the cherubim; let the earth quake!
The LORD is great in Zion;
  he is exalted over all the peoples.
Let them praise your great and awesome name.
  Holy is he!
Mighty King, lover of justice,
  you have established equity;
you have executed justice
  and righteousness in Jacob. (99:1–4)

The theme of God's kingship is, along with the related themes of God's goodness, justice, and faithfulness, central to the psalms: God is praised as good, as just, as faithful, and as kingly. If it is clear from Scripture that we are to understand God as king over all of creation and for all time,[5] and the only or the most adequate way of understanding God's eternal and extensive kingship is through God's possessing the authority of one of the three authority theses, then we have an adequate basis within orthodox Christianity to hold that one of the three authority theses is true. But both of these premises are problematic. First, we have no choice other than to hold that the claim that God is king over all the universe, and at all times, is to some degree metaphorical; and so it is less than clear that we can reliably infer that God is strictly speaking king over all created rational beings. Second, even if we put to the side the worry about the metaphorical character of "God is king," to read it as implying God's authority over all created rational beings is neither the only nor the most adequate interpretation available. So even the direct scriptural testimony offered for God's kingship does not support the authority thesis.

First: the notion that God is king over everything in the universe must be, to some extent, metaphorical. Kingship is a relationship between rational

---

5. We should also keep in mind those texts from Scripture that suggest that God's kingship had a beginning, e.g., Deuteronomy 33:4–5. O'Donovan cannot make intelligible to himself the notion of Yahweh having become a king (1996, p. 34), but offers no account of what is absurd about this notion.

beings, one rational being over another; it holds, strictly speaking, only between rational beings. One cannot literally be a king over mountains, over the ocean, over the stars, over the laws of nature, over sheep, and so forth. Any use of "king" as applied to any other than rational beings, then, must be metaphorical. It is, I of course do not deny, an *apt* metaphor: just as a king controls to some extent the free actions of those subject to his governance by giving commands upon which those subject his governance have reasons to act, God controls in deep and important ways, the existence and the (contingent) activity of all created beings. (See also 7.3.)

So I say that we must allow that the notion of kingship is frequently used metaphorically as applied to God's relationship to creation. But once we allow that the notion of God's kingship is frequently employed metaphorically, we lose much of the motivation to say that God must have practical authority over every created rational being. For it could be that God is king over some set of *rational* beings in only a metaphorical sense, as well. Even if, then, the only permissible interpretation of kingship in the strict sense is that of practical authority, the fact that God might be said to be king over some rational beings only metaphorically should make us doubt that the presence of "God is king" in the Scriptures commits the orthodox Christian to, or even gives the orthodox Christian very strong reasons for, the view that one of the authority theses is correct.

Now, one might deny that the only way to understand God's kingship over all of creation is metaphorically. There is, one might claim, an entirely literal understanding of "God is king of all the earth" that is available. One might claim that what this literally means is that God's *jurisdiction* extends over the entire universe; the territory over which God is sovereign extends over the entire world. Any created rational being within this jurisdiction— that is, of course, every created rational being—is therefore subject to God's kingship. But this is a strained reading of Scripture. The first basis for thinking that it is a strained reading of Scripture is that the notion of territorial sovereignty is a relatively recent phenomenon—authority, prior to the advent of the state system in modern times, is a matter of personal or role relationships rather than a matter of jurisdiction over a certain territory. It is therefore certainly not what the composers of the psalms had in mind as models for kingship. The second basis for finding this a strained reading is that there are so many references in Scripture to nonrational, even inanimate, beings as subject to God's kingship that we really gain very little by holding that the claim that God is king over all the universe really means only that God's jurisdiction is over the entire world. It is inescapable that the notion of the divine kingship is used as a metaphor for God's control over the entirety of creatures, and so it remains a pointed question whether God's kingship must be understood in the strict sense in relation to all *rational* creatures.

The first reason to think that the frequent references to God's eternal kingship do not militate in favor of the authority thesis is that there is a serious question as to whether God is literally a king over all rational creatures. Here is the second: that even if we were to allow that "God is king" is to be taken literally when applied to the relationship between God and all created rational beings, it is far from clear that taking it thus provides much in the way of evidence for the authority thesis. For there are at least two statuses that God could have that would justify the Psalmist in calling God "king." If God held the sort of extensive practical authority attributed to God by any of the three authority theses, it would be perfectly appropriate for the Psalmist to call God "king." But the Psalmist would also be justified in calling God "king" if God were what I will call a 'just rule-imposer.' (I will define 'just rule-imposer' momentarily.) So we face a choice in interpreting the Psalmist's words: should we interpret "God is king" to mean that God is a practical authority over all created rational beings, or should we interpret "God is king" to mean merely that God is a just rule-imposer? While the thesis that God is a practical authority over all created rational beings lacks support from other widely affirmed theses about the divine nature (see Chapters 3, 4, and 5), the thesis that God is a just rule-imposer is well supported. Unless we can provide an argument, then, that God's being a just rule-imposer gives us reason to think that God is a practical authority, the repeated affirmations in the psalms that God is king do not give us reason to think that any of the authority theses is true.

We have already considered what it would be for God to be a practical authority over all created rational beings (1.1). What would it be for God to be a just rule-imposer? A just rule-imposer is a person who lays down rules for others to follow, and whose rules and rule-giving meet the following conditions: (1) the content of the rules must be just, that is, those who follow the rules do no wrong; (2) the imposition of the rules must be just, that is, the rule-imposer does no wrong in laying down the rules for others to follow; and (3) there is decisive reason for those upon whom the rules are imposed to follow the rules. (Condition 3 entails condition 1 if, as I take it, one cannot ever have decisive reason to do something that is wrong.)

Now, if God is a practical authority over all created rational beings, then it would be appropriate to say of God that God is king. But it would also be appropriate, if God were a just imposer of rules, to say that God is king. Think about it this way: if one understood God to be a supreme practical authority, and one were casting about for language familiar to one's audience to describe, in a song of praise, what God is, one would likely choose the term 'king.' But, equally, if one understood God to be a supremely just imposer of rules, and one were casting about for language familiar to one's audience to describe, in a song of praise, what God is, one would likely choose the term 'king.' And so we cannot assume straightaway that when the Psalmist says that God is king, we should interpret the Psalmist to be claiming that God is authoritative over all created rational beings.

We would have to look for help elsewhere to show that "God is king" should be interpreted as the claim that God is practically authoritative over all created rational beings rather than that God is a just imposer of rules upon created rational beings. But our inquiry up to this point has offered no reason to think that any help is forthcoming. We have not found any successful arguments to support the interpretation that God's kingship consists in God's being authoritative. We do have, however, arguments to support the interpretation that God is a just imposer of rules. Since the compliance thesis is true (Chapter 2), it is certain that there will be decisive reason to comply with any rules that God lays down for created rational beings; and if we assume, plausibly, that one cannot have decisive reason to do what it is morally wrong to do, we can conclude from this that the content of God's dictates is just. Conditions 1 and 3 for being a just rule-imposer are therefore met. And we can also be sure, that since God is a perfectly morally good being, that God would not act wrongly in imposing a rule: so condition 2 must be met as well. So, while perfect-being theology offers no basis for thinking that the authority thesis is true, it does offer a basis for thinking that God is a just rule-imposer.

There are, then, only two ways to appeal to the scriptural affirmation of "God is king" in order to establish the authority thesis (assuming for the moment, as I have granted for the sake of argument, that this affirmation is to be taken literally with respect to God's relationship to all created rational beings). One can push the line that being a just rule-imposer entails being a practical authority. Or one can hold that, given the particulars of God's rule-imposition, we can make sense of God's being a just rule-imposer only if we make the further claim that God is a practical authority.

It is not plausible to hold that being a just rule-imposer entails being a practical authority. Here are two situations in which one could be a just rule-imposer without being such that one's dictates constitute reasons for action for others. One is a situation of *moral laxity*. In such a case, a person of superior moral knowledge and persuasive power could justifiably lay down a set of rules for the group's common life that they not (for example) assault or defraud each other. "Look," this person might say, "here is how we are going to live." In imposing these rules, the rule-imposer would be laying down rules that there was already decisive reason for those present to follow. But the acknowledged superiority in moral knowledge possessed by the rule-imposer, and the persuasiveness possessed by that person, could motivate those upon whom the rules are imposed to act better. I see no reason to think that such an imposition of rules, rules with which those present have decisive reason to comply, is itself unjust, and so this counts as a case in which one could be a just rule-imposer without being a practical authority.

Here is a second case. This is a case of *coordination problems*. If a fire breaks out and panic ensues, it is often crucial that people exit the building in a coordinated way. What is needed is a salient coordination pattern. If, in a fire, someone takes charge and lays down an at least minimally acceptable coordination pattern with which folks might comply, there may well be decisive reason for the endangered to follow it. But the reason for adhering to that pattern is that being burned is terrible and, given how others are likely to react to the command, the act most likely to minimize the suffering is to adhere to the pattern. New reasons for action emerge from the commands of those that take charge in such situations. But the role played by the commands in generating these reasons is causal, not constitutive: the commands make a pattern of coordination salient. This is, then, another case in which there is decisive reason to comply and the imposition of the rule is perfectly just. (See also 5.5.)

A more promising line of argument holds that even if just rule-imposition does not entail practical authority, the particular rule-imposition that God has in fact performed makes better sense if we take God to be not merely a just rule-imposer but a practical authority as well. One might put it the following way: look at the rules that God actually laid down to the Jews. These are rules with which there are not always independent moral or prudential reasons to comply; and for the most part they do not appear to be responses to coordination problems. So the Jews would have had decisive reason to comply with these rules only if God were authoritative over them. So even if just rule-imposition in general does not imply practical authority, these particular instances of rule-imposition could have been instances of just rule-imposition only if God were practically authoritative.

I have two lines of response to this suggestion. First, any argument that the particular instances of God's rule-imposition need to be accounted for by appeal to divine authority is hampered by the fact that the vast majority of these instances of rule-imposition concern rules imposed on the *Jews*. This was a people with whom God had (and continues to have) a special relationship, and as I argued in the last section, it is highly plausible to suppose that God was a practical authority over them. God picked them out; and they entered into a covenant with God. So one might well allow that the decisive reasons for the Jews to adhere to these rules is their source in divinely authoritative dictates, without allowing at all that this suggests that God is authoritative over *all* created rational beings.

Second, we can also appeal to the fact that God often stipulates that rewards will be associated with the fulfillment of, and punishments will be associated with violations of, divine commands. These associated rewards and punishments can present, of themselves or in conjunction with other considerations, decisive reasons for compliance with God's commands. Now, one might wonder whether it is consistent with God's goodness to punish persons for failing to comply with a command that they did not otherwise have a reason to obey. But I do not see that this is always wrong, though we can allow that they are not paradigmatic cases of punishment. Suppose, for example, that you customarily do me some good turn, and I customarily reciprocate with a kindness, yet neither of us is obligated to perform these acts. If you refrain from doing me a good turn, I may respond by failing to do a kindness for you: I impose a deprivation upon you for failing to perform a certain action. What makes this sort of act on my part not necessarily vicious is that I have a prior right to give or withhold the favor. Similarly, if there are goods and evils with respect to which God has discretion about whether they are to be bestowed or withheld, then it does not seem that God must act wrongly in punishing or failing to reward persons for refusing to act in accordance with God's commands. Any attempt to show that this is out of line with God's goodness presupposes a prior account of what, if anything, is due to created rational beings from God.

The argument from scriptural affirmations of the divine kingship fails: it points to God's status as just rule-imposer, but not beyond that to God's status as a practical authority. And while I of course accept that appeals to the tradition of the Church are important in understanding what is or is not a part of orthodox Christian doctrine, I will note here my conviction that tradition is no clearer than Scripture on this matter. If it were an established view of tradition that God has natural authority over all humans, then we might appeal to tradition to resolve any uncertainty in the face of scanty or ambiguous scriptural evidence in favor of one or another of the authority theses. Given the paucity of the evidence from Scripture for the authority thesis, the guidance from tradition must be fairly straightforward. But tradition does not provide guidance in any straightforward way. What tradition provides unambiguously are claims such as: God is to be obeyed; God is sovereign; one cannot be morally upright while failing to obey God; and the like. It does not appear to me that these first-order moral claims discriminate between a view in which God naturally possesses authority over humans and a view in which God does not naturally possess authority over humans but in which humans are morally bound to place themselves under God's authority; and it does not appear to me that these first-order moral claims discriminate between a view on which God necessarily possesses authority over created rational beings and a view on which God necessarily imposes rules justly on created rational beings. On any of these interpretations, it is true that the person who does not adhere to God's will is in some way deeply morally deficient; and that is all that Scripture and tradition unambiguously support concerning the relationship between divine commands and creaturely action.

6.5 THE PRESUMPTION AGAINST BELIEF IN AUTHORITY RELATIONSHIPS

Suppose that what I have said about the Strongest, Stronger, and Strong authority theses is true: that we lack adequate argumentative support for any of these claims. What epistemic stance ought we to take with respect to them? Should we simply withhold our assent from them, holding no view whatever on whether God is or is not practically authoritative over all created rational beings? Or should we go further than mere withholding, and actually disbelieve these claims, actually think them false?

There are strong reasons to think that in the absence of good arguments for any of these authority theses, we should deny those theses rather than simply withhold belief with respect to them. We should do so because there is, in general, a reasonable presumption toward disbelief in authority relationships. This is the presumption: if A and B are both rational beings, then in the absence of evidence to the contrary, we should disbelieve the claim that A is a practical authority over B. What I have tried to show up to this point is that we lack evidence that God is a practical authority over all created rational beings. If my argument up to this point is correct, and if the presumption is true, then we ought to reject all of the authority theses.

Is the presumption true? Here are two points in its favor.

First, if we exclude God from consideration, and restrict its scope to existing rational beings, it is overwhelmingly plausible. If I were to claim that *Will Clark*[6] is a practical authority over you, yet were to fail to offer you any evidence for this claim, you would not merely withhold belief on the question of Clark's practical authority over you: you would deny it. If I were to tell you that a certain angel was a practical authority over you, and were to fail to offer you any evidence for this claim, you would not merely withhold belief on the question of the angel's practical authority over you: you would deny it. This is not to say that this presumption is irrebuttable, or even that it is very weighty. I might be able to offer you some argument that remarkably talented ballplayers naturally have authority over the less gifted, and overcome the presumption against the view that Clark has authority over you; and I might be able to offer you arguments that God has, through some special intervention, made this angel an authority over your conduct. But an argument would be needed. And it would not be only an argument to push you from withholding belief on the authority claim to believing it; it would be an argument to push you from disbelieving the authority claim to believing it.

Second: when one considers that all that is essential to being a rational being is that one is the sort of being that can assess, decide about, and act on

---

6. Retired: first baseman, San Francisco Giants, Texas Rangers, Baltimore Orioles, St. Louis Cardinals. Lifetime batting average of .303. Homered off Nolan Ryan in his first major league at-bat.

reasons, it appears wildly improbable that any particular rational being would be a practical authority over any other particular rational being. If some race of rational beings were discovered somewhere else in the universe, we would think it entirely improbable that their commands to us would partially constitute reasons for action for us. Again: it may turn out that, wonder of wonders, they are indeed authoritative over us. But we would need an argument toward this conclusion to shake us from our disbelief; we should reject the notion that they are authoritative over us until we are given reasons for thinking otherwise.

So in the vast run of cases the presumption seems just right. The argumentative burden thus is on those who would reject it in the case of God's alleged authority over created rational beings: for, unless one provides an argument for why the presumption applies to all other rational beings, but not to God, one would be arbitrarily limiting the presumption's scope.[7] But this burden will be a difficult one to meet. For one who wishes to point out a relevant difference between God and created rational beings, a difference that would justify applying the presumption to created rational beings' alleged authority but not to God's, cannot appeal to just any of the many extraordinary divine properties that God exhibits but created rational beings do not. Rather, he or she will have to show how one or another of these divine properties is relevant to the rejection of the presumption. (Most of us would not find illuminating or persuasive the claim that, for example, God's being eternal is the reason that the presumption should not apply to God.) The property will have to be somehow relevant to authority: the presence of that property will make it appropriate not to disbelieve authority claims about a being that exhibits that property, even in the absence of evidence for that authority claim. But we know, if the arguments in Chapter 3 are on tar-

---

7. This appeal to arbitrariness is important. For one might think that my affirming the presumption is a case of affirming a stronger claim when a weaker one will do. After I have spent so much time pushing the merits of the weaker compliance thesis over the stronger authority thesis, primarily on the basis of the compliance thesis's capturing the 'data' of God's relationship to created rational beings' reasons for action with a less controversial thesis, it might seem out of place for me to employ the presumption that I in fact employ rather than a weaker presumption, one that is concerned only with what we should believe about *created* rational beings' authority. But the cases are dissimilar. There are no concerns about arbitrariness in affirming the compliance thesis but refusing to affirm the authority thesis; the former is about a constraint on God's commanding activity, the latter is about a power exhibited by God's commanding activity. But there are genuine worries about arbitrariness if one holds that a certain presumption should apply to every rational being that one can think of—but one.

get, that the properties to which one might appeal will not be enough to establish God's authority. So, if we are to be justified in not applying the presumption to God, then we will have to believe that there is some property that God exhibits that is important enough with respect to authority that it warrants our not affirming a presumption that applies to authority claims about every other possible rational being but not important enough with respect to authority that it warrants our affirming that a being exhibiting that property will be authoritative. I do not see any reason to believe that there are divine properties that meet these criteria.

Nor can I see why one who is concerned to rescue the authority theses would be preoccupied with quibbling with the presumption. The extraordinary divine properties to which we might appeal in order to justify the claim that the presumption does not apply in this one case, the case of God, are just those properties that would be relied upon to overcome the presumption. If it turns out that the properties to which one would have to appeal in order to explain why the presumption does not apply to God are the very same properties that defenders of the authority thesis have tried to rely upon in order to show that God is authoritative—omniscience, omnipotence, etc.—then those friendly to the authority thesis would probably want to say not that the presumption is false but that, in the case of God, it can be overcome. And this is just what I have denied: the presumption against authority relationships is, despite any initial appearances to the contrary, not overcome with respect to God's relationship to created rational beings. All three authority theses are false.

A Solution to the Problem of Divine Authority

7.1 A MORE MODEST ACCOUNT OF DIVINE AUTHORITY

Thus far I have argued that we lack reasons to affirm the Strongest, Stronger, and Strong authority theses (2.1–6.4). I have also argued that when we lack reasons to think that one rational being has authority over another, we should not merely withhold belief in the existence of that authority relationship; we should deny it (6.5). And so the upshot of the argument thus far is that we should deny that God has the authority over created rational beings ascribed to God by the three authority theses.

The aim of this essay is to solve the problem of divine authority—to provide an account of the existence, extent, and explanation of God's authority over created rational beings. It of course does not follow from the rejection of all three of the authority theses that God entirely lacks practical authority over created rational beings, so that the solution to the problem of divine authority is that divine authority does not exist, that its extent is nil, and that it thus requires no explanation. In this concluding chapter I offer a solution to the problem of divine authority that affirms the following five theses:

> *DA1.* God has authority, loosely speaking, over the whole world, and over all created rational beings.
> *DA2.* God does not have authority, strictly speaking, over all created rational beings.
> *DA3.* Those who are under divine authority, strictly speaking, are those who have submitted to that authority.
> *DA4.* There are good reasons to submit to God's rule, so that one is under divine authority, strictly speaking.
> *DA5.* God does have authority, strictly speaking, over some created rational beings.

According to this more modest account of divine authority, we humans are not born under God's authority, but each of us is bound to submit to the divine rule and to make God authoritative over him or her. Each of us builds up God's kingdom by taking his or her place in it as a divine subject.

7.2 DIVINE AUTHORITY, LOOSELY SPEAKING, IS UNIVERSAL

God has authority, loosely speaking, over the whole world, and over all rational beings. As I argued in the first chapter (1.1), to have practical authority over another is for one's dictates to constitute for another decisive reasons for action. But we can understand authority in looser, indeed metaphorical senses. One can understand authority more loosely as a causal control over another's reasons for actions, and not necessarily constitutive control. And one can understand authority metaphorically as any sort of control over some feature of the world.

It is clear from remarks in the previous several chapters that on the view I have defended thus far God has authority over the whole world in these metaphorical senses. I have allowed that God has causal control over agents' reasons for action in a number of ways. First, it was up to God what rational beings to create: and if, as is likely, the nature of the reasons for action that rational beings have depends on the nature of those beings and there are a number of different natures that rational beings might have, God would have control over what are created rational beings' basic reasons for action. Second, it is up to God, to a great extent, what environments created rational beings will inhabit, and thus how those beings' reasons for action bear on the situations in which they find themselves. Insofar, then, as what counts as reasonable conduct depends on the environment that created rational beings inhabit and on the nature of those beings, God has enormous control over created rational beings' reasons for action. Authority in this loose sense is a result of God's omnipotence and God's freedom in creating. It is also God's omnipotence and creative freedom that make the ascription to God of authority over all rational and nonrational creation, metaphorical as that ascription must be, an apt one: God determines what natures are instantiated in the world and the character of the environments in which those created natures operate. So God has, loosely speaking, authority over the whole world, and over all rational beings.

7.3 DIVINE AUTHORITY, STRICTLY SPEAKING, IS NOT UNIVERSAL
God does not have authority, strictly speaking, over all created rational beings. Here I understand 'authority strictly speaking' as the state in which one's dictates at least partially constitute decisive reasons for action for another (1.1). So understood, this claim is simply the denial of the Strong authority thesis, the denial of which I argued for in Chapters 3 through 6.

7.4 DIVINE AUTHORITY ARISES THROUGH SUBMISSION
Those who are under divine authority, strictly speaking, are those who have submitted to be ruled by God. I put this claim forward not as a necessary truth about whatever rational beings might be created, but rather as a truth about us humans; the only way for human beings to become subject to divine authority is through individual or corporate submission to the divine rule. (I take no stand on whether angels are naturally subject to divine authority.)

This claim is a conjunction of two subtheses: that it is possible for humans to become subject to divine authority through submission to God, and that it is not possible for humans to become subject to divine authority other than through submission to God. My rejection of any way of coming under divine authority apart from submission to that authority is not premised upon a general rejection of obligations to others that are not the result of voluntary undertaking. While I have denied that there is a nonvoluntaristic source of divine authority that must apply to all created rational beings, or which in fact applies to all actual created rational beings or even all human beings, I have not shown that any successful account of divine authority must be voluntaristic. I simply do not know of any nonvoluntaristic account.[1] So in defending the view that divine authority results from submission it should be understood that I am proceeding largely on the basis of an argument from ignorance: I do not know of any way for us to come under divine authority except through submission to the divine rule, and I am proceeding on the assumption that there are no other ways.

More important from my point of view is to explain how one might come under divine authority through submission to the divine rule and why there is nothing intrinsically unreasonable about placing oneself under divine authority. Begin with the question of the mechanism of submission: How might one submit oneself to the divine rule? This question might appear to be easy to answer. Just as theorists of political obligation have characteristically held that promise, or consent—even if actually a relatively infrequent occurrence within political communities as presently constituted— is *in principle* an ideal way for citizens to become bound to obey the law, we can say that it is by way of something like a promise that one can become subject to divine authority. Surely it would be possible for one to make a vow of obedience to God, to promise God one's obedience, and in virtue of the binding force of this vow one would have a decisive reason to act in accordance with God's commands.

But the notion that one can employ a vow to establish divine authority over oneself is highly problematic. A vow is but a promise to God. But the most plausible accounts of why promises are binding are incapable of showing that a vow to God would produce a decisive reason to adhere to that vow.

Standard accounts of the moral wrongness of violating one's promises can be divided, roughly, into two classes (following Scanlon 1998, pp. 295–296). Social practice accounts of the wrongness of promise-breaking begin by noting the existence of a social practice of promising, with certain constitutive rules, according to which one who performs a promising act undertakes an obligation to perform that act. The moral requirement to adhere to such

---

1. I do take infant baptism to be a way of coming under divine authority, but it is not clear to me that the binding character of infant baptism is nonvoluntaristic: what occurs in baptism may be a transformation of the will of the baptized such that God becomes authoritative over that infant. The account of consent in the acceptance sense later in this section, if successful, makes clear how one could become subject to another's authority through the will's being disposed in this way.

promissory obligations is resultant upon a moral principle applied to one who inhabits an environment in which such a practice exists: one is required to support practices that are generally beneficial, and the practice of promising is such a practice; or one is required to adhere to the rules of fair practices, and the practice of promising is such a practice; and so forth. The moral principle takes up the rules of the practice as a whole and gives them a moral force that they would otherwise lack (see, for example, Rawls 1971, pp. 344–350).

Now, a social practice account of the requirement to keep promises is singularly unlikely to provide what we are looking for with respect to a requirement to keep one's vows to God. For, first, it is far from clear that any moral requirement that is invoked to give moral force to the practice of promising is going to render a decisive reason to keep one's promises. Reasons of utility, or fairness, are employed only to show that there is a prima facie reason to keep promises, not to show that there is a decisive reason to do so. Second, the force of a promise and the circumstances in which a putative promise is held to produce an obligation depend on the particulars of the social practice. While there are certain broad parameters to which we can appeal to classify a practice as one of promising, there is a great deal of variation with respect to what might count as a valid, obligation-engendering promise, with respect to what counts as occasions in the future on which the promise would no longer bind, and with respect to what reason-giving force the promise has, and with respect to which promissory obligations can be satisfied only by performance and which can be satisfied by performance or by some sort of compensation. But the contingent character of such features makes it hard to see how any promise, tied to existing social practices, would be capable of underwriting a decisive reason to obey God in all things not otherwise ruled out.

If the binding force of promises can be understood only through the vehicle of social practices, we have grounds to doubt that vows can serve to provide us with decisive reasons to obey God. But there are accounts of the wrongness of promise-breaking that make no essential appeal to the existence of such a social practice. Scanlon, for example, argues that there is nothing to the wrongness of promise-breaking accounting for which requires mention of the social practice of promising. What is essential to the wrongness of promise-breaking is its involving the inviting of others' reliance upon one and subsequently failing to deliver that upon which others have relied. But we could invite such reliance, albeit with greater difficulty, even without the existence of a social practice of promising. So there is a way to explain why promise-breaking is wrong without appeal to contingent social practices (Scanlon 1998, pp. 296–309).

Put to the side the issue of whether the reason for action generated by this account of the wrongness of promise-breaking will be sufficiently strong to underwrite divine authority; there is a deeper problem. The moral force of promises, on this view, results from the fact that one who expresses one's intentions to perform certain actions, assures others that he or she plans to preserve that intention, and invites others to rely upon that assurance characteristically acts badly if he or she fails to follow through by performing the intended act. There are a number of ways to explain why one acts badly by failing to follow through. To make a false promise, by inviting reliance that one has no intention of satisfying, is to be objectionably manipulative. Such a rationale may not explain why one should not, after making a sincere promise, later change his or her mind. But considerations of fairness do seem important here: it is unfair, at least in normal circumstances, that one should invite such reliance and fail to supply what one has guaranteed to provide. Or one can appeal to strictly utilitarian considerations: it is generally for the best that people be able to rely upon what others induce them to believe, so that they can formulate their plans of action around others' guarantees.

Central to all of these arguments for keeping promises is that it is the possibility of the promisee's being caught unawares that makes promise-breaking an objectionable act. For the arguments all take the reliance of the promisee on the promisor as key to the badness of promise-breaking: but reliance results only from the promisee's forming the belief that the promise will be, or is likely to be, carried out. But if this is right, then the notion that we are bound by an obligation to obey God through a vow becomes problematic. For if we make a promise to God, there can be no illusions for God with respect to whether or not we will carry through on our promise. (At least if the orthodox conception of God, on which God has foreknowledge of future free actions, is correct.) God will not rely on a promise that we are ultimately not going to keep, because God knows already whether we are going to keep it. So no argument that we ought to keep our promises to God that relies on such an account of why promise-breaking is objectionable is going to succeed.

Scanlon recognizes that accounts of promising that make the reliance of the promisee central are going to have trouble with cases in which such reliance is absent. Scanlon's own case is that of the Profligate Pal (1998, p. 312). The Pal has for years borrowed from you and others, always promising to repay his debts, but never doing so. Finally his friends resolve not to make any further loans, and the Pal is filled with shame. In great need of money, he comes begging for forgiveness, full of heartfelt assurances that he has turned over a new leaf and will repay any loans. Though you do not believe him, you think it would be more cruel to refuse his promise and offer charity than to accept the promise at face value and give him the money. There is no reliance, but nevertheless it appears that there is some sort of obligation on the Pal to fulfill the promise. We do not need to believe Scanlon's own diagnosis—that an obligation of gratitude is what underwrites the requirement to repay—to think that there is genuinely an obligation here, and we might hope that whatever the source of this deviant promissory obligation is, it can be employed to explain the binding force of a vow. But there is a relevant disanalogy. In the case of the Profligate Pal, the Pal's promise is used to induce you to grant some benefit, and it is the benefiting that produces the obligation. We have not assumed, though, that the vow of obedience to God is being used to induce God to grant some sort of benefit, and it would be an untoward result if it turned out that we could subject ourselves to God only by inducing such a benefiting act, an act that God would not have performed were it not for the vow of obedience.

It is important that I am not claiming here that one cannot have a duty to keep promises to God. My preference would be to take the requirement to keep vows to be a requirement stemming from divine command: we are bound to keep vows because God has told us to be faithful in such matters. Needless to say, one could not place vows at the *source* of divine authority on such a view. But even if there is some way to establish the requirement to keep one's vows to God in a way that does not presuppose divine authority, it appears that the explanation will not be one familiar from extant accounts of promissory obligation. The existence of a moral requirement to keep our vows to God cannot be explained in the way that more standard promissory obligations can be explained, and so the appeal to vows as the mechanism by which persons can subject themselves to divine authority is more problematic than it might initially be thought to be.

Scanlon's account of promising is very much akin to the account offered by Neil MacCormick (1972). Like Scanlon, MacCormick is concerned to

reject a two-level view, on which promising is located within a social practice, which social practice is then elevated to the status of morally obligatory
by some normative principle. And like Scanlon, MacCormick argues for the
wrongfulness of promise-breaking by appeal to the wrongfulness of inviting
reliance without carrying through. Against this view Raz argues, with some
plausibility, that the MacCormick account does not get at what is distinctive
about promising: when one promises, one's speech-act is not causally but
normatively powerful; one brings into existence a new norm, a norm with
reason-giving force, by making a promise (1972, pp. 98–101). Raz argues for
this view in part by analogy from the law of contracts and in part by direct
appeal to the facts that one can make binding promises without inducing reliance (such as Scanlon's Profligate Pal case) and that one can induce reliance
without having made any promise. All of this seems plausible enough, and
if Raz's view offers an account of promising alternative to the social practice
and the MacCormick–Scanlon model, we might be able to appeal to it here
to show that we can rely on a promise to God to establish divine authority.
Remember, though, that what makes trouble for the social practice and the
MacCormick–Scanlon accounts is that we cannot see how the binding
power of promises to God is to be made out on those views. But it seems to
me that the problem is even worse with respect to Raz's position: I do not
see how, on Raz's view, *any* promises are binding.

Raz sometimes speaks as if his account of the binding character of promises is that because there are good reasons for people to have the normative
power to make new reasons for action for themselves by promising, people
have this normative power. But this is very strange. Normative powers are,
after all, powers, abilities to make some states of affairs obtain. In no other
case, though, is it true that its being good to have some power makes it the
case that anyone has that power. (It would be good for me to be able to make
ham sandwiches ex nihilo: I'd save myself trips to the delicatessen, and I
would never need fear going hungry. But this gives me no power to make
ham sandwiches ex nihilo.) Sometimes Raz suggests that its being good *to
regard ourselves* as having this power makes it the case that we have it: we have
practical reasons to regard ourselves as having the normative power to bind
ourselves by promises, and so we are able to bind ourselves by promises. But
this is no more plausible: in no other case is it true that its being good to regard oneself as having some power gives one that power. (It is probably good
for me to think of myself as more able to improve my work through revi-

sion than I in fact am—but that does not give me the power to improve my work to that degree through revision.)

The problem with Raz's view is the same problem that I identified with the improved coordination argument for authority (5.5). (This should not be surprising, because both the power to make binding promises and the power to issue binding dictates are normative powers.) We cannot in any case make a legitimate inference from x *is needed* alone to x *exists*. What the coordination argument from authority and Raz's argument for the binding character of promises have in common is that each attempts to move from the fact that it would be good for a person to have a certain normative power to its being the case that the person has that normative power. But this is illegitimate: all that follows from its being good for a person to have a certain normative power is that we should try to put the conditions into place requisite for the person to have that power.

The failure of the attempt to understand submission to divine rule in terms of a promise suggests that there is a dilemma in the vicinity. One serious problem with the promises picture is that the reason to keep promises is due to a human imperfection, and since God does not have such an imperfection, it is hard to see how we could explain being bound to keep promises to God apart from a prior appeal to divine authority. But this is generalizable: our requirements to others are characteristically due to our imperfections and infirmities, ways that we can have our situations worsened by others; but God lacks such imperfections and infirmities, so it is hard to see how to account for moral requirements toward God. The only place where we might be able to allow that God is in an unproblematic way vulnerable to human choices is simply through the possibility of human choices not being in accord with the divine will respecting those choices: if God chooses to make free rational creatures, and has intentions with respect to their action, then God's will is at some level subject to frustration. But this cannot be the infirmity that could be the basis of a moral requirement to God from which we could then derive the authority thesis, because any decisive moral requirement to choose in accordance with the divine will would be enough, by itself, to constitute divine authority.

So we are looking for an account of submission to the divine rule, I suggest, that meets at least the following constraints. First, keeping in mind the difficulties encountered in relying on the social practices account of promising, we would like an account that does not essentially appeal to contingent social practices. Second, the account must be capable of underwriting a decisive reason for adherence to divine commands. And, third, it should be one that escapes the dilemma by locating the requirement to adhere to divine commands other than in terms of a divine vulnerability.

The only way of submitting to the divine rule that I know of that satisfies these criteria is that of taking a practical stance toward God's commands that I call *consent in the acceptance sense*, or simply *acceptance* (see Murphy 1997 and Murphy 2001c, though the account of consent in the acceptance sense offered in this essay to some extent differs from, and to that extent supersedes, the accounts offered in these earlier papers). In showing how consent in the acceptance sense can generate divine authority, I begin by considering how acceptance in more limited cases is able to provide reasons for action; I then show how acceptance can be of the thoroughgoing sort that would make for divine authority.

Here are the basics of the argument, for each step of which I will, in a moment, offer a defense. (1) When a practical principle is indeterminate in its application, agents often have strong reason to *render a determination* of that principle: that is, to decide on a more precise rule that will from that point specify how one will act so as to satisfy that practical principle.[2] (2) When an agent renders a determination of a practical principle, that agent has reason to act on that determination. (3) It is possible for one to render a determination that dictates that the manner in which one will act to satisfy that practical principle is to be specified by another party's dictates. One can, that is, take a practical stance toward some party's dictates on which one accepts another party as the appropriate specifier of how one is to act on that practical principle. This practical stance I call 'consent in the acceptance sense.' (4) Since one has reason to act on one's determinations of practical principles, when one takes a practical stance toward another party's dictates on which that party's dictates form part of one's determination of a practical principle, one has reason to act on that party's dictates. Where there is consent in the acceptance sense, then, the dictates of the party to whom one consents partially constitute reasons for action for the one who consents. If

---

2. The idea of determination has its source in Aquinas, *Summa Theologiae* IaIIae 95, 2. I am also much indebted here to my colleague Henry Richardson's work on specification of moral norms (see Richardson 1990 and Richardson 2000), though the notion of specification and the notion of determination are importantly different. For a brief discussion of the differences, see Murphy 2001c, p. 74 n. 10.

these reasons for action are decisive, then the party to whom one consents has, in the domain of that principle, authority over one (1.1).

(1) Suppose that you are the named the beneficiary of the will of a wealthy and now deceased uncle, and will receive the uncle's entire estate if you are willing to accept a single condition. Your uncle was balding, and often thought that he had been belittled because of his baldness. Your receiving the estate is dependent on your promising to give five dollars to every bald person that you run across in the course of your life. You make this solemn promise—the estate is huge—and are on your way, beholden only with respect to a single moral requirement: to give five dollars to each bald person that you encounter. Here is your problem. You have taken on a reason to act on a certain abstract principle; but your action must take place in the concrete. Your job is to give five dollars to every individual who counts as bald; but the principle does not tell you whether to count someone with half a head of hair, or with a receding hairline, as bald. So, in order to do what you are bound by your promise to do, you have to make this vague principle more precise. You will have to decide whether a person with half a head of hair, or even with a receding hairline, will count as bald.

Now, there are a couple of ways that you could carry out your responsibility to make these decisions. You could decide on a case-by-case basis whether a person is to count as bald, and award the five dollars accordingly. Or you could make a decision about how you plan to act on that principle from that point on, forming a determination that makes more precise the criteria by which you will classify a person as bald or nonbald. I want to say that there is prima facie reason in favor of the latter route: you would be better able to act on the requirement to give five dollars to every bald person in a way that adequately responds to its character as a moral principle by rendering a determination of it.

This claim might seem immediately implausible. What basis is there for rational criticism of the case-by-case method, so long as the person employing it never refrains from giving five dollars to a person who is clearly and unambiguously bald? After all, if the user of the case-by-case method decides to give five dollars to someone with half a head of hair, one cannot show by appeal to the requirement to give five dollars to bald people that the giving act was not required, and if the user of that method decides not to give five dollars to someone with half a head of hair, one cannot show by appeal to the requirement that the giving act was required. But we should

not underestimate what is necessary in order to act on a practical requirement in a principled way. It is not sufficient to show that for any particular
act, that act cannot be shown of itself to be within the range of what the
practical requirement forbids. Acting on a moral requirement in a principled
way necessitates a certain *pattern* of compliance, one that conforms to canons
of consistency in action. It is true that you could not be criticized simply for
giving the five dollars to a person with half a head of hair and that you could
not be criticized simply for refusing to give the five dollars to a person with
half a head of hair. But you could be rationally criticized for counting a person with half a head of hair as nonbald while counting some other person
with half a head of hair as bald. If one is to act in a principled way, one must
act *consistently*, so that like cases are treated alike. A highly effective way of
honoring this requirement of consistency in acting on a principle is to set
for oneself a determination: a version of the principle made more specific,
so that it can be a clearer guide to action, but universal in scope, so that by
adhering to it one can satisfy the demands of consistency.

The promise to give five dollars to every bald person that you encounter
is of course a rigged case, exploiting a stock example of a vague predicate.
But there are plenty of less contrived and more momentous examples ready
to hand. Consider, for example, the following practical principle: *one ought
not drink to excess*. Surely this is a reasonable principle. But on its own it is
not sufficiently determinate to provide an adequate guide for conduct. In
order for it to guide one's conduct adequately, one will have to provide
some sort of further content for the principle, deciding more precisely how
that principle will figure in one's deliberation. This decision will not be an
indifferent one: for it is not as if, within the range of minimally acceptable
determinations of 'excess,' we have no reasons to prefer some over the others. If we tighten up the constraint, allowing less drinking, we are threatened with the loss of some of the goods of drinking: conviviality, gusta-
tory pleasure, and so forth. If we loosen it up, allowing more, we are
threatened with some of the evils of drinking: impaired comic timing,
weepiness, car wrecks, and so forth. To act faithfully on the principle one
needs to choose a determination of it, something that settles the limit one
should observe with respect to the consumption of alcohol (see Murphy
2001c, pp. 85–86). Or consider the 'common good principle': that one
ought to do one's share with respect to the promotion of the common
good of one's political community. This principle is indeterminate in a

number of ways: we would need not only a determination of what is to count as the common good of one's community, but also a determination of what counts as one's share in promoting that end (Murphy 2001c, pp. 87–88). Again, surely a great deal rides on how this principle is specified; there is good reason to come to a more specifically formulated but nevertheless universal rule concerning how one is to act on it rather than merely to decide on a case-by-case basis how one will act on it. It seems to me that the sort of indeterminacy that makes determination a good idea is a ubiquitous feature of practical principles.

(2) One who has rendered a determination of a practical principle has, I say, reason to act on that determination. By rendering a determination of a practical principle, one makes the way of acting on that practical principle specified by the determination *privileged*.

The basis for the claim that agents have reason to act on their determinations of practical principles is that determinations are just one kind of decision—a decision that if one is to act on a practical principle, then it will be in this specific way—and agents have reason to act on their decisions. There are a number of things that I might choose to do with my Saturday afternoon: I might take my children to the park; I might mow the lawn; I might read a book. There may be, prior to my deliberation and decision, no one of these options that is privileged with respect to reasons to choose it; there may be no rational basis for criticism of my choice to go to the park and no rational basis for a criticism of my choice to mow the lawn. But matters are different once I have made my choice: once I have decided to take my children to the park, it would be a failure of reasonableness for me not to go to the park, and I would be open to rational criticism for failing to do so. Decision is normatively effective; it can privilege an option that was, prior to one's choice, just one option among others. Matters are no different with respect to long-term rather than short-term decisions. We are agents that must make choices whose execution is extended over time, and it is just as unreasonable to fail to carry out one's long-term decisions as it is to fail to carry out one's short-term decisions. Those who make decisions yet fail to carry through on them are, practically speaking, pathetic (see also Murphy 2001a, p. 212).

Because to render a determination is to make a decision, a decision about how one will act on a practical principle, and because decisions enter into reasons for action, one who renders a determination of a practical principle has reason to act on that determination. The reason is the practical principle itself, together with the decision that if one acts on the practical principle, then it will be in this specific way. By making the promise to give five dollars to every bald person, one takes on a certain reason for action; but the range of acts of giving five dollars that this reason requires is indeterminate. By rendering the determination that persons with a half a head of hair or less are to count as bald, however, one now has a reason that consists of the facts that one is bound to give five dollars to every bald person *and* that one has decided, for the purposes of the principle, to count all and only those with less than half a head of hair as bald. This reason directs one to give five dollars to every person with half a head of hair or less. It may not have been, prior to one's decision, unreasonable for one to fail to award the five dollars to someone with two-fifths of a head of hair. But one's determination has changed matters; one's determination has made that choice an unreasonable one.

The claim that one has reason to act on one's determinations is not, of course, the claim that one never has reasons to reconsider, revise, or even revoke those determinations. To say that one has reason to act on one's determinations is to say that so long as one renders a certain determination of a given practical principle, one has reason to act in accordance with it; it is not to say that one must never renounce a determination, or that one is bound by that determination even if one were to renounce it. It may sound as if one can evade the requirements of a determination at will. But this is not so, for decisions made by rational agents stand until there is adequate reason to revisit them, where by 'adequate reason' I mean considerations that were not appropriately considered in the deliberation that led to the initial decision. If there was some sort of infirmity in the deliberation upon which one based one's decision—if there was an error in reasoning, or the agent was unaware or inadequately appreciative of some relevant fact—then there may well be adequate reason to reconsider one's decisions. And if there was a relevant change in one's circumstances of action, then, too, there may well be adequate reason to reconsider one's decisions. The case of determinations is no exception to this generalization that decisions of rational agents are not to be revisited without adequate reason. There may well be reason for an agent to reconfigure his or her determinations of practical principles due to mistakes in the deliberation by which he or she came to a determination, or due to alterations of the environment in which he or she is acting. But to alter

one's determinations in the absence of such rational considerations is to engage in an unreasonable flightiness. (See also Murphy 2001a, pp. 210–212,
and Murphy 2001c, p. 86.)

(3) Consider the principle forbidding drinking to excess, and suppose
that one is attempting to settle on a determination of that principle. There
are a couple of important options here. The content of that determination
might involve merely descriptions of certain situations and rates of alcohol
consumption—'during the work week I am to drink no more than one beer
an hour, and on weekends no more than one-and-a-half,' that sort of thing.
But from what I have said so far about determinations there is no basis to
suppose that such determinations might not include within them references
to another party's dictates. I might be impressed by the fact that mechanical
specifications of the principle against drinking to excess often do not capture the nuances of the different situations that one might find oneself in,
and by the fact that, when in such situations, I am a bad judge of what is a
good limit to set to my drinking, and by the fact that my wife both has solid
prudence in these matters as well as a thorough knowledge of my character
and predilections. I might very well decide, in light of these facts, to render
an at least partial determination of the principle forbidding drinking to excess along the lines of 'do not drink past the point at which your wife tells
you to stop.' My wife then has the ability to *complete a determination* of mine,
to specify by her say-so the point at which my drinking is excessive.

There is nothing in the very idea of a determination that militates against
the possibility of determinations including such reference to other persons'
dictates. The general form of the case that would have to be made in favor
of rendering such determinations is that in some contexts there is some reason to leave the content of one's determinations open-ended, to be filled
in by others, and that in those contexts the reason to fill in the content of
the determinations for oneself is not so strong. I allow that there may always be *some* reason to complete one's determinations for oneself: there is
a good in reasonable autonomous choice that is forgone to some degree
when one allows another to make such decisions for one. But over and
against this reason of autonomy for not rendering determinations that must
be filled in by others' dictates, there may be very strong reasons for forgoing one's autonomous choice and for allowing others to complete one's determinations. Here are a few such reasons. First: it may be the case that in
some contexts it is terrifically important to make correct choices, and one

may know that he or she has trouble rendering complete determinations of normative principles in those contexts in a reasonable way. One might then have good reason to render determinations that allow others—others who are, presumably, better equipped to choose rightly in those contexts—to complete one's determinations for one. (The determination that I rendered in which my wife specifies, in some contexts, my drinking limits might be justified along these lines.) Second: it might be that allowing another to complete one's determination for one is itself a benefit to that other; or, if it is not exactly a benefit, an expression of one's regard, respect, or love for the other. (If my wife is worried about how much I might choose to drink, I might, even if I disagree with her estimation of my own capacities to judge well in such matters, allow her to specify what counts as excessive drinking.) And third: it might be very important for persons to have determinations that are coordinated in some way. If it is crucial that you and I attempt to satisfy normative principles so that our activities are not mutually frustrating but are instead mutually reinforcing, one way to try to ensure coordination of our determinations is to have them completed by a single party that is adequate to this coordinating task. (Such a determination of the common good principle might be justified in this way: if all of us are to act on the principle that we are to do our share in promoting the common good, it would surely be important to coordinate our understandings of what is to count as common good and what is to count as our shares in promoting that good.) So: not only is there nothing in the notion of a determination that rules out determinations that must be completed by others, there is reason to think that in some cases rendering such determinations might be the wisest course.

(4) One has reason to act on one's determinations of normative principles. And one's determinations can allow another party's dictates to specify how one is to act on those normative principles. It is possible, then, for another party's dictates to at least partially constitute reasons for action for one as a result of one's rendering a determination that allows that other party to complete that determination. If I rendered a determination of the principle concerning drinking to excess that directed me to stop drinking at the point at which my wife tells me to stop, then if I were to fail to act on her directives, then I would be failing to do what I have reason to do; and that reason is constituted, in part, by the fact that my wife told me to stop drinking at that point. If, in that context, the reason not to drink to excess were a de-

cisive reason, then my wife would have a limited kind of authority over me: her dictate concerning when I should stop drinking would partially constitute a decisive reason for me to stop drinking at a certain point; her telling me to stop drinking would constitutively actualize a decisive reason for me to act (1.1).

Now, all of the cases of consent in the acceptance sense that we have considered here are very limited. We have considered a very specific promise to give five dollars to bald people, a requirement not to drink to excess, and a principle that mandates that one do one's part for the common good of one's political community. Even if it is true that through rendering determinations one can install another as a practical authority over one, how can we go from these highly circumscribed cases to the wide-ranging and final authority that God is supposed to have over at least some created rational beings?

Consider the set of *all* correct practical principles for some rational being, the set of *all* principles that state what that rational being has reason to do or refrain from doing. Call this master set of practical principles R. It is possible that R just precludes the reasonableness of certain courses of action in certain situations, but it is overwhelmingly likely that in many cases there will be a number of minimally reasonable choices that could be appropriate determinations of R. Now, in making an all-things-considered decision about what to do, agents are determining, in light of R, what is to be done; and for the reasons given with respect to a single practical principle, one is bound by one's rendering a certain determination of R to act in accordance with that determination.

Now, each agent has reason to come to determinations of the practical principles that govern his or her conduct. And each agent is bound by the determination that he or she renders. But, as we have seen, it is possible for one's determinations to be such that others' dictates specify how one must act to fulfill those principles. And it does not seem impossible for one to take this practical stance not only with respect to some other party's dictates concerning some particular practical principle but with respect to the *totality* of practical principles. One could, I say, consent to God's authority in the acceptance sense with respect to all practical principles that apply to that agent. If one inhabited that practical stance, then any dictate that God were to render would be binding for that agent. Any dictate rendered by God, adherence to which was not otherwise ruled out by these practical principles, would be authoritative for that agent.

Consent in the acceptance sense is a way of becoming subject to divine authority that does not essentially appeal to contingent social practices: I appealed at no point to any sort of institutional rules to account for the binding force of such consent. It is able to provide decisive reasons for action. For one has a decisive reason to adhere to the totality of practical principles—what reason could there be not to adhere to that totality?—and thus one has decisive reason to act on one's determinations of that totality of principles. And the account of why one should adhere to God's commands on this view is not that one would be damaging God thereby, but that one would be failing to respond adequately to the totality of reasons for action that there are. We thus do not find ourselves trapped in the dilemma about submission to divine authority.

7.5 SUBMISSION TO DIVINE AUTHORITY IS REASONABLE

There are good reasons to submit to God's rule, so that one is under divine authority in the strict sense. I want to defend a particularly strong version of this thesis, that is, that the good reasons to submit to God's rule are indeed decisive reasons; one who fails to submit to divine authority is unreasonable for failing to do so. My defense will proceed in two stages. I will first respond to arguments that consent in the acceptance sense to the divine rule is as such deeply unreasonable, even vicious. Only after I respond to that criticism will I turn to positive reasons for subjecting oneself to God's authority.

Against consent views of political authority Wolff has argued that while political authority could in principle be generated by a citizen's consent, the act of consent would itself be morally objectionable. The reason that such consent would be objectionable is, on Wolff's view, that the authority is legitimated at the cost of the citizen's forfeiting his or her autonomy (1970, p. 70). But Wolff's argument has little to recommend it as a criticism of consent views in general. There is an ambiguity in Wolff's notion of autonomy concerning whether being autonomous consists in acting in accordance with one's own best assessment of what ought to be done or, rather, in acting in accordance with one's own best assessment of what ought to be done, discounting certain considerations—for example, that someone commanded one to do something—that are unworthy to be treated as reasons for action by a moral agent (see, for example, Sterba 1977). If Wolff means the former, then there is nothing objectionable about consenting: for if the consent makes it the case that a reason-candidate (1.1) will be elevated to the status of a reason by the giving of a command, the autonomous agent can take the resultant reasons into consideration in deciding what to do. He must therefore have the latter meaning in mind: the objection is that consent would require an agent to take another's will as a reason for action—which is something that a morally autonomous agent would not do. But this is an overstated conception of moral autonomy, as is made clear by the fact that Wolff's argument proves far more than that political authority should not be generated: not only would it militate against consent that establishes the existence of political authority, it would militate against *any* sort of agreement to comply with another's will, for example, "I promise to go with you to whatever movie you want to see." This strikes me as a *reductio* of Wolff's view. Since morally autonomous beings can have good reasons to create reasons for action, as we can imagine might be the case in the example, and there are no grounds for holding that such created reasons could not include reasons to adhere to another's decisions, Wolff's view that the creation of authority by consent is an objectionable process is unjustified.

Even if Wolff's criticism is, as stated, a failure, there are some serious concerns raised by those criticisms that are worth examining in a bit more detail in relation to consent in the acceptance sense. For this kind of consent involves a thoroughgoing willingness to surrender one's decision-making to God: it is allowing God entirely to complete one's determinations for one that gives him or her decisive reason to act in accordance with God's dictates. Unlike the cases of the principle concerning alcohol consumption or even that concerning the promotion of the common good of the political community discussed in the previous section, in the case of submission to divine authority the surrender of decision is *maximal*. These are serious concerns. The notion that we might accept another's decisions as our own often has, it must be admitted, an unsavory air about it, and this unsavoriness undoubtedly derives at least in part from the sorts of considerations that Wolff's criticisms raise.

Worries about submission to God's rule by consent in the acceptance sense can be deflected by two different sorts of response. One sort of response directly attacks the idea that consent in the acceptance sense is an intrinsically unreasonable stance to inhabit. The other sort of response acknowledges that in certain cases it is unreasonable to consent to another in the acceptance sense, but rejects the notion that submission to God is a case in which such submission is unreasonable.

The rejection of the intrinsic unreasonableness of consent in the acceptance sense rests on two points. First, there can be very strong reasons for one
to consent to another in the acceptance sense. I mentioned three in the previous section: first, the great need in some contexts to make determinations
in a reasonable way, a way that outstrips one's powers of deliberation; second, the desirability of expressing love, respect, or trust in another through
surrendering one's decision-making to him or her; and third, the need to
coordinate one's determinations with others'. Second, even though such
consent pretty much guarantees some loss of autonomous decision-making,
to allow another's determinations to take the place of one's own involves a
forgoing of, rather than an intentional attack upon, one's autonomous decision-making. So one cannot claim that even if there are great goods to be
realized through consent in the acceptance sense, it is nevertheless unacceptable because it involves an attack on one good for the sake of another.
Instead, one good is forgone in pursuit of another. The only way to show
the intrinsic unreasonableness of consent in the acceptance sense would be
to show that the goods of autonomy inevitably outweigh others: and this
would be very hard to believe.

On the other hand: it is true that there are prudent and imprudent instances of consent in the acceptance sense, and one might rightly harbor
worries that even the most careful parties might find themselves in a bad situation through the inhabiting of this practical stance. A decision maker
might lay down unreasonable dictates, or those that go beyond the bounds
of that decision maker's authority, and so forth. But note that no objection
to submission to God by consent in the acceptance sense can gain any pur-
chase by this sort of criticism. For God lacks all of the imperfections that are
present in every limited rational being to whom we might consider giving
some allegiance, imperfections that render dubious to some extent acceptance of any limited agent's authority. (This is not to say that one could not
be imprudent in deciding what sources should be recognized as correctly
containing the content of God's commands.) So the content of God's dictates will be entirely reasonable, and God's decisions about when and how
often to lay down such dictates will be entirely reasonable.

Such thoroughgoing consent will not be reasonable, it may be conceded,
unless there are very strong reasons for one to consent to God's authority.
None of the reasons for submission to divine authority that I present here
will be unfamiliar: each of them arose in our consideration in Chapter 5 of

moral arguments for the Strongest authority thesis. In the discussion of the property argument (5.3), I noted that we might be better off under divine authority than not, and suggested that this might provide us with reason to submit to divine rule. In the discussion of the arguments from gratitude (5.4) and coordination (5.5), I argued that these arguments show not that rational beings are under divine authority but at most that they ought to place themselves under divine authority. I want to reconsider these arguments briefly here, and show that they present a powerful cumulative case that we have decisive reasons to submit to divine authority.

The argument from good practical reasoning. Suppose that you have the aim of filing a successful tax return, where a successful tax return is one in which you pay the smallest amount of taxes consistent with full compliance with the letter and the spirit of tax law. You know, though, that you are susceptible to errors in such matters: you often miss legal deductions, and you have a tendency to dupe yourself into thinking that an illegal deduction is a legal one. You would succeed better in your aim of filing a successful tax return if you were to defer to the judgments of an expert, someone highly trained in tax preparation. But knowledge of this person's expertise may very well not be virtue with respect to it: you may have a regrettable tendency to second-guess, to circumvent, to avoid following this expert's advice. It would be better with respect to your aim if you had further reason to do what this person advises you to do with respect to the preparation of your taxes.[3] You could promise yourself to do what the person advises, or follow some other route to attach additional reasons to follow the person's advice: you might even accept that person's authority with respect to tax matters (7.4).

Now, we all have tendencies to failures with respect to practical reasoning, failures with respect to acting on the totality of practical principles that apply to us. So, if our aims were simply to make no incorrect decisions, it would be a good idea to give ourselves additional reasons to adhere to God's dictates about what we are to do: because God makes no mistakes with respect to reasons for action, and God would not intentionally misdirect our conduct. So we can make an initial case in favor of submission to divine authority concerning how we are to act on that totality of practical principles.

---

3. Raz emphasizes that the normal way to justify authority (I would say submission to authority) is that one better complies with the reasons that apply to one if one is under authority than if one is not under authority. See Raz 1986, p. 53.

The relevant disanalogies between giving ourselves reasons to follow the tax advisor's advice and giving ourselves reasons to adhere to God's commands are the following. First, we may have no interest in making decisions for ourselves about our tax returns, but may have an extensive interest in making decisions for ourselves in some life matters. Perhaps if deliberation and choice were mere means to making no incorrect decisions, submission to divine authority would be the way to go. But if there is an intrinsic good to deliberation and choice, then the argument from good practical reasoning would seem to be substantially weakened. Second, we have allowed that there is normative openness in the totality of practical principles, for there are a number of incompatible yet reasonable ways to act on that totality of principles. Why does the interest in good practical reasoning militate in favor of entire submission to divine authority rather than merely in matters in which the totality of practical principles fixes what is to be done?

With respect to the first worry, the difficulty is eased by the fact that the party whose authority one is accepting is one who is intensely interested in one's good. So God's selection of the occasions on which God has chosen to give commands will necessarily constitute an appropriate response to the good of making decisions for oneself about life choices. So: though there is a good in making decisions for oneself in such matters, one can be sure that God would make due allowance for that good in deciding whether to issue a directive concerning one's conduct.

Here is an analogy. It is reasonable for a child to have a thorough trust in his or her parent's dictates, on the assumption that the parent knows much better what is to be done than the child does. The child may form the thought: "But wait . . . there is a good in thinking through and acting on these decisions for myself, and this is a good that *competes* with my placing trust in my parents." But if the child believes that his or her parents are practically wise, the child will further recognize that the parents are as cognizant of this good as the child is, and that the parent will thus limit his or her commanding activity in light of this. Good parents know that they have reason to keep their commands few and strategic. God is apparently of the same mind, having given few but strategic commands, and having otherwise left us humans to our own counsel.

With respect to the second worry, the difficulty is eased by the fact that we are likely to have enormous problems determining for ourselves the range of what counts as the domain in which the exhaustive set of practical principles fixes what is to be done and what counts as the domain in which those practical principles allow for normative openness. So the only way to receive the full benefits of God's complete practical knowledge is to submit entirely to divine authority. And since we know that God would not take advantage of us, would not use us as mere tools, we can trust that any demand that God lays upon us due to our submission will not be an unreasonable one.

To sum up, then: There is a great good in right choice, and submission to divine authority is a powerful way of realizing that good in one's life. So there is strong reason to submit to divine authority. Of course, there are potential drawbacks to submitting oneself to authority, but the fact that it is *God* to whom one is submitting prevents these potential drawbacks from becoming actual.

The argument from gratitude. The substance of the argument from gratitude appeared in 5.4, and we need only recapitulate it briefly here. According to the principle of gratitude, one who has received gratuitous benefits from another ought to perform beneficial acts for that other. But each created rational being has received all good that he or she is and has from God, and it thus is plausible to hold that all created rational beings are maximally obligated to perform beneficial acts for God. Now, it is hard to see precisely how to understand the idea of benefiting God: there are insuperable difficulties with the notion that God could be made better or worse off. But there is one sense of 'benefiting God' that, even if only an analogous one, is relevant here: that of freely yielding what God has bestowed on one back unto God. But one of the things that God has bestowed on us is practical freedom. So to act in accordance with one's debt of gratitude, one must yield one's practical freedom by submitting oneself entirely to divine authority.

The argument from coordination. God is traditionally understood as both loving and provident: God has an intense yet impartial love for the good of each and every person, and cares for the world by ordering it providently. There is an instructive comparison to be made here between the activities of political authority and the intentions of God with respect to human action. Just as political authority, when functioning properly, has the capacity to promote the common good through coordinating the activity of political agents, God has the power and will to order the action of created rational beings to the overall good of the universe. Of course, God is not subject to the same failings to which political authority is subject: God's capacity to direct agents extends to all agents; God's care for the overall good does not fail; and God's wisdom to decide how to direct human agents is insusceptible of error. Thus, if there was an adequate basis to suppose that practical reason pressures one to submit to a sufficiently effective political authority in order to promote the common good (5.5), there is a much stronger reason to consent to God's governance.

The arguments from good practical reasoning, gratitude, and coordination provide in my view decisive reasons for rational beings to subject themselves to divine authority. It is important to note that these reasons are not merely contingent. The argument from good practical reasoning appeals only to rational beings' interest in reasonable conduct, the limitations of practical knowledge inherent in being created rational beings, and the absence of limitations in practical knowledge present in the divine nature. The argument from gratitude appeals to God's necessarily being the source of all goods that any created rational being enjoys. And the argument from coordination appeals to God's necessarily possessing all of those perfections—being perfectly good, knowing, powerful, provident—that make God supremely worthy to coordinate the activities of rational beings toward the achievement of the good. (Of course, this does not mean that there will not be in some possible worlds *contingent* reasons to submit to divine authority; if, say, God were to inform rational beings that God has chosen to make it possible for them to enjoy forever a good far outstripping any goods that they could hope to obtain through their efforts in this life, a good the ordinary path toward which includes submission to the divine rule.)

The decisive character of the reasons for submission to divine rule dulls the force of a couple of likely objections to this conception of divine authority. One might think that, given the rejection of the Strong, Stronger, and Strongest authority theses, there is too little that we can say in criticism of one who takes up a disobedient stance toward God. Surely, given the compliance thesis, we can say that such persons would be wrong to fail to comply with God's commands, since God only gives commands when those commanded would have sufficient reason to comply. But the disobedient stance would not be *in itself* objectionable, since God does not naturally possess authority over us. This line of criticism turns out to be too hasty, though. For one's taking a stance of disobedience toward God's commands can be criticized even if God lacks authority over one; for it might be that there are strong reasons to place oneself under divine authority by occupying such a stance. One who defies the divine rule is not necessarily in error for failing to recognize God's prior authority, but he or she is necessarily in error for failing to recognize or to respond adequately to the strong reasons to place him- or herself under that authority.

Along similar lines, one might worry about consent in the acceptance sense as a way of placing oneself under divine authority. Consider one way in which consent in the acceptance sense compares unfavorably with vows. A vow, once taken, can have binding force that persists into the indefinite future, even if one changes one's attitude toward the subject-matter about which one has made the vow. But with consent in the acceptance sense, the decisive reason to adhere to the dictates of the party to whom one has consented in this way persists only so long as one occupies that practical stance. This has the unfortunate result that one who no longer consents to divine, or any other, authority, is no longer bound to act in accordance with that authority's dictates. One who submits to divine authority through consent in the acceptance sense is under divine authority only so long as that consent is present. Again, though, the force of this worry is blunted by the fact that whether one is under divine authority is not a practically neutral matter; one is *required* in reason to subject oneself to God's rule. And so while it is always open to one to free oneself from divine authority, one can do so only by engaging in the deepest unreasonableness. When such defiance occurs, and God fails to have the status of authority over the one who defies, the defect is not in God, but in the defiant.

7.6 CHRISTIAN ETHICS AND DIVINE AUTHORITY

Before turning to a discussion of *DA5*—the claim that there are some persons under divine authority—I want to consider some of the resources this theory of divine authority offers for furthering our understanding of theistic, and in particular Christian, ethics. I want to argue that this solution to the problem of divine authority promises an interesting, plausible, and attractive way for one to interpret the *distinctiveness* of Christian ethics.

There are weaker and stronger versions of the view that Christian ethics is distinctive. More weakly, it can mean simply that those who are Christians tend to have a fairly distinctive set of moral beliefs, or perhaps that the content of Christian revelation supplies premises for a set of moral theses that could not be provided by natural reason. On either of these views, what matters about Christianity with respect to morality concerns simply moral *belief*: that it modifies the content of one's moral beliefs, or extends the range of moral beliefs that might be warranted. These views are compatible with the claim that one's forming the beliefs and undertaking the commitments consonant with orthodox Christianity do not alter a whit what one is in fact morally required to do. It would be a stronger form of distinctiveness if one's being a Christian were not simply a matter of one's being better positioned to know what it is morally right for one to do but were instead a matter of changing in some way what it is morally right for one to do. And it is this stronger form of distinctiveness that is suggested by this theory of divine authority. For if this account of divine authority is true, then it may well be that there are certain obligations that bind only those that have formed the beliefs and undertaken the commitments of Christianity, obligations that bind such persons to a higher demand ethically speaking than that to which human beings generally are bound.[4]

How the theory of divine authority that I have defended can underwrite this sort of distinctiveness in Christian ethics is fairly straightforward. Suppose that, as I argued in 7.4, the principles of reasonable conduct that bind human beings generally have some openness to them: there are a number of principled ways to set about acting on this set of directives. But one who submits to another with respect to how this set of directives should be acted upon makes that other authoritative with respect to the fulfillment of these directives. But Christianity requires of a believer the entire submission to God that would make God authoritative over that believer. In submitting to the divine rule, believers make themselves subject to divine commands whose content may well go beyond what is contained in the principles of rational conduct that govern all human beings; and if God lays down any such commands, then those who have submitted to the divine rule will be subject to moral demands that go beyond those that bind human beings generally speaking. There will be included in a correct and comprehensive

4. There are, I allow, some puzzles here concerning the way that Christian submission to divine authority may or may not differ from Jewish or Muslim submission. One might, reasonably enough, think: members of all three Abrahamic faiths submit to one God. As a result, even if they differ in their interpretations of what God has in fact commanded, the obligations that they are under as a result of divine commands are the same. But there is a complication here. Submission to authority is often a matter of submission to persons; and the Christian believes that God is not one person but three. Thus it seems possible that a Christian might well submit him- or herself to the authority to all three members of the Trinity, and would rightly understand Jews and Muslims as submitting only to the Father.

Christian ethics some moral demands that are not demands on all human beings, but only on those that have surrendered their discretion about how to act on these principles to God's choice and command.

The extent of the distinctiveness of the content of the moral demands on those subject to divine authority would likely depend, on this view, on the extent of the natural demands of practical reasonableness on human beings as such. One's views on the distinctiveness of the content of the moral demand on those subject to divine authority would of course be influenced by one's views in moral theory. So any illustration of the distinctiveness of Christian ethics that I offer here is bound to be controversial, presupposing certain views in normative ethics. In considering the examples that I will offer below, then, it should be kept in mind that these examples are here as possible instances of the general claims about the distinctiveness of Christian ethics; a full defense of the claim that these genuinely are instances of those claims would depend on a fuller defense of the normative viewpoint that I take as my starting point. (My starting point—a natural law approach to normative ethics—is defended in Murphy 2001a.)

A narrow application: homosexual conduct. Consider the vexed issue of homosexual sodomy. A number of contemporary moral theorists—most prominently, Germain Grisez and John Finnis—have recently turned their attention to providing a decisive *natural law* argument against homosexual conduct. Such an argument appeals only to principles of rational conduct that bind all human beings as such. As Christians, these writers take the moral requirement against homosexual sodomy to be given by Scripture and tradition. But these writers have been concerned to show that the view that homosexual conduct is intrinsically immoral does not require any premises drawn from revelation in order to be defensible.[5]

According to this natural law argument—developed initially by Grisez and Finnis, but also defended by Robert George and Gerard Bradley—homosexual conduct is an intrinsically unreasonable response to certain natural human goods. On the Grisez–Finnis argument, the list of fundamental

---

5. It seems that what initially motivated their attempts to exhibit the capacity of a natural law view to provide an argument against homosexual sex that does not rely upon revelation are the recent disputes over whether homosexual conduct should be outlawed, or officially discouraged, by the secular state. Thus these natural law theorists, relying on the premise that state action should have a secular rationale, have been concerned to show that there exists such a rationale.

human goods includes, among others, both the "marital good" and the good of "self-integration" (as Grisez calls it) or "integrity" (as George and Bradley call it). The marital good is the "many-faceted good" which is constituted by a "one-flesh unity" of two persons (Grisez 1993, p. 568 n. 43); this one-flesh unity is only a real possibility for a male and a female member of the species, who can be made one through acts of a reproductive type. The good of self-integration, or integrity, is the good of "harmony among all of the parts of a person which can be engaged in freely chosen action" (Grisez 1983, p. 124); it is the good of acting as "a dynamic unity of body, mind, and spirit" (George and Bradley 1995, p. 314).

Here, then, is their argument against homosexual sodomy. Insofar as those engaging in homosexual sodomy pursue it qua unifying, they engage in it as a pursuit of the marital good. But the marital good can be participated in only by a male and a female of the species by performing an act of the reproductive type. Thus, those engaging in homosexual conduct are pursuing an *illusion* of a genuine good, which is intrinsically unreasonable (Grisez 1983, p. 652). On the other hand, if homosexual sex is not pursued as a participation in the marital good, then it is sought for the sake of the pleasure to be gained from it. Thus homosexual conduct is in this way on a par with any other sex act whose aim is simply self-satisfaction; as Finnis strikingly puts it:

> [Homosexual acts] cannot express or do more than is expressed or done if two strangers engage in such activity to give each other pleasure, or a prostitute pleasures a client to give him pleasure in return for money, or (say) a man masturbates to give himself pleasure and a fantasy of more human relationships after a gruelling day on the assembly line. (Finnis 1994, p. 1067)

But such acts invariably instrumentalize the human body, which is intrinsically good. This is an "existential separation" which "disintegrates the acting person as such" (George and Bradley 1995, p. 314). To flout the good of integrity by choosing such disintegrity is intrinsically unreasonable (Grisez 1993, p. 650). There is, then, no possibility of engaging in homosexual sodomy in a practically reasonable way.

Suppose that both of the goods upon which the Grisez–Finnis argument relies are genuine basic goods. Suppose further that if one chooses to engage in sodomy in order to gain pleasure, one chooses self-disintegration in a way that is of itself unreasonable. Granting the truth of these claims, it is clear that one who rejects the conclusion of the Grisez–Finnis argument will have to provide an account of the goods at stake in homosexual conduct that characterizes homosexual sex neither as a deluded attempt to participate in the marital good nor as merely a use of one's body for the pleasures result- ant from such sex. What would this account look like? I suggest the follow- ing. Homosexual sex is, or can be, an expressing and fostering of intense friendship, which expressing and fostering is carried out through the partic- ipation of the partners in unifying goods. Of course, the marital good, which would be a premier unifying good, is unavailable in homosexual sex. But there are other goods that can unify besides the marital good. Play is an obvious candidate: the good of play involves activities chosen for their own sake; and these activities can include more than one agent in ways that unify those taking part. One can hold, then, that homosexual sex is a kind of play, sought in part because of its expressing and fostering the friendship of the persons involved.

In presenting his argument against homosexual sodomy, Grisez antici- pates a response of this sort, and attempts to show that such responses must inevitably be unsuccessful. Whatever the apparent or alleged motives of those engaged in homosexual conduct, their "true motive" (Grisez 1993, pp. 653) is the pleasure gained from the act.

> Someone who admits that sodomy necessarily lacks the unitive signifi- cance of heterosexual intercourse which makes a couple a single repro- ductive principle might nevertheless suggest that a couple can choose such sodomitic intercourse as a way of communicating good will and af- fection. However . . . sexual intercourse is not chosen by sodomites in preference to conversation and mutually beneficial acts because it is the more expressive means of communicating affection. Rather, it is chosen because it provides subjective satisfactions otherwise unavailable. (Grisez 1993, p. 654)

It is hard to see, though, what Grisez means here. Surely he is not arguing that since a sexual act cannot express a proposition with the sort of exact- ness that the utterance of sentences can, it follows that a sexual act cannot be more expressive than the utterance of sentences. This much is clear from

Grisez's allowing that the performance of mutually beneficial acts can express the friendship of two persons of the same sex. What, then, can Grisez have in mind here? Perhaps it is this: that it is impossible to explain why in particular homosexual sex is chosen as a peculiarly appropriate way of expressing and fostering friendship except by reference to the pleasure, the subjective satisfaction, to be gotten through those acts. The only other way to explain its peculiar appropriateness would be to liken it to the peculiarly unitive character of the marital good; but to go this route would be to indulge irrationally in the illusion that homosexual sex is marital.

This, then, is the challenge posed by Grisez's argument: to show why homosexual sex conceived as a kind of play would be a peculiarly appropriate way for homosexuals to express friendship and affection without attributing to them delusions about achieving the marital good. Otherwise, says Grisez, it is clear that the homosexual sex is chosen because of the pleasure generated by it. But Grisez's challenge can be met: we should affirm that homosexual sex is chosen because of the pleasures present in it, and is a peculiar appropriate unitive activity because of the pleasures present in it; we should deny, though, that homosexual sex need be chosen *for the sake of* the pleasure to be gotten out of it. Homosexual sex need not, that is, have pleasure as its aim, even though the pleasures of sex are essential to its being a peculiarly unitive form of play and therefore an especially appropriate expression of friendship.

Nagel's account of paradigmatic sexual encounter (1979b) is helpful here. Without rehearsing that account in detail, we may note a couple of points emphasized by Nagel that help to explain the particular appropriateness of the sexual act, even if not of the reproductive type, as a unitive act. First, sex involves what Nagel calls "mutual reflexive recognition": "it involves a desire that one's partner be aroused by the recognition of one's desire that he or she be aroused." Second, "In sexual desire and its expression the blending of involuntary response with deliberate control is extremely important"; while Nagel holds that "This is to some extent also true of an appetite like hunger," with respect to other desires "the takeover there is more localized, less pervasive, less extreme. One's whole body does not become saturated with hunger as it can with [sexual] desire" (1979b, p. 47). These two features in tandem suggest, at least in outline, an account of why sex is a peculiarly appropriate unitive activity, even when engaged in without possibility of realizing what Grisez calls the marital good: it involves an intricately structured play activity requiring of the participants a tremendous sensitivity and responsiveness to the other's reactions; further, the depth of the sexual response is such that it holds those experiencing it so completely in its sway, makes those experiencing it so vulnerable, that it could only be appropriate for those that are expressing and fostering an intimate friendship.

This outline of a response answers Grisez's challenge to explain why sexual interaction will be central to the life of homosexual partners in a way that does not make the point of such interaction merely subjective satisfaction. It is clear that, on this view, this particular unitive activity is chosen in part *because of* the pleasures involved. But it does not follow from this that the activity is chosen *for the sake of* the pleasures involved: it is the way that humans can experience pleasure in sex, responding and reacting to others' pleasures, that makes it possible for sexual interaction to be not just brute coupling but rather the intricate pattern of mutual responsiveness discussed by Nagel.[6]

Once Grisez's challenge is answered, this natural law argument for the intrinsic immorality of homosexual conduct fails.[7] I have no way of doing better than Grisez and Finnis: they do the best that can be done with the natural law premises available to them. Does it follow, then, that, contrary to centuries of received Christian moral teaching on homosexual sodomy, homosexual sodomy is a morally licit activity? No: for while a moral theory

6. Nagel's account of sexual desire is framed within a discussion of sexual perversion, and it is interesting to note the suggestion that he offers with respect to the status of homosexual sex. On his view, it seems unlikely that homosexuality is as such a perversion: "Nothing rules out the full range of interpersonal perceptions between persons of the same sex" (Nagel 1979b, p. 50).

7. One might suppose that George and Bradley suggest an alternative line of response when they write that "We reject the proposition that sex can legitimately be instrumentalized, that is, treated as a mere means to any extrinsic end" (1995, p. 305). It might be thought, then, that we could draw from this an argument that homosexual sex, because it is instrumental to the genuine goods suggested above, would fall prey to this line of response. But to think this would be an error and I doubt that George and Bradley had this in mind as an independent argument against the view I have offered. For, first, when they say that sex can never be treated as a mere means, they must have in mind sexual intercourse of the reproductive type; for only that sort of sex, on their view, instantiates the marital good, and thus should always be treated as an intrinsic good and not merely as a means to some other end. Thus, the proposition as expressed says nothing about homosexual sex. Second, even if homosexual sex were included here, it is not as if it is a mere *instrument* to the goods of friendship and play: it would be an *expression* of friendship and a way of *constituting* the good of play. There is no way to transform George and Bradley's initial thought, even if correct with respect to the instrumentalizing of reproductive-type sex acts, into a criticism of the account presented in my text of how homosexual sex could be reasonable.

unsupplemented by an account of divine authority would be unable to explain the truth of the moral precept against homosexual sodomy, a natural law theory that has a place for divine authority can affirm the truth of this moral proposition by appeal to divine command. If God has commanded those subject to God's authority not to engage in such acts, then they are bound not to engage in those acts. Homosexual sodomy is wrong because it is contrary to divine command, not because it is contrary to the principles of natural practical reasonableness.

It is important to see that this appeal to divine authority is not a desperate turn to divine authority as a stopgap where a theory of normative ethics has failed, any more than an appeal to the existence of a civil law prohibiting driving over sixty-five miles per hour is a desperate turn to the civil law to remedy normative theory's 'failure' to explain why certain people are bound not to drive more than sixty-five miles per hour. Just as human legislators can give reasons rooted in the human good for laying down such a human law, even if the human good does not dictate a particular speed limit, we can provide some account, grounded in the good of rational creatures, of why God would lay down this sort of command. The reasons forwarded by Grisez, Finnis, and George and Bradley are, while inadequate as grounds for affirming a moral absolute against homosexual sodomy, good reasons to view homosexual sex (as well as other kinds of nonmarital sex) as morally problematic. The pleasures of sex are not its intelligible point but render it a peculiarly appropriate unifying activity for those in intense and dedicated friendships; but a sad consequence of this is that there is a powerful tendency for sexual relationships to become instrumentalizing, manipulative, to the point at which self-satisfaction does become the ultimate aim of that activity. Now, those that recognize this powerful tendency would not be unreasonable to decide, for themselves, not to enter into any sort of sexual relationships except in the context of a lifelong union the conditions of which hinder this tendency. (This is not to deny that sex can be terribly manipulative within marriage.) But if it can be a reasonable choice for a human agent to restrict his or her sexual relationships in this way, then there is little to bar the possibility that God, who is perfectly practically wise, might decide that those in God's particular care are not to engage in sexual conduct except in the context of lifelong marriage.

Note the scope of the moral prohibition on sodomy that results from this theory of divine authority. On this account, God is not a natural practical authority over human beings; God has practical authority only over those agents that have submitted themselves to divine authority. It follows, then, that since the moral prohibition on sodomy results from the expressed will of an authoritative being, only those humans that have submitted themselves to divine authority are morally wrong to violate the divine command against sodomy. *This is not to say, though, that there are any that engage in homosexual sex that are not practically unreasonable in some way.* Those who are subject to divine authority and violate the proscription of sodomy are guilty of flouting God's authoritative command. Those who are not subject to divine authority and perform acts of sodomy are morally guilty, but not for disobeying God's command; they are guilty of practical unreasonableness for failing to submit themselves to divine authority. On this account, the sin of those who engage in homosexual sodomy outside the range of divine authority is not unchastity, but pride: the wrongful refusal to submit to God's will in all things.[8]

This account of the way that homosexual sodomy is wrongful provides, in my view, the most adequate Christian response to the growing awareness that there are homosexual couples the partners of which are extremely devoted to each other, set on building for themselves a common life of mutual love, respect, and dignity, and who as part of that common life engage in one kind of sexual act that Christian morality forbids. Such cases are troubling. We find no successful argument from natural reason that sodomy is inevitably morally illicit. If we were to note the dangers present in a sexual life outside of a traditional Christian marriage, those in homosexual partnerships may very well reply that they are well aware of such dangers, guard against them vigilantly, and seem to be faring well—no worse, at any rate, than a number of couples in traditional Christian marriages. There is, after all, no guarantee that their sexual lives will degenerate into the sort of instrumentalization toward which sex has a tendency. I suggest that a Christian response to this situation should be guided by an awareness that all positive law—divine and human alike—that does not simply reproduce the contours of practical reasonableness but goes beyond them by rendering undetermined yet nonarbitrary decisions is *bound* to rule out some actions that, viewed apart from that positive law, seem untainted by practical un-

---

8. The ascription of pride is warranted, of course, only on the assumption that one's wrongful refusal to submit is culpable.

reasonableness. Instead of searching further for ways that the sex lives of those in homosexual unions must be deficient, or rejecting a teaching of Christian morality, we should instead defer to God's decision in these matters: apparently God has decided—in a way compatible with God's supreme practical wisdom and love for us—to accept a loss of goods, that is, those goods that these homosexuals might be able to achieve through their union, by favoring a particular form of life with its attendant restrictions on sexual conduct. Thus, without degrading the character of any particular homosexual relationship, or ignoring the goods to be lost by those whose inclinations make any heterosexual marital life closed to them, Christians may say simply that, for those that have accepted divine authority, this is not a matter for them to decide: sexual union, by divine will, is to be pursued only in a certain kind of heterosexual marriage. For those that have not accepted divine authority, by contrast, the central issue is not the failure to adhere to this particular command not to engage in homosexual conduct; the central issue is the failure to submit oneself completely to *all* of God's dictates.

A broad application: love of neighbor. Consider another Christian moral norm, not merely for the sake of further illustrating the contribution to Christian ethics that this theory of divine authority can make but also in order to examine the precept that has the best claim to be the supreme Christian moral principle governing relationships between humans: the requirement to love one's neighbors as oneself (Matthew 22:39; Mark 12:31; Luke 10:27; see also John 15:17). Before we consider how this precept might be understood within this account of divine authority, I need to make a few remarks about how I interpret it, however brief and unfair to the richness of philosophical and theological commentary these remarks are bound to be.

First, on what is commanded: what is required by this commandment is a matter of the will, and not the sentiments. It is what Kant called practical (rather than pathological) love (*Grounding*, p. 399). We are not fundamentally required to have any particular feelings for our neighbors, but are only (!) required to will their good.

Second, on the object of the commanded love: what is required by this commandment is, obviously, that we love our neighbors; but the notion of "neighbor" is to be construed very broadly. The scope of our practical love includes—as Kierkegaard powerfully argued—not just our friends, or those near to us in other ways (blood relatives, coreligionists, fellow citizens), but everyone (*Works of Love*, p. 55). *Agape* is universal love.[9]

Third, on the nature of the commanded love: the requirement to love one's neighbor as oneself does not involve merely the elevation of a particular descriptive claim into a universal normative one. It does not function, that is, by transforming a proposition about how one in fact responds to one's own good into a proposition about how one should respond to everyone's good. The reason that the precept cannot function in this way is just that the practical stances that agents take toward their own good are too variable, and can be deficient in too many ways, to serve as an adequate reference point for appropriate love of neighbor. Now, writers have drawn different morals from this assessment. Kierkegaard argued, for example, that the neighbor-love commandment teaches us what appropriate self-love is: we learn about how properly to love ourselves by seeing what such love would look like if made into universal love (*Works of Love*, pp. 17–18). I draw from it a different moral: that the commandment presupposes that those to whom it is addressed have access to certain normative truths—perhaps as thin as 'each person ought to love him- or herself,' perhaps as thick as a cluster of more particular precepts concerning reasonable ways to respond to one's own good—about appropriate love of self. These particular normative claims about proper self-love are transformed by the neighbor-love commandment into principles that require precisely this love for all human beings.[10]

This cursory, unnuanced treatment of *agape* as universal practical love will be sufficient for our consideration of the way that rival moral theories have understood this principle of Christian morality. Quinn takes it that the neighbor-love commandment, understood in this way, is a remarkable and unique moral thesis. Indeed, Quinn holds that its uniqueness provides a basis for a defense of the divine command conception of morality that he favors. For since no secular moral conception forwards an account of dutiful love like this one, and since this dutiful love is the object of a divine command,

9. Given that the love required of us is practical, oriented to action, why is the scope of the commandment everyone, rather than merely those whom we can affect by our conduct? But given the possibility of efficacious prayer, everyone can enter the scope of one's practical concern.

10. If this reading is correct, then the neighbor-love commandment is not fundamental in the sense that all Christian moral claims concerning treatment of human beings are derived from it. It is fundamental in the sense that it regulates the normative force possessed by other principles.

those Christians that affirm the correctness of this precept have reason to think that divine command theory is true. For if one affirms the neighbor-love commandment and recognizes that there is no other plausible way to explain its truth except by way of Christ's command to love one another, then one has reason to accept a divine command conception of morality (P. Quinn 1992, pp. 503–508).[11]

This theory of divine authority offers a different explanation. While the precept of neighbor-love is not required by natural practical reasonableness, to live as that precept dictates is, in itself, a reasonable commitment: the reasons to live this way are simply the goods to be promoted in all of the persons capable of enjoying those goods. Given the eligibility of this sort of life, we lack grounds to hold that God could not impose an obligation to that sort of life on all those that are subject to divine authority. While Quinn is right to hold that the correctness of the precept can be established only by appeal to the command of an authority, he is wrong to think that the pre-

11. I agree with Quinn that there is no adequate defense of this precept within philosophical ethics. But it is surprising that Quinn dismisses the possibility of such a defense so quickly, given the existence of normative theories that take themselves to be establishing something like that precept. For Quinn, the distinctiveness of the neighbor-love commandment comes from its binding humans to an utterly uncompromising universal love, a love for our enemies and those on the other side of the world just as much as for our friends and next-door neighbors. But given that the love involved here is practical, requiring us to will others' good, it seems strange to say that no secular moral conception lays down such a requirement. Isn't this one of the charges leveled against utilitarianism, that it requires an unreasonable or unnatural amount of love of neighbor from humans? Indeed, it is the very demandingness of the requirement of universal practical love that led Mill to assert that utilitarianism is a profoundly Christian doctrine: " 'To do as you would be done by,' and 'to love your neighbour as yourself,' constitute the ideal perfection of utilitarian morality" (*Utilitarianism*, pp. 16–17). There is also a case to be made that a natural law view like John Finnis's has the resources to affirm, independently of divine command, the commandment to love one's neighbor as oneself. Finnis posits as a principle of practical reasonableness that agents must display a "fundamental impartiality" among all those that can participate in the basic goods. Given that Finnis defends this principle by appealing to the status of the basic goods as having their value independently of the particular identity of the person participating in them, it seems clear that Finnis's principle requires the sort of equal regard demanded by this commandment—one's practical love is to extend to all that can partake in the basic goods. The universal practical love required by Finnis's natural law view and the universal practical love required by utilitarianism differ only in their conceptions of the goods to be promoted and their views on the constraints imposed by practical reasonableness on the promotion of those goods. If utilitarianism is a secular moral conception that affirms the neighbor-love commandment, then Finnis's natural law view is surely one also (1980, pp. 106–109). My reasons for rejecting the love commandment as an implication of natural practical rationality are noted in Murphy 2001a, pp. 201–204.

cept's being part of Christian morality gives us reason to move to a divine command conception of ethics.

Because this requirement of universal practical love has its normative force through divine command, it binds only those persons that have submitted themselves to divine authority. Though all humans are called to submit themselves in this way, those that have not submitted are—absent other special commitments they have made—under no requirement to love their neighbors as themselves. Christians are thus under a weighty moral burden that persons generally are not, one that requires us to sacrifice our own good in ways that most of us would not choose to sacrifice it were it up to us. But this moral burden should be cause for joy, not despair.[12] For it is plausible to interpret *agape* as another aspect of Christian witness: apart from proclaiming the good news, Christians are bound to make manifest as well as they can the intensity and universality of God's love for human beings through the carrying out of this commandment. (See also Grisez 1983, pp. 555–557.)

7.7 DIVINE AUTHORITY IS ACTUAL

God does have authority, strictly speaking, over some rational beings. Even with the now more fully developed account of divine authority and how one might become subject to it, it is extraordinarily difficult to gauge the extent to which divine authority over created rational beings has been realized in the actual, fallen world. I will not attempt to gauge it too finely: to make such judgments would involve the inspection of the hearts of believers, and it is an inspection that I am unqualified and (fortunately) forbidden to undertake. It is plausible to say this: that many people, to some extent, and in some areas of their lives, place themselves under divine authority. It even seems plausible to say that there are persons in the actual world who have, over stretches of their lives, managed (undoubtedly with divine assistance; see J. Hare 1996, pp. 263–275) the complete submission to the divine will that makes God fully authoritative over them. God's authority will be, we may hope, fully actualized in the next life: Thy kingdom come.

---

12. We might also note here Christ's guarantee that His yoke is easy (Matthew 11:30)—which refers, I take it, not to the capacity of unaided human nature to live out the demands of a Christian life, but to the gracious help that Christ will give us in carrying out these burdens.

Works Cited

Works are cited by the author's last name and the year of publication. Exceptions include classic works by Anselm, Aquinas, Kant, Kierkegaard, Locke, and Mill: all of these texts are cited by abbreviated title. References are given by page number in the cited edition unless otherwise indicated in the bibliographical entry. All biblical quotations are from the New Revised Standard Version.

Adams, Robert M. 1973. "A Modified Divine Command Theory of Ethical Wrongness." In Helm 1981, pp. 83–109.

——. 1979. "Divine Command Metaethics Modified Again." *Journal of Religious Ethics* 7, pp. 71–79.

——. 1987. "Divine Commands and the Social Nature of Obligation." *Faith and Philosophy* 4, pp. 262–275.

——. 1999. *Finite and Infinite Goods: A Framework for Ethics.* Oxford University Press.

Alston, William P. 1990. "Some Suggestions for Divine Command Theorists." In Beaty 1990, pp. 303–326.

——. 1999. *Illocutionary Acts and Sentence Meaning.* Cornell University Press.

Anselm. 1995. *Proslogion.* Trans. Thomas Williams. Hackett. References given by chapter number.

Aquinas, Thomas. 1975. *Summa Contra Gentiles.* Trans. Anton Pegis. University of Notre Dame Press. References given by book and chapter number.

——. 1981. *Summa Theologiae.* Trans. Fathers of the English Dominican Province. Christian Classics. References given by part, question, and article number.

Austin, J. L. 1962. *How to Do Things with Words.* Ed. J. O. Urmson and Marina Sbisà. Harvard University Press.

Beaty, Michael, ed. 1990. *Christian Theism and the Problems of Philosophy.* University of Notre Dame Press.

Becker, Lawrence. 1977. *Property Rights: Philosophical Foundations.* Routledge and Kegan Paul.

Berger, Fred R. 1975. "Gratitude." *Ethics* 85, pp. 298–309.

Blackburn, Simon. 1988. "Supervenience Revisited." In Sayre-McCord 1988, pp. 59–75.

Broad, C. D. 1953a. *Religion, Philosophy, and Psychical Research.* Routledge and Kegan Paul.

——. 1953b. "Arguments for the Existence of God." In Broad 1953a, pp. 175–201.

Brody, Baruch. 1981. "Morality and Religion Reconsidered." In Helm 1981, pp. 141–153.

Donagan, Alan. 1977. *The Theory of Morality.* University of Chicago Press.

Finnis, John. 1980. *Natural Law and Natural Rights.* Oxford University Press.

——. 1984. "The Authority of Law in the Predicament of Contemporary Social Theory." *Notre Dame Journal of Law, Ethics, and Public Policy* 1, pp. 114–137.

——. 1993. "Is Homosexual Conduct Wrong? An Exchange." *New Republic* 209, p. 12.

——. 1994. "Law, Morality, and 'Sexual Orientation.'" *Notre Dame Law Review* 69, pp. 1049–1076.

Flew, Anthony, and Alasdair MacIntyre, eds. 1955. *New Essays in Philosophical Theology.* Macmillan.

Garcia, J. L. A. 1998. "Lies and the Vices of Deception." *Faith and Philosophy* 15, pp. 514–537.

Geach, Peter. 1969a. *God and the Soul.* Routledge and Kegan Paul.

——. 1969b. "The Moral Law and the Law of God." In Geach 1969a, pp. 117–129.

——. 1973. "Omnipotence." *Philosophy* 48, pp. 7–20.

Gellman, Jerome I. 1997. *Experience of God and the Rationality of Theistic Belief.* Cornell University Press.

George, Robert P., and Gerard P. Bradley. 1995. "Marriage and the Liberal Imagination." *Georgetown Law Journal* 84, pp. 301–320.

Goodman, Lenn E. 1995. *God of Abraham.* Oxford University Press.

Green, Leslie. 1990. *The Authority of the State.* Oxford University Press.

Grice, Paul. 1989a. *Studies in the Way of Words.* Harvard University Press.

——. 1989b. "Logic and Conversation." In Grice 1989a, pp. 22–40.

Grisez, Germain. 1983. *The Way of the Lord Jesus,* vol. 1: *Christian Moral Principles.* Franciscan Herald Press.

——. 1993. *The Way of the Lord Jesus,* vol. 2: *Living a Christian Life.* Franciscan Herald Press.

Guest, A. G., ed. 1961. *Oxford Essays in Jurisprudence.* Oxford University Press.

Guleserian, Theodore. 1985. "Can Moral Perfection Be an Essential Attribute?" *Philosophy and Phenomenological Research* 46, pp. 219–241.

Hare, John. 1996. *The Moral Gap.* Oxford University Press.

Hare, R. M. 1952. *The Language of Morals.* Oxford University Press.

——. 1963. *Freedom and Reason.* Oxford University Press.

——. 1981. *Moral Thinking.* Oxford University Press.

Hasker, William. 1989. *God, Time, and Knowledge.* Cornell University Press.

Helm, Paul, ed. 1981. *Divine Commands and Morality.* Oxford University Press.

Honoré, A. 1961. "Ownership." In Guest 1961, pp. 107–147.

Howsepian, A. A. 1991. "Is God Necessarily Good?" *Religious Studies* 27, pp. 473–484.

Idziak, Janine Marie, ed. 1979a. *Divine Command Morality: Historical and Contemporary Readings*. Edwin Mellen.

Idziak, Janine Marie. 1979b. "Divine Command Morality: A Guide to the Literature." In Idziak 1979a, pp. 1–38.

———. 1989. "In Search of 'Good Positive Reasons' for an Ethics of Divine Commands: A Catalogue of Arguments." *Faith and Philosophy* 6, pp. 47–64.

Jackson, Frank. 1998. *From Metaphysics to Ethics: A Defence of Conceptual Analysis*. Oxford University Press.

Kant, Immanuel. 1993. *Grounding for the Metaphysics of Morals*. Trans. James Ellington. Hackett. References given by Academy numbers.

Kierkegaard, Søren. 1972. *Works of Love*. Trans. Howard V. Hong and Edna H. Hong. Princeton University Press.

Kim, Jaegwon. 1993a. *Supervenience and Mind*. Cambridge University Press.

———. 1993b. "Concepts of Supervenience." In Kim 1993a, pp. 53–78.

Kretzmann, Norman. 1991. "A General Problem of Creation: Why Would God Create Anything at All?" In MacDonald 1991, pp. 208–228.

La Croix, Richard. 1977. "The Impossibility of Defining 'Omnipotence.' " *Philosophical Studies* 32, pp. 181–190.

Lafollette, Hugh, ed. 1999. *Blackwell Guide to Ethical Theory*. Basil Blackwell.

Locke, John. 1988. *Second Treatise of Government*. In *Two Treatises of Government*, ed. Peter Laslett. Cambridge University Press. References given by section number.

Lombardi, Joseph L. 1991. "Filial Gratitude and God's Right to Command." *Journal of Religious Ethics* 19, pp. 93–118.

MacCormick, Neil. 1972. "Voluntary Obligations and Normative Powers—I." *Proceedings of the Aristotelian Society* 46 (suppl.), pp. 59–78.

MacDonald, Scott, ed. 1991. *Being and Goodness: The Concept of the Good in Metaphysics and Philosophical Theology*. Cornell University Press.

MacIntyre, Alasdair. 1971a. *Against the Self-Images of the Age*. University of Notre Dame Press.

———. 1971b. "Imperatives, Reasons for Action, and Morals." In MacIntyre 1971a.

———. 1986. "Which God Ought We to Obey and Why?" *Faith and Philosophy* 3, pp. 359–371.

———. 1995. "Truthfulness, Lies, and Moral Philosophers: What Can We Learn from Mill and Kant?" In Peterson 1995, pp. 309–361.

Mann, William E. 1975. "The Divine Attributes." *American Philosophical Quarterly* 12, pp. 151–159.

McLeod, Owen. 2000. "Is There a Moral Obligation to Obey God?" *Philo* 3, pp. 20–31.

Mill, John Stuart. 1965. *Principles of Political Economy*. University of Toronto Press. References given by book, chapter, and section number.

———. 1979. *Utilitarianism*. Ed. George Sher. Hackett.

Mitchell, Basil. 1955. "Theology and Falsification." In Flew and MacIntyre 1955, pp. 103–105.

Morris, Thomas V. 1987a. *Anselmian Explorations*. University of Notre Dame Press.

——. 1987b. "Perfection and Power." In Morris 1987a, pp. 70–75.

Murphy, Mark C. 1994. "Acceptance of Authority and the Requirement to Comply with Just Institutions: A Comment on Waldron." *Philosophy and Public Affairs* 23, pp. 271–277.

——. 1996. "Natural Law and the Moral Absolute against Lying." *American Journal of Jurisprudence* 41, pp. 81–102.

——. 1997. "Surrender of Judgment and the Consent Theory of Political Authority." *Law and Philosophy* 16, pp. 115–143.

——. 1998. "Divine Command, Divine Will, and Moral Obligation." *Faith and Philosophy* 15, pp. 3–27.

——. 2001a. *Natural Law and Practical Rationality*. Cambridge University Press.

——. 2001b. "Divine Authority and Divine Perfection." *International Journal for Philosophy of Religion* 46, pp. 155–177.

——. 2001c. "Natural Law, Consent, and Political Obligation." *Social Philosophy and Policy* 18, pp. 70–92.

——. 2002. "A Trilemma for Divine Command Theory." *Faith and Philosophy* 19, pp. 23–31.

Nagel, Thomas. 1970. *The Possibility of Altruism*. Princeton University Press.

——. 1979a. *Mortal Questions*. Cambridge University Press.

——. 1979b. "Sexual Perversion." In Nagel 1979a, pp. 39–52.

Nowell-Smith, Patrick. 1976. "What Is Authority?" *Philosophic Exchange* 2, pp. 3–15.

Nozick, Robert. 1974. *Anarchy, State, and Utopia*. Basic Books.

O'Donovan, Oliver. 1996. *The Desire of the Nations: Rediscovering the Roots of Political Theology*. Cambridge University Press.

Parfit, Derek. 1984. *Reasons and Persons*. Oxford University Press.

Peterson, Grethe, ed. 1995. *Tanner Lectures on Human Values,* vol. 16. University of Utah Press.

Plantinga, Alvin. 1967. *God and Other Minds*. Cornell University Press.

——. 1970. "World and Essence." *Philosophical Review* 79, pp. 461–492.

——. 1974a. *God, Freedom, and Evil*. William B. Eerdmans.

——. 1974b. *The Nature of Necessity*. Oxford University Press.

——. 1983. "On Existentialism." *Philosophical Studies* 44, pp. 1–20.

Pollock, John. 1986. *Contemporary Theories of Knowledge*. Rowman and Littlefield.

Quinn, Philip. 1978. *Divine Commands and Moral Requirements*. Oxford University Press.

——. 1979. "Divine Command Ethics: A Causal Theory." In Idziak 1979a, pp. 305–333.

——. 1990. "An Argument for Divine Command Ethics." In Beaty 1990, pp. 289–302.

——. 1992. "The Primacy of God's Will in Christian Ethics." *Philosophical Perspectives* 6, pp. 493–513.

——. 1999. "Divine Command Theory." In Lafollette 1999, pp. 53–73.

Quinn, Warren. 1993a. *Morality and Action*. Cambridge University Press.

——. 1993b. "The Puzzle of the Self-Torturer." In W. Quinn 1993a, pp. 198–209.

Rachels, James. 1971. "God and Human Attitudes." In Helm 1981, pp. 34–48.

Rawls, John. 1971. *A Theory of Justice*. Harvard University Press.

Raz, Joseph. 1972. "Voluntary Obligations and Normative Powers—II." *Proceedings of the Aristotelian Society* 46 (suppl.), pp. 79–102.

——. 1975. *Practical Reason and Norms*. Hutchinson.

——. 1979. *The Authority of Law*. Oxford University Press.

——. 1984. "The Obligation to Obey: Revision and Tradition." *Notre Dame Journal of Law, Ethics, and Public Policy* 1, pp. 139–155.

——. 1986. *The Morality of Freedom*. Oxford University Press.

Richardson, Henry S. 1990. "Specifying Norms as a Way to Resolve Concrete Ethical Problems." *Philosophy and Public Affairs* 19, pp. 279–310.

——. 2000. "Specifying, Balancing, and Interpreting Bioethical Principles." *Journal of Medicine and Philosophy* 25, pp. 285–307.

Sayre-McCord, Geoffrey, ed. 1988. *Essays on Moral Realism*. Cornell University Press.

Scanlon, T. M. 1998. *What We Owe to Each Other*. Harvard University Press.

Schlesinger, George N. 1985. "Divine Perfection." *Religious Studies* 21, pp. 147–158.

Searle, John, and Vanderveken, Daniel. 1985. *Foundations of Illocutionary Logic*. Cambridge University Press.

Simmons, A. John. 1979. *Moral Principles and Political Obligations*. Princeton University Press.

Smith, Michael. 1994. *The Moral Problem*. Basil Blackwell.

Sober, Elliot. 1982. "Why Logically Equivalent Predicates May Pick Out Different Properties." *American Philosophical Quarterly* 19, pp. 183–190.

Sterba, James P. 1977. "The Decline of Wolff's Anarchism." *Journal of Value Inquiry* 11, pp. 213–217.

Swinburne, Richard. 1977. *The Coherence of Theism*. Oxford University Press.

——. 1996. *Is There a God?* Oxford University Press.

Taliaferro, Charles. 1992. "God's Estate." *Journal of Religious Ethics* 20, pp. 69–92.

van Inwagen, Peter. 1995a. *God, Knowledge, and Mystery: Essays in Philosophical Theology*. Cornell University Press.

——. 1995b. "Introduction." In van Inwagen 1995a, pp. 11–21.

——. 1995c. "The Place of Chance in a World Sustained by God." In van Inwagen 1995a, pp. 42–65.

van Til, Cornelius. 1955. *The Defense of the Faith*. Presbyterian and Reformed Publishing Company.

Wielenberg, Erik. 2000. "Omnipotence Again." *Faith and Philosophy* 17, pp. 26–47.

Wierenga, Edward. 1989. *The Nature of God*. Cornell University Press.

Wolff, Robert Paul. 1970. *In Defense of Anarchism*. Harper and Row.

Wolterstorff, Nicholas. 1995. *Divine Discourse: Philosophical Reflections on the Claim That God Speaks*. Cambridge University Press.

Index

Cornell Studies in the Philosophy of Religion
A SERIES EDITED BY WILLIAM P. ALSTON

The Nature of God: An Inquiry into Divine Attributes
by Edward R. Wierenga